Harry Goffin
Taylor Univ.
3-14-66

THE CRISIS IN
PSYCHIATRY AND RELIGION

by

O. HOBART MOWRER
University of Illinois

AN INSIGHT BOOK

D1250166

D. VAN NOSTRAND COMPANY, INC.
PRINCETON, NEW JERSEY
TORONTO   LONDON
NEW YORK

D. VAN NOSTRAND COMPANY, INC.
120 Alexander St., Princeton, New Jersey
(*Principal Office*)
24 West 40 Street, New York 18, New York

D. VAN NOSTRAND COMPANY, LTD.
358, Kensington High Street, London, W.14, England

D. VAN NOSTRAND COMPANY (Canada), LTD.
25 Hollinger Road, Toronto 16, Canada

COPYRIGHT © 1961, BY
D. VAN NOSTRAND COMPANY, INC.

Published simultaneously in Canada by
D. VAN NOSTRAND COMPANY (Canada), LTD.

No reproduction in any form of this book, in whole or in part (except for brief quotation in critical articles or reviews) may be made without written authorization from the publishers

Preface

One day, while this book was still in preparation, I was chatting with a student who, amiably but not very discerningly, asked if it would be the first to appear in the psychiatry-religion area. In reply I pointed to two piles of books, each nearly two feet high, on a nearby table and suggested that he run his eye down over the titles. Here, I told him, was only a part of my personal collection of such books and added that there are many more which I do not possess.

The more pertinent question, therefore, is why should I, why should anyone, write yet *another* book in this area? The answer, to which the prospective reader is immediately entitled, is that this book is different—in a way which, at least crudely, can be quickly stated. The typical psychiatry-religion book, subtly or boldly, promises "peace of mind" to the reader on the premise that psychiatry is wonderful, religion is wonderful, put them together and you get something better still! More accurately, the situation might be likened to that of two aging lovers who have married, each with the illusion that the other has "resources" which have been implied but, thus far, not concretely exhibited. The thesis of this collection of articles and lectures is that the honeymoon is now coming to an end and that crisis, not connubial bliss, is the term we need to describe the resulting situation.

This book contains, therefore, no "prescription for anxiety," according to the familiar formula. Here we shall proceed on the assumption that our problems in this area are not purely "personal" but have instead broadly social, historical, scientific, and professional dimensions. And the invitation to the reader is thus to join in a quest and a commitment which, while not immediately "anxiety reducing," may, in the long run, be more so than the soothing, personalized approaches

which are today being offered in such profusion. In other
words, to borrow a useful distinction from the sociologist
C. Wright Mills, it seems that instead of merely having
troubles—of a highly particularized sort, to which there
are known, readily available, standard solutions—we here
face broad and complex *issues*, which must be recognized,
openly and honestly, and dealt with accordingly.

Until roughly a century ago, psychology, philosophy,
and religion, in both the popular and academic mind,
were essentially one discipline. But then, in an attempt
to separate the empirical from the speculative, the scientific from the metaphysical, psychology and its medical
counterpart, psychiatry, made a determined effort to
establish themselves as independent enterprises. In certain
limited respects, this separation or fissioning has been
successful; but in other, perhaps more important ways,
it has brought serious difficulties in its wake. Human
beings, whether in sickness or in health, are manifestly
not divided into clear-cut psychological, philosophical,
and religious entities. And our efforts, in the separate
professions, to understand and minister to human need
have been far less effective than we would like. In light
of this situation, it is understandable that, for some years
now, there has been a tendency, particularly on the part
of psychiatry and religion, to "get together" again.
Certainly there is much to commend and support such
a movement; but there are also some major complications
—which constitute the crisis with which this book is
centrally concerned.

Traditionally, it has been recognized that man is pre-
eminently a *social* being—or, in theological phrase, a
"child of God." However, clinical psychology and psychiatry, in an effort to consolidate their separation from
religion, have been powerfully attracted by the alternative emphasis of Freudian psychoanalysis upon the *biological*, rather than social and moral, nature of man's
deepest aspirations. Currently, in this area, we are hearing a good deal about a new interest in *values*. More
precisely, we should refer to this as merely a *change* in
our conception of the good, the valuable. Psychoanalysis
has always had (at least tacitly) a "value system," one
in which "adult genital sexuality" (capacity for lusty
heterosexual orgasm) and unencumbered "assertiveness"

(which often eventuates as frank hostility and aggressiveness) occupy positions of supreme importance.

In psychiatry and clinical psychology there is now, belatedly, a growing realization that such a disingenuous amorality is more likely to *cause* than cure personality deviation and disorder. But, paradoxically, this re-awakening on the part of the secular professions concerned with healing is currently a barrier, rather than an asset, in their efforts to interact with religion; for the latter has also been deeply saturated with this same disingenuous doctrine and is having a hard time shaking free of it. A major objective of the present collection of recently published papers and lectures is to facilitate the process of disenchantment and thus help liberate religion for the more substantial accomplishments, both in conjunction with psychology and psychiatry and in its own right, which seem to be clearly within its reach—and also, hopefully, to help psychology and psychiatry, in whatever collaboration with religion may be logically indicated, to develop in more promising and effective directions.

This book is therefore addressed primarily to psychologists and psychiatrists, on the one hand, and to seminarians and clergymen, on the other, but also to the members of such "intermediate" professions as education, social work, and law. Manifestly it is not a textbook, in the conventional sense of the term; yet, on two different occasions, a mimeographed version thereof has served very satisfactorily in this role. During the Spring semester of this year, Dr. Perry London and I gave an advanced graduate seminar on "The Nature and Management of Guilt," with these materials as the focus of our attention; and during the summer I also used these materials as a "text" in a course on "Mental Hygiene for Teachers." But this book will very likely find its greatest academic usefulness as supplementary reading and as the basis for special discussions in a variety of subject-matter areas.

This is not to say, of course, that more systematic and elaborate treatises will not ultimately be written from the standpoint of the general position which is here roughly delineated. We are, I believe, definitely in process of abandoning psychoanalysis, both as personality theory and as would-be therapy—and also, very possibly, those forms of theology which have allowed themselves to become most seriously adulterated by it. To the extent, then, that this book expedites such developments, it is admittedly "negative," "destructive." But it also points, hopefully and unequivocally, to the *social* basis of both the genesis and correction of psychopathology and thus provides the basis for a broad and potentially very powerful and constructive attack upon our problems in this area.

Some readers will, I imagine, sense a similarity between this approach and that somewhat amorphous but presently vigorous movement known as Existentialism. To the extent that the latter is in revolt against the denial and debasement of human responsibility which have been foisted upon us alike by Calvinist theology, Freudian psychoanalysis, and academic Behaviorism, the present approach is indeed similar. But here the reader will, I trust, find none of the cultishness and mysticism which so often characterize Existentialism, in its various forms. Here the aim is to keep well within the bounds of common sense and scientific thought, but at the same time to take a sufficiently broad view of the human enterprise to include also a considerable segment of what is ordinarily termed "morality" and "religion."

Much of the incentive for bringing this collection of documents together in book form comes from the friendly, yet thoughtful and concerned way in which they have been received, as articles and lectures, by the various professional and lay groups to which they have been addressed. These reactions have been both an encouragement and a challenge, for which I am extremely grateful. The title of each chapter is followed by a footnote which indicates the chapter's origin: if an article, the place of prior publication; if a lecture, the circumstances of its delivery. And at the outset of each chapter there is also a brief introductory statement, designed to highlight the argument of the book as a whole and to link successive chapters together. However, it is here that I wish to express my very warm appreciation to the Pacific School of Religion for the invitation to deliver the E. T. Earl Lectures for 1960 and to North Park College and Seminary for a similar opportunity to

give the David Nyvall Lectures for 1960. These lectures
are reproduced in full, as Chapters 8, 9, and 10, and
11 and 12, respectively. And in September, the latter
were presented, as the first of the Geehns Lectures for
this academic year, at the Southern Baptist Theological
Seminary, in Louisville, Kentucky. I shall long remember,
with much pleasure, the many personal courtesies extended to me on these occasions and the helpfulness of
the comments and criticisms which I thus received.

Also, I take pleasure in acknowledging the generosity of those authors and publishers who have granted
permission to quote from other works, and in expressing
my gratitude to Miss Leona D. Pedigo and Mrs. Donald
W. Keefer for highly competent secretarial assistance in
the preparation, proofing, and indexing of this book.

Although the materials here assembled were originally
directed, in most instances, to professional audiences—
psychiatrists, psychologists, educators, and theologians,
the language is essentially nontechnical and can be understood by any interested layman. And because the issues
under discussion are so vital to our very existence, both
as individuals and as a people, I believe that many laymen, as well as specialists, *will* be interested. To this
end, the book has been deliberately kept small and the
format inexpensive.

O. H. M.

Urbana, Illinois
December, 1960

Contents

To
CRYSTAL MOWRER SMITH
and
GLADYS DURDEN COOK
with gratitude for their faith in
the ultimate unity of psychology and religion

I

Some Philosophical Problems in Psychological Counseling*

This paper is centrally concerned with certain historical and cultural dimensions of the crisis in psychiatry and religion. Academic psychology (particularly here in America) and Freudian psychoanalysis (an indigenous European movement) were both powerfully influenced by the Darwinian conception of organic evolution, which regarded mind as essentially an "organ of adaptation." This type of approach has, in some ways, been extremely useful. However, there are today signs of acute unrest in both psychiatry and psychology. Personal disorganization and psychopathology persist as great unsolved problems in our time; and there is growing conviction that the principles and conditions of biological adaptation and survival do not necessarily provide the understanding needed for psychological survival. Human beings are more than mere bodies, organisms, physiological entities; they are also persons. And personality, it seems, can be

* Previously published in the *Journal of Counseling Psychology,* 1957, 4, 103–111; also read, under a different title ("A Practical, Contemporary Aspect of the Mind-Body Problem"), at the Eighth Annual Institute in Psychiatry and Neurology held, under the auspices of the Veterans Administration, in North Little Rock, Arkansas (March, 1956). Between then and the time of original publication, a number of other pertinent references came to the writer's attention and were listed, for the reader's convenience, as follows: Blake (1955), Fingarette (1955), Gallagher (1956), Hobbs (1956), Liften (1953), Maslow (1956), Roberts (1956), Schneiderman (1954), Shoben (1955, 1956), Walters (1955), White (1952), and Williamson (1956). And to this list a comment was added, "Although these papers do not by any means all take the same position as does the present author, they are unanimous in calling for a re-appraisal of the philosophical premises on which contemporary psychotherapy, counseling, and even diagnosis are predicated."

properly understood and appreciated only in terms of sociality, i.e., interpersonal and moral values systems.

Religion is, of course, deeply concerned with man as person and personality; and in their shifting perception of man-as-body to man-as-person, psychology and psychiatry find themselves looking again, with renewed interest and respect, at religious precept and practice. Whatever may be the incompatibility of religion and these secular disciplines in the metaphysical realm, here, in the study of personality in its social and ethical dimensions, is a natural and favorable meeting place. Although it is at present impossible to foresee how far the rapprochement of religion and psychiatry, broadly conceived, will eventually go, here, manifestly, is the place to start.

Is mind designed to serve the body or is body designed to serve the mind? During the last half century, assent has been so nearly universally given by psychologists to the first of these possibilities that the alternative view has hardly been considered at all.

But there are signs that all is not well with psychology, either as science or as profession, and that we may need to re-examine some of our most basic assumptions. Ask a representative sample of bright, young clinical psychologists who got their doctorate degrees at our best universities four or five years ago and who have since been on the clinical firing line, ask them what they now think of their training in light of their attempts to make application thereof. Without bitterness, self-pity, or even undue pessimism, they commonly express doubts of the most profound and far-reaching nature. They question both the instruments and the categories of diagnosis; they feel that the rationale and results of psychotherapy and counseling are uncertain; and they divergently evaluate the significance of recent contributions to psychology as a science.

Or, listen to what some of our elder statesmen have to say in this connection. In 1955 the American Psychiatric Association sponsored an all-day symposium, by psychiatrists and psychologists, on psychotherapy—later published in book form under the title, *Progress in Psy-*

chotherapy (Fromm-Reichmann and Moreno, 1956).
Here are some of the comments made on this occasion:

> Psychiatry has a great need for a clear and rational
> understanding of the process of recovery. . . . Hypotheses
> we have, . . . but none has gained that degree of validation
> which should serve to command general acceptance in the
> medical profession as a well-established theory (Whitehorn,
> p. 62).
> Psychotherapy has many more variants than psychoanalysis
> and what constitutes psychotherapy, and what does not, is
> even less clear than what is, or is not, psychoanalysis. . . .
> The time has come to investigate not the differences but the
> similarities, and to formulate common denominators among
> the bewildering array of different methods and procedures
> (Hoch, pp. 72–73).
> It is discontent which drives me in my approach to this
> problem. Only a few years ago (although it seems a long
> time in my life as a psychoanalyst) I harbored the comfort-
> ing expectation that increasing analytic sophistication and
> experience would yield a higher percentage of therapeutic
> successes. . . . My reluctant impression is that this hope
> has not been realized (p. 87). I am impatient with any
> propagandish approach to the problem from any point of
> view. We have no right to be for or against anything in
> this field. We have a right only to the most complete
> humility—humility that says we still know practically nothing
> about many important elements either in the neurotic process
> or in the psychotherapeutic process) (Kubie, p. 101).
> Psychotherapy is today in a state of disarray, almost ex-
> actly as it was two hundred years ago (p. 108). At this stage
> we seem to be fighting each other to attain some sort of
> theoretic throne, and we often forget that that throne is as
> unsteady as a three-legged chair (Zilboorg, p. 110).

Or, take still a different sort of evidence that we have
failed to meet manifest social need in this connection.
One of the most remarkable and unanticipated developments on the whole contemporary human scene is the
extent to which religious leaders are thinking about and
actively working at the problem of personality disorder.
Books on religion and pastoral counseling are being published at an unprecedented rate, and if one takes the
trouble to examine them, one finds that they are sometimes quite thoughtful, informed, and creative. "Mental Health" is a common pulpit topic; and to the twin

concepts of "Sin and Salvation" has been added, "and Sanity." Moreover, and even more remarkable, it seems that the profession of psychiatry is now beginning to think in a new way about the role of religion in mental health and illness: witness the just-published books by Viktor Frankl of Vienna (1953) and by the English psychiatrist, Ernest White (1955). For similar trends in this country, see *The Church and Mental Health* (Maves, 1953) and *Ministry and Medicine in Human Relations* (Galdston, 1955). And the same trend is also conspicuous in *Progress in Psychotherapy* (Fromm-Reichmann and Moreno, 1956).

Granted, then, the reality of psychology's ailment, what precisely is the diagnosis, what the remedy?

THE "BIOLOGIZING" OF AMERICAN PSYCHOLOGY

The writer has just read Boring's paper (1950) on "The Influence of Evolutionary Theory upon American Psychological Thought." It is most suggestive. Boring begins by noting a paradox, that in the latter part of the nineteenth century, American psychologists were busy ostensibly imitating and importing one kind of psychology from Germany while, almost unwittingly, creating something very different. This was Functionalism and, a little later, Behaviorism. Here Darwinian thought was the touchstone. Says Boring:

> To his thinking about psychology Dewey brought the concept of functional use for the events of the mind, and thus, closely related to functional use, the notion of functional activity. The way to express this matter is to say that both consciousness and activity function *for* the organism—the use of consciousness is to produce activity which "saves" the organism. That is the essential tenet of the Chicago school of functional psychology which Dewey started, and which Angell carried on. In the doctrine of this school behavior and physiology and conscious states are mixed in with each other because they are unified, not by their essential natures, but by their common aim for the survival and use of the organism (p. 277).

Boring then goes on to say that, in his judgment (Watson to the contrary), Behaviorism was a direct outgrowth "of Dewey's functionalism and of Cattell's capacity psychology. . . . Watson's view was essentially American, a psychology consistent with the [pioneer and democratic] belief in necessity of struggle for survival" p. 288).

Radical Behaviorism is today antiquated, on two scores. (a) Its adherents, in the pursuit of their own objectives, have found it increasingly necessary to make use of "intervening variables." And (b) the spread of interest in clinical psychology has, again of necessity, focused interest upon mind rather than upon body, upon disturbances of consciousness rather than upon questions of biological adaptation. As Boring observes:

> Behaviorism was itself too unsophisticated to last. It has now given place to positivism or operationism or whatever one prefers to call the newest psychological objectivism. The operationist argues that all the data of psychology, including the data of consciousness, are to be defined by the operations which are used to observe them. You can know nothing more about mind than you can find in the evidence for the existence of mind. This movement gets its sophistication from the logical positivism of the Vienna Circle and from the operational physics of P. W. Bridgman, but this is not the place for its full consideration. It is sufficient here to point out that the epistemology of operationism was already implicit in the faiths of behaviorism, functional and capacity psychology, the basic American psychological faith (p. 288).

It is not the purpose of the present paper to suggest that this faith, this "basic American psychological faith," has been completely misplaced or entirely unfruitful. The present author (Mowrer, 1960a); has spent the past several months reviewing the research and theoretical literature to which this faith has given rise in the field of learning; the results are undeniably impressive. The question is whether this faith is as broad, as inclusive, as far-reaching as it ought to be.

> Functional psychology becomes the study of the organism in use. Functional psychology is thus practical through and through in the way that Darwin's theory was the greatest practical theory of living that has ever been put forth (Boring, 1950, p. 277).

Here, then, is the crux of the issue. Is it indeed true that mind is designed to serve the body (which is presumably what is meant here by "practicality")? Or is there a reciprocal relationship of some sort, in which the body must become obedient, even subservient to mind? One hesitates to ask this question because of its clearly anachronistic ring. Religion has always insisted that soul is more important than body, that the flesh should be subjugated by the spirit. And the "old psychology," against which Functionalism and Behaviorism were so strenuously —and not without reason—rebelling, was based upon presuppositions closely akin to those of theology. Boring calls attention to "the influence of seventeenth century theology upon Descartes, an influence abetted by language." In French *l'ame*, he notes, may be interpreted either as *mind* or *soul*, and the same is true of the German word, *Seele*. Since one does not attribute a "soul" to animals, there was, then, a tendency to deprive them of "mind" (and consciousness) as well.

> The Darwinian theory, on the contrary, asserted the existence of continuity between man and animals, continuity in all respects, mental as well as physical, since man is believed to be derived from animals by continuous change (Boring, 1950, pp. 284–285).

There is no doubt that much has been accomplished by the Darwinian, the organic, the mechanistic approach to mind. Many things of a psychological nature are now clearly and systematically understood in objective terms which were simply given, seemingly unanalyzable, in a psychology which made conscious experience all important. And with the physical models and thought forms provided by modern servo theory, it seems that we have by no means yet fully exploited or exhausted what can be done along these lines. But we must return to the thesis that all is not well with contemporary psychological science. To assume otherwise, in face of the manifest realities, is hazardous—and a betrayal of the ideals of science itself.

BIOLOGICAL VERSUS PSYCHOLOGICAL SURVIVAL

The fact, the decidedly inconvenient but seemingly inescapable fact, is that man must be concerned with the struggle for *psychological survival*, as well as with physical, organic, bodily survival. Indeed, he has already succeeded so well in the latter respect that his very success now constitutes one of our most pressing dilemmas (waning natural resources and a world population that is increasing at the net rate of 75,000 persons per day) [cf. also Chapter 13]. But in the struggle for psychological survival, we seem to be groping for first principles. Whether, in absolute terms, there is more "mental disease" in this country than formerly is perhaps open to question; but relatively—relative, that is, to physical illness and incapacity—psychological and emotional disorders are so clearly in the lead that it is now trite to refer to them as "the nation's number-one health problem," the *plague* of modern times.

We have remarked upon the considered skepticism and disillusionment of our bright young men in clinical psychology. And we have also seen what some of our more mature writers have to say about the field of psychotherapy. Moreover, under the urgency of the growing popular demand that "something must be done," men in positions of responsibility and public trust have openly declared that if a new "breakthrough" does not soon come in the field of mental health, they will be forced, by the very nature of their social obligations, to start supporting research and training outside the acknowledged professions of psychiatry, clinical psychology, social work, and psychiatric nursing—not, perhaps, with much conviction but out of sheer desperation.[1]

The professions just mentioned have, by and large, pinned their hopes to psychoanalysis. This body of theory and practice needs no criticism here; the logic of events seems to be making purely verbal objections gratuitous. While the present writer has previously joined in the attack upon psychoanalysis, he now has no zest for further criticism. If one can correctly interpret the course of on-going developments, they clearly signify the failure

[1] Since the above was written, the National Institute of Mental Health (of the U. S. Public Health Service) has approved several "pilot study" grants for training of personnel in psychopharmacology, neurophysiology, sociology, theology, and other "peripheral" professions. Note also the work of the newly established Joint Commission on Mental Illness and Health.

of this movement, leaving one only to say, perhaps, "More's the pity. Things would have been so much simpler, so much easier if Freud had only been right!" But if reality is not as he thought, then the sooner and more completely we recognize his errors the better.

We need hardly remind ourselves that Freud was strongly influenced by the same forces that shaped the "new psychology" in America. We know, by his own repeated statement, that as a youth Freud read and greatly admired Darwin, and the influence is evident: for Freud, neurosis was the result of cultural (moral, religious) interference with normal physiological (instinctual) processes. The mind, if dominated by certain mistaken social values, may cease to serve the body and obstruct its functions. The body then protests and retaliates. *That* is "neurosis," and the crux of Freudian psychopathology. Here we see Functionalism and Scientific Materialism applied to Twentieth-Century man's most pressing problem. Are they indeed so eminently practical? Are they really the greatest "theory of living that has ever been set forth"?

Let us not sell them short. Functionalism and Scientific Materialism provided the intellectual climate and basic premises which have made possible unprecedented advances in our knowledge of animal behavior and have laid the foundation for attacking some distinctively human problems—for example, the psychology of language—with new insights and confidence (Mowrer, 1960b). Perhaps we merely lack patience. Give them time and opportunity to demonstrate their ultimate potency. Indirect report has it that one of the few remaining extreme Behaviorists has recently begun researches with severely disturbed psychiatric patients and that the therapeutic results already obtained are remarkable. All power to this project. But sanguine hopes were expressed decades ago for what the New Psychology would do for the field of mental hygiene (Angell, 1907). It has not, sad to say, borne the hoped-for fruit. Let no hunch go neglected here. But neither history nor the contemporary scene provides grounds for much confidence that the solution, if solution there be, lies in that direction.

What other alternatives are there?

THE NEED FOR A TRULY MENTAL HYGIENE

Is it, then, improper to explore the possibility that the body must serve the mind, as well as mind serve the body? While mind presumably evolved because, as Boring observes, it "saves" the body, yet once evolved it appears that mind has its own special needs, its own conditions for survival, *its own hygiene and culture.* And we must then ask, How and in what sense the body can serve and "save" *the mind?*

For psychologists, this is a dangerous question to consider; for if it is answered at all affirmatively—if we conclude that body must serve mind, it brings us immediately into a domain where we are by no means authorities, but rank amateurs. Religion has steadfastly said, save in its weaker moments, that conduct must be guided by the needs of the spirit as well as those of the body. And some of the best minds of all ages have devoted themselves to working out patterns and precepts of conduct which are "holy" (integrative, redemptive, health-giving, therapeutic). Here, not only are we psychologists relatively uninformed; we have sat, alas, in the seat of scorn and have barriers of pride and deep bias to overcome before we can become even apt students, much less teachers and trustworthy leaders in this area.

Let it be at once granted that religion has sometimes taken an extreme and indefensible position in this connection. Sometimes it has said that not only must the body be subservient to mind and soul; the body must also be despised and continually chastized. No greater or more clarion voice ever cried out against this perversion than that of Martin Luther. Said he:

> No Christian should despise his position and life if he is living in accordance with the word of God, but should say, "I believe in Jesus Christ, and do so as the ten commandments teach, and pray that our dear Lord God may help me thus to do." That is a right holy life, and cannot be made holier even if one fast himself to death. . . .
>
> Huss has been burned, but not the truth with him (Stuber, 1952, p. 213).

Although Luther successfully launched the Protestant Reformation, the philosophy of asceticism is still alive within but under debate by the Roman Church. Gold-brunner (1955), an ordained priest and scholar well known in Europe, has recently stated the growing sentiment within the Church *against* asceticism, in a most interesting and energetic manner. But we need not here pursue his argument in detail. Asceticism is clearly in retreat. Moreover, it is not indigenous to or an intrinsic part of the Christian "way" or life style. The founder of the movement did not say, Do not eat at all. He even taught his students and followers to give thanks for their "daily bread." But he did insist that man *does not live by bread alone*. And he spoke of a more abundant life, a life of the spirit, which was to be achieved by relatedness, reconciliation, fellowship—with man and God. What does it profit a man, he asked, if he gain the whole world but lose his mind, his soul? Truly a life with a permanently disordered mind ("unredeemed soul") is a "life worse than death." In insanity there is physical, biological survival; a compassionate society sees to that. But to what avail?

It has been common for us objectivists to psychologize religion, to write about the "psychology *of* religion." And Freud (1928), as we know, went a step further and reduced it to a form of psychopathology, often relatively benign but sometimes thoroughly malignant. How helpful, how constructive, how genuinely scientific have such forays been? Psychoanalysis as a movement is in trouble. Church attendance in this country, by contrast, is rapidly increasing, well beyond population growth. In other words, Freud's "reality principle" appears to be doing less well than the "illusion" with such an unpromising future. Perhaps Freud was still, in one sense, right: maybe he was wrong only in his estimate of man's growing capacity to live *without* illusion. Or, can it be that he himself misperceived "reality"?

Under the sway of Darwinian thought, we practical, functional, behavioristic psychologists have tended to dismiss religion as irrelevant to both the scientific and human enterprise, or, with Freud, to regard it as actively inimical to soundness of body and mind alike. We have analyzed, psychologized, pathologized religion, ignoring the possibility that it is, in and of itself, a *psycho*logy, *soulo*logy of the profoundest sort. By our own stated premises, our science is a species, a derivative of biology, physiology, even physics. Religion represents man's attempt, through the ages, to meet mind on its own terms. Can this be a truer, more genuine psychology than our own?

How to decide? The antiquity and continued vitality of religious thought and action may be said to bear upon the question. Freud argued to the contrary. It was something, he said, that had simply become lodged, adventitiously, in man's "unconscious" and was perpetuated like some congenital physical weakness or disorder. But contemporaneous, as well as historical, evidence suggests that religion, as an institution, has survived for the reason that it often has unique *psychological survival value* for the individual. That it gave early Christians the capacity to handle not only the ordinary conflicts and tensions of life but enabled them to persevere in the face of and eventually to overcome the most powerful political opposition on the face of the earth is established history. And in our own time the evidence from case-histories of "brain washing" successfully withstood on religious grounds is steadily growing (see, for example, Perkins, 1956).

The English psychiatrist, Ernest White, (1955, p. 11) takes this position:

> One often finds that questions do not admit of a clear answer because the assumptions on which they rest are false. For example, after an address had been given on the subject of Psychology and Religion, a member of the audience asked why it was that so many more neurotic people were found inside the churches as compared with people outside. Now it is not possible to answer such a question unless it has been first demonstrated by special investigation that there are in fact more neurotics in proportion among churchgoers than among the general population. As far as I know, no such investigation has been made.

Preliminary attempts, apparently not known to White, have been made in this country to get empirical evidence on this point, with results that give church members a comparatively clean bill of emotional health (Link, 1936, Chap. 1 and p. 99). But much more searching study of the issue, at the empirical level, is obviously needed. From one point of view, no neurotic individuals at all should be found in a church-going population. If religion offers an assured salvation, this might seem to follow axiomatically. But it would be absurd to condemn hospitals, as institutions of physical remediation, because one finds so many *sick* people in them. The appeal of religious institutions has always been addressed to "poor, sick souls," and Christ himself said that he did not come to call the righteous. Hence, a study which would be faithful to both sides of the argument needs to be carefully interpreted, as well as meticulously impartial.

COMMON GROUND: THE STUDY OF INTERPERSONAL AND GROUP RELATIONSHIPS

It has already been noted that psychologists, for reasons given, have been hard to interest in religious psychology, as opposed to objective psychology and psychoanalysis. Indeed, as Roberts (1956) has observed, "A psychologist who is suspected of being religious is at once under suspicion of scientific incompetence," although the same suspicion does not attach itself to a physicist, a chemist, or an engineer. But there are signs of change. A number of national organizations (typified by the National Academy of Religion and Mental Health) have recently sprung up with the avowed purpose of unifying, or at least relating, psychology, psychiatry, and religion; and, within the American Psychological Association itself, there is now a "special interest group" in this area which has held meetings at our two most recent conventions.

Perhaps most auspicious of all is the fact that so many psychologists are now turning their research interests toward problems which have long been of concern to religious and church leaders, notably problems having to do with social affiliation and what Foote and Cottrell (1955) have aptly termed *interpersonal competence*. Here it is inevitable that psychologists should encounter many of the same realities as have interested religious thinkers and practitioners throughout history. This point is well illustrated in a paper recently published by Corsini and Rosenberg (1955). These writers did a sort of informal factor analysis of the contents of some 300 contemporary books and articles on the subject of group psychotherapy and emerged with "ten classes of mechanisms" commonly emphasized therein.

All of these mechanisms, or principles, need not be considered here; but the two which head Corsini and Rosenberg's list are these:

Acceptance. This statistically most frequent concept was taken to mean respect for and sympathy with the individual. Acceptance implies belongingness, a warm, friendly, comfortable feeling in the group.

Altruism. Closely related to acceptance but in addition involving wanting to do something for others is the mechanism of altruism. The essence of this mechanism is the desire to help others (p. 107).

Are these two mechanisms so salient because the authors of the works thus analyzed have a basically religious orientation? Or have the authors, with an initially neutral or perhaps even unsympathetic attitude, empirically rediscovered the therapeutic potency of "fellowship" and "charity"?

Whatever the answer to this question, the fact stands out that, increasingly, psychologists are joining psychiatrists and clergymen in looking for both the cause and cure of personality difficulties in the social, interpersonal, moral, or "spiritual" realm. But what of those most welcome advances recently made in drug therapy? As May (1955) has cogently observed, these drugs—merciful as they are for use with persons in terror states and agitations—leave essentially untouched the problem of prevention and personality reorganization.

In our neighbor discipline, Sociology, there has long been a tendency to view mind, or "self," as much more of a *social* than biological phenomenon. Here the influence of Mead (1934) is already strong, and becoming increasingly so. Thus the confluence of thought noted above gains yet another tributary.

The centrality of religious tradition and practice is obvious here. But there was a manifest difficulty. Let one highly placed within organized religion, itself, speak on this score. Says Rev. James A. Pike (1954), Dean of the Episcopal Cathedral of St. John the Divine, in New York:

The Biblical writers are, by and large, short on concepts, long on concern as to the human situation. The early Church carried this tradition forward: the articles of the Creeds are not just intellectual speculations. They are affirmations wrought out in the fire of personal and corporate experience and found to be abiding answers to perennial questions which affect the nature and direction of human life under God (p. 6).

The Biblical writers emphasize, not "theory," but *testimony*. Make an "investment," "experiment," "try it" say characters in Lloyd Douglas' novels. Or, in Pike's own colorful phrase, in order to find out you have to "bet your life." *Prove* all things, said the Apostle, Paul.[2] Perhaps psychologists can ultimately help provide a clearer, more naturalistic, more rational explanation and understanding of these pragmatic varieties. This would be an undertaking of first-rate importance and magnitude. But before psychologists and religionists can thus creatively collaborate, both must change from what they have earlier been. Contemporary religious writers now seem increasingly aware of errors into which religion fell during the nineteenth century. One of these errors was obstinacy in accepting the clear evidence for organic evolution. But ever more grievous, perhaps, was a later willingness to go *too far* in accepting the psychological view of man seemingly dictated by evolutionary considerations. In the introduction to Alexander Miller's recent book, *The Renewal of Man*, Reinhold Niebuhr (1955) has said:

> Christianity has tried rather too desperately to accommodate itself to modernity. In its desperation it frequently sacrificed just those points in the Christian Gospel which would throw light on mysteries which modern learning left obscure (p. 8).
> The present age, though incredulous toward the chief affirmations of this faith, is bound to find it more relevant than previous ages, which conceived their own schemes of salvation. Our age is the inheritor of the confusion and the evil which proceeded precisely from these schemes of salvation (p. 9).

[2] *Walters (1955) has pertinently observed that Freud, while condemning religion, took the same position in holding that no one could properly evaluate or criticize psychoanalysis who had not himself had such an experience.*

There are many indications, over and beyond those cited in this paper, that we are now well into a religious reformation comparable in scope and significance to that of four hundred years ago. Institutionalized religion had stagnated. Within the past century, science in general and biological science in particular, threatened its very life. Now religion appears to be recovering and, in that process, has gained new vitality and validity. What are the implications of this unexpected turn of events for psychology? Although we may feel uncertain of the answer, we cannot complacently ignore the question.

SUMMARY

There is clear indication that the theory of organic evolution has profoundly and pervasively influenced American psychology during the past three-quarters of a century. Mind, rather than being something to be studied in its own right, has been conceived as "an organ of adaptation," an appendage of the body instrumental to the achievement of bodily ends.

Thanks to the stance of the "New Psychology" (Functionalism, Behaviorism), it has proved possible, for the first time, to develop a systematic, essentially objective understanding of many basic psychological processes. Behavior theory is now a relatively unified assembly of fact and principle which commands respect in any scientific company.

Nor was the influence of Darwinian thought restricted to psychology in this country. Equally potent was its impact upon Freud and the school of psychopathology which he founded. Here the "neuroses," both mild and severe, were seen as springing from the fact that the mind, under the sway of unfortunate or misdirected *social* experience, has, in effect, *turned against* the body and is no longer ministering to its needs.

But there is increasing evidence that neither the original Freudian formulation nor its attempted restatement in terms of contemporary behavior theory gives us the answer to some of man's most profound, and uniquely human, problems. Today we are probing the future (through research) and searching the past, through historical studies, for leads to a better and psychologically more abundant life. What do we find? Growing indication that the *human mind, in its towering complexity, long ago reached the point where it has its own special conditions for "survival,"* conditions which are not only different from those of physical comfort and well-being but which may on occasion be in conflict therewith. Both ongoing researches and a re-examination of history point to the conclusion that religious precepts and practices, over the centuries, have grown up largely in response to man's unique psychological needs and that there are insights and prescriptions for action here which contemporary man may, with profit, reconsider.

Such a reconsideration seems now to be well under way, mainly by theologians, naturally enough, but also, and to a surprising degree, by psychiatrists. Psychologists, in their increasing interest in group psychotherapy, are also showing a new awareness of social values; and several interprofessional groups have recently been formed for a concerted confrontation of the problem at the level of research and practice.

The burden of the present paper is that it will greatly hasten this readjustment if we can succeed in seeing the proper relationship between man's needs for physical and *psychological* survival and can transcend the tacit assumption that mind is merely servant of the body and that, if it serves this master well, it will itself necessarily prosper. Long ago we were reminded that man does not live by bread alone; and it is none too early for us to turn our attention to the identification and better understanding of this "something more."

2

Changing Conceptions
of the Unconscious*

Perhaps more than anything else, the feature of Freudian psychoanalysis which has given it an air of mystery and its practitioners a presumption of esoteric knowledge and power is its doctrine of "The Unconscious." In the present chapter we see that this doctrine is in process of radical revision and re-evaluation, along lines more congenial to common sense and traditional moral and religious ideology. Now it is possible, in terms of this evolving conception of psychopathology, for the average person not only to know something about such matters but also to do something, i.e., take initiative and responsibility in their prevention and correction.

In the preceding chapter, we have postulated that personality disturbance can be adequately understood only in an interpersonal, social, moral matrix. But in order for this conception to hold, we must also be able to account for the purely internal, intrapsychic—as well as external, interpersonal—phenomena which characterize those states we call neurosis and psychosis. The critical consideration here is the way in which that remarkable agency known as conscience operates. If our present analysis is correct, personality disturbance is less an "illness" than an effort, on the part of "The Unconscious," to bring about personal change and growth. Can it be that much of our current therapeutic and preventive endeavor in this area is ineffective (even harmful) because it is predicated on a contrary set of assumptions?

INTRODUCTION

In a field which otherwise abounds with confusion and uncertainty, there is one rock-ribbed fact: namely, that the hallmark of psychopathology is a feeling, on the part of the afflicted individual, that he is having experiences

17

which he himself did not plan or "will" and which he does not at all understand. The ubiquity of this observation, therefore, makes entirely plausible the impression that personality disturbance is somehow associated with the presence and activity of an alien, dissociated, unknown, and ominous force or set of forces within the personality which is currently known as *The Unconscious*.

But beyond this point, there is scant agreement. What is *in* the Unconscious? How did it get there? What is it trying to *do*? Should it be assisted or opposed? These are questions to which, in our time, we have had no assured answers. The purpose of the present paper is to look at these questions and at the overall problem of psychopathology in historical perspective and to suggest, tentatively, a way of reinterpreting and, hopefully, integrating the presently discordant array of fact, theory, and practice.

FREUD ON REPRESSION AND THE UNCONSCIOUS

From the point of view of this inquiry, 1915 was an eventful year. In that year Freud published two papers, one on "Repression" and the other on "The Unconscious" which epitomized his theoretical system or so-called "metapsychology" and which set forth ideas that have gained world-wide currency and influence. In the second of these papers, Freud argued persuasively that the concept of mind or mental activity should not be confined to those processess which are at any given moment conscious or likely to become conscious, but should instead include forces or processes which are unconscious but which are not, for that reason, to be thought of as dormant or ineffectual in determining experience and action. He said:

> In many quarters our justification is disputed for assuming the existence of an unconscious system in the mind and for employing such an assumption for purposes of scientific work. To this we can reply that our assumption of the existence of the unconscious is *necessary* and *legitimate*, and

---

* Prepared and delivered, by invitation, as a lecture at the 1958 meeting of the American Personnel and Guidance Association, in St. Louis, and subsequently published in *The Journal of Nervous and Mental Diseases*, 1959, 129, 222–232.

that we possess manifold *proofs* of the existence of the unconscious. It is necessary because the data of consciousness are exceedingly defective; both in healthy and in sick persons mental acts are often in process which can be explained only by presupposing other acts, of which consciousness yields no evidence. These include not only the parapraxes and dreams of healthy persons, and everything designated a mental symptom or an obsession in the sick; our most intimate daily experience introduces us to sudden ideas of the source of which we are ignorant, and to results of mentation arrived at we know not how. All these conscious acts remain disconnected and unintelligible if we are determined to hold fast to the claim that every single mental act performed within us must be consciously experienced; on the other hand, they fall into a demonstrable connection if we interpolate the unconscious acts that we infer. . . . We become obliged then to take up the position that it is both untenable and presumptuous to claim that whatever goes on in the mind must be known to consciousness (1915b, p. 99).

While Freud did not hold that the unconscious mind is created solely by repression, he did hold that repression is a potent source of unconscious energies and a prime cause of psychopathology. The mere fact that an idea or impulse has been banished from consciousness does not at all mean that it has lost its dynamic properties; and its continued striving for recognition and expression constitutes, according to Freud, the principal basis of anxiety and ensuing symptom formation. More specifically Freud believed that the mental processes which are most likely to undergo repression are the instinctual forces of sexuality and hostility and that repression occurs, typically, when the ego, under the sway of socially instilled moral precepts, rejects and condemns these impulses.

Two forms or stages of repression were to be distinguished. There was, first of all, what Freud called *primal repression*, "a first phase of repression, which consists in a denial of entry into conscious of the mental (ideational) presentation of the instinct" (1915a, p. 86). But, continued Freud, "repression does not hinder the instinct-presentation from continuing to exist in the unconscious and from organizing itself further, putting forth derivatives and instituting connections" (p. 87).

The second phase of repression, *repression proper*, concerns mental derivatives of the repressed instinct-presentation, or such trains of thought as, originating elsewhere, have come into associative connection with it. On account of this association, these ideas experience the same fate as that which underwent primal repression. Repression proper, therefore, is actually an after-expulsion (pp. 86–87).

Therefore, continued Freud,

The process of repression is not to be regarded as something which takes place once for all, the results of which are permanent, as when some living thing has been killed and from that time onward is dead; on the contrary, repression demands a constant expenditure of energy, and if this were discontinued the success of the repression would be jeopardized, so that a fresh act of repression would be necessary. We may imagine that what is repressed exercises a continuous straining in the direction of consciousness, so that the balance has to be kept by means of a steady counter-pressure. A constant expenditure of energy, therefore, is entailed in maintaining a repression, and economically its abrogation denotes a saving (pp. 89–90).

The resolution of a conflict between instinct and moral scruple by means of repression is thus unstable and debilitating; and from this it followed, reasonably enough, that the sovereign aim of therapy was to undo repression and permit sexual and hostile impulses to find freer, less encumbered routes to gratification. Such a program called upon the psychoanalyst to align himself with and to speak for the instincts, in opposition to the moral or pseudomoral forces within the personality which have instituted the repression. Hopefully, these forces can be held back by the combined strength of the patient and the analyst so that the blocked instincts can find more adequate expression; and, more than this, it was believed that, by working through the so-called transference neurosis, the severity and irrationality of these forces might be permanently lessened so that, following analysis, the individual could function, more naturally and more comfortably, without the analyst's continued presence or assistance.

For all practical purposes, Freud's theory was herewith complete. In the 1915 papers he still regarded anxiety as a direct "transformation" of the repressed impulses, a view which was to be somewhat modified in his "second theory" of anxiety. And he was still to introduce the term, superego, although he was already speaking of a "censorship" function (1915b, p. 105). But, in broad outline at least, the theory was fully developed and was later to be changed in only minor ways. With his special gift for graphic similes, Freud summarized his discussion of repression thus:

> In general, repression of an instinct can surely only have the effect of causing it to vanish from consciousness if it had previously been in consciousness, or of holding it back if it is about to enter it. The difference, after all, is not important; it amounts to much the same thing as the difference between ordering an undesirable guest out of my drawing-room or out of my front hall, and refusing to let him cross my threshold once I have recognized him (1915a, p. 91).

To which we need only add that the unwelcome "guest" does not, after his ejection, quietly go away, but instead continues to try to find other means of re-entry and, much in the manner of a restless ghost, haunts the abode which it feels to be rightfully its own, to the dismay and discomfiture of the dominant occupant.

THE ALTERNATIVE VIEW
OF STEKEL, BOISEN AND OTHERS

In his recently published three-volume biography, Ernest Jones defends Freud against the common surmise that he was a difficult man to get along with and argues that those who were first attracted to but then, sooner or later, turned against him were themselves unstable or of doubtful character. On the other hand, Ira Progoff, in his book *The Death and Rebirth of Psychology*, suggests that the difficulty was not basically one of "personality" at all, on either side, but was rather ideological. At least in the case of Adler, Jung and Rank the final rupture, Progoff holds, came because these men were keenly aware of incongruities between the clinical facts and Freud's theories and were compelled to withdraw from the orbit of his influence in order to be true to their own developing ideas and convictions [cf. Chapter 13].

Among the less well known but most interesting of those men who first joined and then left Freud was Wilhelm Stekel. In his autobiography, published in 1950, Stekel gives the details of his break with Freud, over apparently personal and practical matters; but a study of

Stekel's other published works reveals a deep and, for our purposes, highly significant theoretical deviation.

In the preface of a book first published in German (1938) and later translated into English (1950), with the title *Technique of Analytical Psychotherapy*, Stekel indicated just how complete his break with Freud had been by remarking:

> I contend that orthodox analysis has reached a crisis which betokens that the end is near, that collapse is approaching. Clinical records of its successes count for nothing, now. The happy days of interminable analyses are gone for ever (p. xxii).[1]
>
> The medical analysis of tomorrow will have to separate the wheat from the chaff, to combine the various doctrines and schools into an organic whole, and to establish an undogmatic, unprejudiced psychoanalysis. Then the physician will become the educator of mankind (p. xxiv).

The seemingly hasty and bombastic way in which Stekel wrote undoubtedly kept him from being taken as seriously as he otherwise might have been; but in light of subsequent developments, we find a genuinely prophetic element in his work. In *Technique of Analytical Psychotherapy* there is a most remarkable chapter entitled "Diseases of the Conscience" which does not unfold at all the way one might expect it to. Freud—implicitly in his early writings and, later on, quite explicitly—held that repression, as the primal pathogenic act, occurs because the individual's conscience or superego is too severe, unrealistic, and irrational. Therefore, when Stekel refers to "diseases of consciences," one might well expect him to have in mind much the same assumptions as had underlain Freud's conception of the so-called neuroses.

Instead, Stekel's attitude toward conscience is respectful and positive; and by "diseases of conscience" it is quickly apparent that he means diseases or disturbances which are caused by a careless disregard or active defiance of conscience and its urgings. He says:

> My experiences as a psychotherapist have convinced me that many nervous disorders are "diseases of the conscience." Of course it is far from easy to recognize conscience under

[1] Cf. Freud's own paper, "Analysis terminable and interminable" (1937).

the manifold disguises it can assume. But there are stereo-typed ways by which we can be aided in exposing the wiles of conscience, and in discovering when parapaths are play-acting—for they often persuade themselves that they have no conscience, and take refuge in an ostensibly organic disease in order to escape the torment of self-reproach. Some-times, however, such a patient will during the analysis have a bad "fit of conscience," bursting into tears, which may continue for as much as half an hour before the releasing avowal comes (p. 320).

Stekel, as was his literary practice, then plunges into a series of interesting and highly dramatic case histories which we cannot review here. But in summary he says:

All these cases show how grave a blunder we should make were we to accept the one-sided view of those Freudians who hold that lack of sexual gratification is the exclusive cause of psychogenic troubles. In Cases 69, 70, and 71, free rein was given to the sexual impulse, which was adequately gratified, and yet intractable illness supervened, whereas during the periods of abstinence the symptoms disappeared because the conflict-engendering relations were broken off and the con-science was at rest (p. 324).

I have had many cases of the kind, but have merely selected a few to show that parapathic disorders may be diseases of the conscience. The patient suppresses his re-morse, tries to drown the voice of conscience, and feigns immunity. Nature takes vengeance (p. 327).

As long as Freudian theory was in the ascendancy, it is little wonder that Stekel's views remained unknown and without influence. But in 1956 a book entitled *Progress in Psychotherapy* was published in this country (under the semi-official auspices of the American Psychiatric As-sociation) in which many of the forty-odd contributors expressed mounting doubt and disillusionment concern-ing orthodox psychoanalysis and in which there is a chapter, by Lowy and Gutheil, which is devoted to an ex-position and advocacy of Stekel's so-called "active ana-lytic" approach to psychotherapy. Here these authors say:

Stekel's debut as the originator of an independent psy-choanalytic technique was manifested by his thesis that every neurosis—or as he called it "parapathy"—is based on a con-flict between the principles of morality and loyalty and the impulses and tendencies to the contrary. This simple, clinically evolved formula was then not as self-evident as it has become subsequently. . . .

Although essentially a practitioner, Stekel also made a few important contributions to the theory of psychoanalysis. Long before Freud's discovery of the superego, Stekel spoke of the "moral ego" as a factor in the psychogenesis of neurosis. He maintained that a neurotic reaction can ensue not only through the repression of moral tendencies; that on certain occasions, even if the individual appears to be ready to give in to his antimoral and antisocial desires, the moral trends may assert themselves against the patient's will. He [Stekel] quoted the case of a traveling salesman who was always potent with his wife, while being impotent with other women. Cases of this type were considered proofs that neurotic symptoms may be serving the patient's unconscious moral needs, that they may safeguard the individual's intrinsic morality (p. 136).

As Progoff points out in the book previously cited, Adler, Jung and Rank, in abandoning the classical psychoanalytic position, all moved in the direction of a greater emphasis upon the social, moral, or "spiritual" factors in neurosis; but this trend was certainly outstanding in Stekel, as the foregoing quotations indicate.

Also, about the same time and apparently quite independently of any direct connection with Stekel, an American writer by the name of Anton T. Boisen was formulating a very similar point of view. As a result of a brief psychotic experience of his own and of subsequent participation in the Rockefeller-supported study of schizophrenia at the Worcester (Massachusetts) State Hospital, Boisen became convinced that psychosis represents a character crisis, from which an individual may move either in the direction of deterioration or toward personal reorganization on an ethically and socially higher plane. Gentle, soft-spoken, and in no sense given to controversy, Boisen was temperamentally very different from Stekel, yet his ideas about psychopathology are much the same. In his best known book, *The Exploration of the Inner World* (1936), Boisen's views are epitomized by the following excerpts. He says:

The form of psychotherapy now most in the public eye is psychoanalysis. This in its aims is the exact opposite of faith healing. It has often been compared by its proponents to surgery, and major surgery at that. It is an attempt to lay bare and bring into clear consciousness the disowned sexual desires and cravings which it assumes have become detached from the conscious self and are responsible for the neurotic symptoms. Its aim is to make over the harsh conscience and the rigid ethical standards which have led to the disowning of these sex cravings so as to permit of their incorporation in the personality. To this end the psychoanalyst tries to get his patient to live through again his early experiences. The entire procedure is designed to detach the patient from his early loyalties in order to enable him to build up a new philosophy of life in which the dissociated cravings may be properly assimilated (pp. 243–244).

In all my efforts [as a hospital chaplain and therapist] I rely upon a simple principle derived from my theological training which seems to me far too little understood. I refer to the view that *the real evil in mental disorder is not to be found in the conflict but in the sense of isolation or estrangement.* It is the fear and guilt which result from the presence in one's life of that which one is afraid to tell.[2] For this reason I do not consider it necessary to lower the conscience threshold in order to get rid of the conflict. What is needed is. forgiveness and restoration to the fellowship of that social something which we call God (pp. 267–268).

I would furthermore [suggest] that our findings indicate that the sense of guilt, the self-blame and the emotional disturbance which accompany it are not themselves evils but attempts at a cure. The real evil is the failure to attain the level of adjustment called for in some new period of development and the short-circuiting of the vital energies through easy satisfaction (p. 281).

Elsewhere in the same volume Boisen, using a phraseology almost exactly the same as Stekel's, refers to a severely neurotic or psychotic person as one who "has recourse to certain unsatisfactory protective devices, seeking to suppress a troublesome conscience, until the tension reaches the breaking point and the solution comes with cataclysmic suddenness" (p. 78).

Only vaguely aware of the names of Stekel and Boisen and without any detailed familiarity with their writings, the present writer, in 1947, after more than a decade of acceptance of the Freudian view, took the following position:

[2] Somewhere I have recently read that Havelock Ellis, even earlier, once remarked that the problem of psychopathology arises, not from the unconscious, but from the *unuttered!*

By way of recapitulation let it be said that we are here fully accepting the basic theory of Freud concerning the nature of *symptom formation, i.e.,* that a neurotic symptom, so-called, is any habit which resolves anxiety but does not lessen the ultimate, realistic problem which the anxiety represents. And we are also in complete accord with Freud's contention that *repression* is necessary to an adequate theory of anxiety; without this concept a really satisfactory account of anxiety is apparently quite impossible. But it now appears, on both pragmatic and logical groups, that Freud never succeeded in fully apprehending the essential nature of anxiety itself.

It is not possible at this time to give at all completely the evidence on which this statement is based. But what can be indicated, at least briefly, is the direction in which Freud's analysis needs to be modified. In essence, Freud's theory holds that anxiety comes from evil wishes, from acts which the individual would commit if he dared. *The alternative view here proposed is that anxiety comes, not from acts which the individual would commit but dares not, but from acts which he has committed but wishes that he had not. It is, in other words, a "guilt theory" of anxiety rather than an "impulse theory."*

Stated in its most concise but abstract form, the difference between these two views is that the one holds that anxiety arises from repression that has been turned toward the *id;* whereas the other holds that anxiety arises from repression that has been turned toward the *superego* or *conscience* (p. 537).

Naturally, the later discovery of the antecedent works of Stekel and Boisen and the privilege of personal acquaintance with Dr. Boisen have been a source of great personal satisfaction to the writer. But, despite the converging agreements to be found here and elsewhere in contemporary literature, some conceptual difficulties are still to be resolved. These, it so happens, have been neatly summarized by Sidney M. Jourard in his book, *Personal Adjustment—An Approach Through the Study of Healthy Personality.* Here the author says:

Clinical experience suggests that neither Freud nor Mowrer is wholly correct or wholly incorrect. Rather, it can be found that some neurotic patients do indeed have a conscience that is too strict; in order to remain guilt-free, they must refrain from *all* pleasurable activities, including those which society condones. Other patients may be found with the makeup which Mowrer has regarded as nuclear to all neurosis—they repress conscience so they can break social tabooes without conscious guilt.

If we paraphrase Freud's therapeutic aim to read, "change the conscience in lenient directions," and Mowrer's to read, "strengthen the conscience, and help the person to conform with his conscience," we are thrust into an acute impasse: we find that contradictory roles are assigned to the conscience in neurosis, and contradictory therapeutic aims are proposed. This impasse can be resolved if we recognize that consciences *are not all alike* among all members of a given society. Some consciences are stricter than the society requires, some are more lenient, some are quite deviant from the social value system, and many are highly conflicted (p. 366).[3]

This analysis seems by no means unreasonable. It does not, however, accurately represent my own earlier position in these matters, in that *never* did I hold that it was the aim of therapy to strengthen or increase the severity of the conscience, although this has been a common mispreception. All I had said was that perhaps the neurotic's great need was to have his conscience *released*, just as Freud had conjectured that it was certain repressed instincts that were clamoring for freer access to consciousness and a greater share in the control of behavior. In neither case was it suggested or even implied that the repressed part of the personality needed to be *strengthened*. Because Freud did hold that the neurotic's superego needed to be made *less* rigid and *less* severe; and because I had expressed a disagreement with this position, it was an easy but entirely mistaken inference that I was saying just the reverse of this. My difference with Freud's position had to do, explicitly and exclusively, with the question of *what* is repressed or, in other words, with the *direction* of repression and the *content* of the unconscious; and I welcome this opportunity to attempt to clarify the issue (see Levitsky, 1960).

In other respects, Dr. Jourard's formulation is certainly plausible. Consciences *do* vary, from infancy to maturity, from culture to culture, and from individual to individual within the same culture. The sociopath, at least by definition if not in actual fact, is a person with an under-

[3] For a somewhat similar position, see Fenichel (1954), Fromm (1947) and Jung (1938).

developed, weak conscience; and there is certainly no reason, *a priori*, why in other individuals conscience might not be excessively severe. However, it is not my wish here to debate this issue, either on empirical or logical grounds. Rather do I wish to invite attention to a different way of conceptualizing the whole matter of the unconscious, conscience, and the question of repression.

THE UNCONSCIOUS RE-EXAMINED
IN A RELIGIOUS CONTEXT

Psychologists, despite pretentions of open-mindedness and scientific objectivity, have in certain respects been an arrogant and bigoted lot. I recall hearing a colleague, in the mid-1930s, when the question of whether we should include History in the disciplines represented at the Institute of Human Relations at Yale, say that we were not interested in History, that we were not interested even in the History of Science, that we were interested only in *making* Science. And certainly there has been a widespread assumption that the Future was ours alone. Some of us psychologists are now old enough to feel that we have experienced a sizeable piece of this Future, and we are by no means sure that we are necessarily much wiser or more efficient directors of destiny than were some of our forebears. Certainly the phenomena which we today call psychopathology have been known to mankind for a very long time; and it is by no means certain that our progenitors understood or managed them less well than do we.

Thus chastened, I, as a psychologist, have found myself looking with renewed interest and respect at some of the great cultural and historical documents of the past; and here I have found nothing more illuminating than that remarkable collection of writings known as the Old Testament. The language is often metaphorical and poetic; but the basic intent and content of these writings can hardly be missed. And here we find, unmistakably, a psychiatry which is at one with religion.

Old Testament writers interpreted their own and their fellowmen's emotional anguish as a manifestation of the "wrath of God." This idea is found in Ecclesiastes (5, 7), Isaiah (13, 9), Psalms (90), and elsewhere; and Job puts it succinctly when he says, "Have pity upon me, have pity upon me, O my friends; for the hand of God hath touched me" (19, 21). But the theme is perhaps most explicitly and fully developed, in the 4th Chapter of Ist Daniel, in the account of the madness that beset Nebuchadnezzar. Being afflicted by visions and dreams, the King called Daniel in to *interpret* them for him. After much hesitation, Daniel told the King that he had become vain and iniquitous, and that he was going to have to suffer grievously before he found deliverance.

> And at the end of the days [of suffering and humiliation] I Nebuchadnezzar lifted up mine eyes unto heaven, and mine understanding returned unto me, and I blessed the most High, and I praised and honoured him that liveth forever, whose dominion is an everlasting dominion, and his kingdom is from generation to generation; and all the inhabitants of the earth are reputed as nothing: and he doeth according to his will in the army of heaven, and among the inhabitants of the earth: and none can stay his hand, or say unto him, What doest thou?
>
> At the same time my reason returned unto me; and for the glory of my kingdom, mine honour and brightness returned unto me; and my counsellors and my lords sought unto me; and I was established in my kingdom; and excellent majesty was added unto me.

Here, it seems, are implications of a most profound and far-reaching kind. Here, if I understand the stories of Job, Nebuchadnezzar, and other Old Testament characters, there is no intimation that psychopathology necessarily involves repression; surely the very core of the problem is that God has spoken, expressed himself, *touched* the individual in question. And there is accordingly no intention or need to make the unconscious conscious.[4] The question rather is *why* God and conscience have smitten us and what we can *do* about it.

This is not to say, of course, that the now afflicted individual may not have *previously* repressed conscience and "denied God." The wicked are often referred to as "hard of heart," calloused, and insensitive. And as long

----

[4] Cf. Stekel's remark, "After thirty years' experience of analysis, I no longer believe in the overwhelming significance of the unconscious (in the Freudian sense of that term)" (1938, p. xx).

as these defenses hold, there is no manifest disturbance. Rather the "disease," if we may now use that term in a strictly social and moral sense, is to this point a purely *latent* one; and when conscience finally rebels and erupts, when, in Biblical language God's patience is exhausted, the individual is already grappling with a crisis from which he may emerge a chastened, changed, and converted man [see also Chapter 9].

Of course, in a certain limited sense one may say that religious leaders *do* attempt to make the unconscious conscious, do attempt to release repressed, imprisoned, denied forces of personality. To the hard of heart, they continually put forth a "call to repentance," the confession of sin, and reaffirmation of obedience to the good and to the godly. In fact, it would seem that this is one of the main functions of regular worship on the part of the devout, to constantly acknowledge and correct their waywardness and to grow in the "grace and admonition of the Lord."

But it is surely equally, or even more importantly, true that remorse, contrition, and dismay often break out spontaneously in deviant individuals and that it is this state of *manifest* disturbance which we call neurosis or mental illness and which someone is supposed to "treat." Therefore, it would seem to be a real question as to whether efforts at making the unconscious conscious are relevant. If, by the unconscious, we now mean conscience and the "Hand of God," the task would seem to be *quite the reverse*, namely that of helping the individual find what he can do that will please God, satisfy conscience, and thus allow him once more to "go forth in peace."

Steeped as we are, in this generation, in a particular form of naturalism, we do not easily assimilate either the language or the thought forms of the ancient Hebrews; but if the interpretation of psychopathology which has just been suggested be correct, its naturalistic basis is at once apparent. To me it has been helpful to recall that a child can operate in either of two ways: (a) of his own free will and wish or (b) under parental compulsion. By acting "like a big boy (or girl)," that is to say, maturely and responsibly, the child enjoys many privileges and feels and indeed is "free." But if the child "forgets" or ignores what his parents have tried to teach him, they have to reassert their authority, with an ensuing loss of freedom and self-direction on the part of the child.

In like manner, may we not assume that an adult is free, *i.e.*, self-determining and autonomous, only so long as he is *good* and that when he sufficiently violates the trust of conscience, the latter "takes over," perhaps far from gently and almost certainly with a feeling on the part of the individual that "things are happening to me." Like the parents of an earlier day, conscience thus deprives the individual of his freedom and will restore it only when he has shown that he can again be trusted. Thus, the objective of therapy is not to "make the unconscious conscious." If the view just indicated is valid, the very root of the difficulty is that the unconscious (now understood as conscience) is all too much in evidence—and the objective is to get it to subside, retreat, relax; and this it will presumably do only when the ego or autonomous part of the personality has redeemed itself.

Religion, in its most vital and significant form, has always been intent upon saving "lost souls," *i.e.*, in helping individuals regain their sense of peace and freedom through a return to responsible living, integrity, and concern and compassion for others. This, it seems, is "therapy" of the most profound variety; and it is perhaps our great misfortune that this conception is today accepted and practiced with so little confidence.

IMPLICATIONS FOR PSYCHOTHERAPY, COUNSELING, AND "EGO PSYCHOLOGY"

If space permitted, it would perhaps be profitable to try to relate the foregoing discussion to that somewhat chaotic but vigorously growing system of thought known as contemporary learning theory. Starting as it did with just the two concepts of objectively observable stimulation and response, learning theory has gradually incorporated certain subjective, or "intervening," variables, notably those of fear, relief, hope, and disappointment. Karl Muenzinger, at the University of Colorado, has recently suggested a way in which "courage" can be operationally defined and empirically studied in rats or other laboratory animals; and I think it entirely probable that learning theory will soon be elaborated to the point that it can be equally precise and explicit about the phenomenon of *guilt*. Already some progress has been made in this connection, but it would carry us too far afield to discuss this matter further [cf. Mowrer, 1960b; 1961].

Recently I was much interested and, I confess, not a little surprised to hear a physiological psychologist state that there is some evidence that the neurological correlates of the unconscious mind have now been at least roughly identified and that there is apparently here a capacity for gross emotional conditioning which may later affect the individual in ways very similar to those already attributed to conscience in this paper. Here, likewise, we will await further developments eagerly, with the possibility in mind that we may, at long last, be approaching a way of thinking about psychopathology which articulates not only with social psychology and religion but also with learning theory and neurophysiology.

But there is a more immediate consideration before us. A few months ago I heard a theologian say that although he was convinced that religion is relevant to the problem of mental health, he did not regard religion as *sufficient* in this connection. When asked to elaborate, the theologian said that he meant, quite simply, that religion can deal with the conscious personality, but *not* with unconscious forces. This position reflects, of course, one way in which the church has tried to make peace with the secular healing professions; but there is a question as to whether such a "division of labor" corresponds to reality. If the line of thought we have pursued in this paper is even remotely valid, religion, at its best, is always concerned with the unconscious, conceived as conscience and the Voice of God. The God of Moses was known as the *Invisible* God, and the church, quite generally, has been concerned with helping individuals live so that they do not see God as an hallucination or hear his angry voice.[5]

Now if our general point of view here is tenable, one would have to entertain the same misgivings about the

[5] See Boisen's illuminating discussion (1952) of the "externalization of conscience"; also Freud on the "delusion of observation" (1933, p. 85).

attempt which is commonly made to draw a line between psychological counseling and psychotherapy on the grounds that the latter deals with unconscious material whereas the former does not or at least *should* not. In November, 1950, the University of Minnesota was host to a conference on "Concepts and Programs of Counseling"; and at that time I gave a paper entitled "Anxiety Theory as a Basis for Distinguishing between Counseling and Psychotherapy." Much of what was said on that occasion is congruent with the present discussion. Take for example this sentence: "It makes an enormous difference practically whether we, as therapists, are afraid of anxiety in our patients (or in ourselves) [as something malignant and destructive] or whether we see it as essentially a constructive ally both to our therapeutic efforts and to the best trends and forces within the patient" (p. 26).

But I also took the position that we should clearly distinguish between two forms of helping activity—call them what you will—the one of which involves dealing with essentially normal persons, *i.e.*, persons whose conflicts and difficulties are still fully conscious, and the other involving persons in whom dissociation and repression have already occurred and where there is therefore an unconscious to deal with. While such a distinction may still have a limited justification, it would now seem that the psychological counselor, at least in principle, is in much the same position as the religious counselor. If our reasoning has been correct, the normal individual has actually a "larger" unconscious than does a disturbed person; and support, direct admonition, and counsel may be one of the best means, in the latter case, to get conscience to relax and again become "unconscious." As already suggested, the best way for a child to get his parents "off his back," to use a common but graphic expression, is for him to redeem himself with respect to past misdeeds and to regain their confidence and trust for the future. Likewise, surely, the best hope of the conscience-stricken adult is to associate himself with other persons or *ideas* which can encourage and guide him into paths of conduct that will lead ultimately to the approval rather than condemnation of conscience.

Today it is difficult to discern clearly what is happening in the field of psychoanalysis. In general, it is in a state of crisis and uncertainty [cf. Chapter 13]. But one trend stands out rather unmistakably, namely, the growing emphasis upon "ego psychology." I cannot claim to have been a close student of this trend, but even from afar one sees in it developments which are complementary to the thinking we are here exploring. Here, instead of stressing superego over-severity, we find more reference to the importance of *ego adequacy*. Here it is not nearly so much a question, as it was formerly, of how to pare down or reform the conscience; rather the question is, how to get the conscious self-system or ego of the individual to grow and mature, so that it is more responsible and more competent to deal with the manifold demands that impinge upon it. Here, surely, the work of the minister, the counselor, the teacher, and the parent are all highly pertinent; and where intensive, specialized psychotherapy becomes necessary, it is presumably not so much a question of reversing or undoing the work of others but instead a matter of trying to *carry on* where others have left off or have failed.

On the whole, however, one has the impression that the development of ego psychology has not as yet proceeded very far in psychoanalytic quarters. Certainly Federn's 1952 (posthumous) volume, *Ego Psychology and the Psychoses*, cannot be said to have shed any great new light upon these matters. This book is abstruse and still so heavily encumbered with classical psychoanalytic jargon that whatever innovations it contains are very hard to discover. Far more illuminating and, it would seem, more promising is the approach suggested by Shoben in his paper entitled, "Toward a Concept of the Normal Personality" (1957). Although he does not use the term, Shoben here is largely concerned with ego psychology. He says, unequivocally, that the normal, integrated, mature individual must of necessity be concerned with self-control, honesty, personal responsibility, and compassion and affection for others and that how one conceptualizes life and interpersonal relationships is of the essence. "Ideologies are at issue here," he frankly says and argues persuasively for the importance also of values and value systems. Here, surely, is an ego psychology—and one with which the social scientist as well as the theologian can very largely agree [see also Waelder, 1960].

Writing on the Oxford Group movement, in 1950, Walter H. Clark described the difference between the aims of psychoanalysis and religion thus: "Both the psychiatrist and the Group want to reduce the sense of guilt —the former by reducing the aim, the latter by increasing the accomplishment" (p. 238). While there is no denying that we sometimes set for ourselves and for others unrealistic aims, yet it now appears that less harm is usually done on this score than when an attempt is made to be deliberately less, morally, than we potentially are. A scholarly friend tells me that our our word *anthopoid* comes from a Greek word meaning, "with the head up." And we are apparently in the process of discovering that we cannot solve our problems by looking "down" without also losing perhaps the most distinctive aspect of our humanity.

FURTHER IMPLICATIONS
AND CONCLUDING OBSERVATIONS

From the foregoing discussion it would seem that psychology and related disciplines are undergoing a period of painful reappraisal; and our vision and understanding are still far from perfect with respect to the end points of this movement and change. But perhaps the way is sufficiently illuminated for us to see before us a few steps further.

Jourard says that in assuming that repression can be directed toward either id or superego, an impasse has been reached; and we have here tried to cut through that impasse by exploring the proposition that in psychopathology the trouble arises, not from what is being repressed, but rather from what, in the form of a wrathful conscience, is being *expressed*. *Past* disregard, denial, or "repression" of conscience may, to be sure, account for the present outbreak or "attack"; but the very presence of disturbance means that the repression has broken down. And the psychotherapeutic task, it would seem, is much less that of releasing the repressed than of helping the individual *understand* what is happening to him and how he can help make the final outcome constructive rather than destructive.

However, our hypothesis does not at the same time exclude the possibility of impulse repression, in at least a limited sense. For some time now I have been interested in collecting illustrations of seemingly *bona fide* impulse repression but which call for an interpretation rather different from the one Freud proposed. From several possible examples, allow me to select and present the following one, because of its simplicity and brevity. It was reported to me by a colleague. He said (as I later reconstructed an informal conversation):

A week or so ago I had an experience which I think will interest you, as a psychologist. Some two months ago the chairman of the program committee of an organization to which I belong called and asked me to recommend someone as the speaker at the annual meeting of the organization. This I did, and I was pleased, when the occasion arrived, that the person whom I had suggested gave a quite excellent and well-received talk. Afterward, however, when my wife and I went home, I found I was vaguely dispirited; and, during the period of meditation which I practice before going to bed each night, I had a very peculiar experience. It was almost as if there was a "live coal" in a part of my mind, a sort of localized "anxiety" I suppose you'd call it. Then, all of a sudden, I realized that I had been *jealous* of the speaker; and immediately the "burning" sensation within me dissolved. I guess I knew I was now in a situation where I couldn't and wouldn't *act* upon my jealousy so it was safe for me to have the feeling. Needless to say, I was *ashamed* of myself for having had such a feeling.

Here, apparently, was a situation where conscience, far from being repressed, had been instead the repressor. Like a parent who does not entirely "trust" a small child in some crucial social situation, conscience had held my friend, so to say, tightly "in rein" and had released him only when the chance for misconduct had passed. There was, presumably, some history of past ungraciousness and envy in situations such as the one described; and it would only be with improved self-control and a genuine "change of heart" on the part of the individual in question that his conscience could "trust" him to handle such a situation responsibly and well. Here the goal of "therapy" would not be to release the repressed impulse but rather to help the individual grow in responsibility and "ego strength."

The term, ego strength, can of course be easily misunderstood. It can be taken to imply independence, self-sufficiency, and even selfishness and defiance. As we are presently conceiving of it, the term implies instead obedience and dedication to broad social objectives and values. Here the "strong" individual is not an individual who selfishly demands, or refuses but one who instead *serves* and is loyal to a set of high social ideals and values.

The point of view here expressed is, of course, manifestly similar to that of religion. Our generation is one which has been said to have lost its "faith in God." Perhaps this loss of faith is related to a misconception of God, which the church itself, in recent centuries, has inadvertently fostered. God, we have been told, is *something out there:* and we have forgotten that there is excellent precedence for thinking of God also as *something in here,* a part of our own selves and innermost experience. For example, consider this passage from I Kings:

> And behold the Lord passed by, and a great and strong wind rent the mountains, and broke in pieces the rocks before the Lord, but the Lord was not in the wind; and after the wind an earthquake, but the Lord was not in the earthquake; and after the earthquake a fire, but the Lord was not in the fire; and after the fire—a still small voice (18: 11–12).

Can it be that we have lost faith in God because we have *lost faith in conscience?* Our widespread use of alcohol and other so-called "tranquilizers" is surely, from one point of view, an expression of distrust of conscience; and in classical psychoanalysis, with its premise about the over-severity of the superego, the distrust is even more explicit. There, as Boisen observes, the therapeutic aim is likened to that of surgery, with the superego the object of interest. We are now beginning to suspect that where psychoanalysis has been successful in its avowed aim, the result is likely to be, not a normal human being, but a person with manifest tendencies toward psychopathy and acting-out; but psychoanalysis is usually not so effective [cf. Chapter 13]. One of the cases cited by Stekel in his chapter on "diseases of conscience" has to do with a physician from India who had come to Vienna for treatment—and, also, it seems, because of Vienna's reputation for liberality in the realm of sex.

The patient sprang from a pious family [and] I pointed out that his troubles were due to a disease of conscience, and told him that the sleeplessness and pruritus would cease to trouble him if he refrained from the libertinage which was contrary to the principles in which he had been brought up. Realizing that I might be right, he broke off all his liaisons and returned to a fleshless diet. Thereupon the pruritus ceased, and he slept exceedingly well. . . .

Psychologically interesting is the fact that [the physician was, however] extremely dissatisfied with the results of the treatment. He had expected the impossible. I ought to have freed him from his inward inhibitions, so that he could enjoy relations with as many women as he pleased (1938, pp. 322–323).

Conscience would thus seem not readily altered, and perhaps we would do well to rethink and redirect our would-be therapeutic strategies. Certainly it is not easy to be a man as well as an animal, to be dominated by social as well as biological considerations. But the privilege of declining to at least make the supreme effort is apparently no longer ours. Man is that remarkable and paradoxical creature who has, as we may say, domesticated, socialized, and civilized *himself*, historically speaking; and this same drama, struggle, and high calling is one which is repeated, in miniature, in each of us. Therefore, the issues on which our personal success or failure, our humanity or inhumanity, our sanity or insanity hinges are as broad as the total human enterprise; and the prevention or correction of our human shortcomings can hardly be reduced to the level of the services performed by an automobile mechanic, the pharmacist on the corner, or even the surgeon—grateful as we are for their expert and specialized assistance on certain occasions. Surely with the slogan of the National Association for Mental Health we can agree: "Mental health is *everybody's* business." And any attempt, on the part of any professional or special-interest group to claim omnipotence and "full responsibility" in this field is as presumptuous as it is illogical.

Is a society "sick" because it has standards, and rules, and laws and punishes offenders thereof by fines, imprisonment, or even death? Who would care to claim "full responsibility" in *this* area? The problem is neither larger nor smaller than our struggle to be fully human.

And is an individual "sick" because he, too, has standards and punishes himself, sometimes quite severely, for deviation therefrom? A penitentiary is the place we send those whom society condemns; and a mental hospital is the abode of the self-condemned—or, as Boisen has called it, a sort of this-worldly purgatory, from which a person may return, to a more abundant life, or in which he can also sink into the hell of a living death [see Chapter 3].

We thought it a great gain when, a century or so ago, we began to try to perceive the insane as sick rather than as sinful. But we are now wondering, to put it as a quip, if sin is not the lesser of two evils [cf. Chapter 4]. Citing the supporting views of Marzolf and Riese, Shoben says:

> Recently, there has been a considerable dissatisfaction with the whole notion of interpreting psychological states in terms of disease analogies. Maladjustive behavior patterns, the neuroses, and—perhaps to a lesser extent— the psychoses may possibly be better understood as disordered, ineffective, and defensive styles of life than as forms of sickness (1957, p. 184).

One of the features of the Protestant Reformation that gave it such dynamic power and wide appeal was the doctrine of "the priesthood of all believers" and belief in "the sanctity of the common life." Nothing, it would seem, short of a similarly broad and universal invitation and challenge, to each and every member of contemporary society, can represent a fully rational and potentially more effective attack upon contemporary man's faltering faith and tottering reason.

3

Some Constructive Features
of the Concept of Sin*

As long as one adheres to the theory that psychoneurosis implies no moral responsibility, no error, no misdeed on the part of the afflicted person, one's vocabulary can, of course, remain beautifully objective and "scientific." But as soon as there is so much as a hint of personal accountability in the situation, such language is, at the very least, wide of the mark and, conceivably, quite misleading. Therefore, if "moral judgment" does enter the picture, one might as well beard the lion and use the strongest term of all, sin. This is the strategy involved in the present and following chapter.

But there is also a deeper objective here. "Sickness," as we shall see increasingly in later chapters, is a concept which generates pervasive pessimism and confusion in the domain of psychopathology; whereas sin, for all its harshness, carries an implication of promise and hope, a vision of new potentialities. Just so long as we deny the reality of sin, we cut ourselves off, it seems, from the possibility of radical redemption ("recovery").

In some ways it is perhaps not surprising that we are assembled here today to explore the question of whether real guilt, or sin, is relevant to the problem of psychopathology and psychotherapy. For half a century now we psychologists, as a profession, have very largely followed the Freudian doctrine that human beings become emotionally disturbed, not because of their having *done* any-

* One of four papers comprising a symposium on "The Role of the Concept of Sin in Psychotherapy" held at the 1959 meeting of the American Psychological Association, in Cincinnati, Ohio (*American Psychologist*, 1959, 14, 356) and later published in the *Journal of Counseling Psychology*, 1960, 7, 185–188.This paper has also appeared, without authorization, in *Catholic Mind*, 1960, 58, 151–155.)

thing palpably wrong, but because they instead *lack insight*. Therefore, as would-be therapists we have set out to oppose the forces of repression and to work for *understanding*. And what *is* this understanding, or insight, which we so highly prize? It is the discovery that the patient or client has been, in effect, *too* good; that he has within him impulses, especially those of lust and hostility, which he has been quite unnecessarily inhibiting. And health, we tell him, lies in the direction of recognizing and expressing these impulses.

But there are now widespread and, indeed, ominous signs that this logic and the practical strategies it seems to demand are ill-founded. The situation is, in fact, so grave that, as our presence here today suggests, we are even willing to consider the possibility that misconduct may, after all, have something to do with the matter and that the doctrine of repression and insight are more misleading than helpful.

However, as soon as we psychologists get into a discussion of this problem, we find that our confusion is even more fundamental than might at first appear. We find that not only have we disavowed the connection between manifest misconduct and psychopathology; we have, also, very largely abandoned belief in right and wrong, virtue and sin, in general.

On other occasions when I have seen this issue under debate and anyone has proposed that social deviousness is causal in psychopathology, there is always a chorus of voices who clamor that sin cannot be defined, that it is culturally relative, that it is an unscientific concept, that it is a superstition—and therefore not to be taken seriously, either in psychopathology or in ordinary, everyday experience. And whenever an attempt is made to answer these objections, there are always further objections—often in the form of reductions to absurdity—which involve naivity or sophistry that would ill-become a schoolboy. Historically, in both literate and non-literate societies, human beings are supposed to have reached the age of discretion by early adolescence; yet here we have the spectacle of grown men and women soberly insisting that, in effect, *they* cannot tell right from wrong—and that no one else can.

Now I realize how futile it is to try to deal with this

kind of attitude in a purely rational or logical way. The subversive doctrine that we can have the benefits of orderly social life without paying for it, through certain restraints and sacrifices, is too alluring to be counteracted by mere reason. The real answer, I believe, lies along different lines. The unassailable, brute fact is that personality disorder is the most pervasive and baffling problem of our time; and if it *should* turn out that persons so afflicted regularly display (or rather *hide*) a life of too *little*, rather than too much, moral restraint and self-discipline, the problem would take on an empirical urgency that would require no fine-spun argument.

Sin used to be—and, in some quarters, still is—defined as whatever one does that puts him in danger of going to Hell. Here was an assumed cause-and-effect relationship that was completely metaphysical and empirically unverifiable; and it is small wonder that it has fallen into disrepute as the scientific outlook and method have steadily gained in acceptance and manifest power. But there is a very tangible and very present Hell-on-this-earth which science has not yet helped us understand very well; and so I invite your attention to the neglected but very real possibility that it is *this* Hell—the Hell of neurosis and psychosis—to which sin and unexpiated guilt lead us and that it is *this* Hell that gives us *one* of the most, perhaps *the* most realistic and basic criteria for defining sin and guilt. If it proves empirically true that certain forms of conduct characteristically lead human beings into emotional instability, what better or firmer basis would one wish for labeling such conduct as destructive, self-defeating, evil, sinful? [1]

If the Freudian theory of personality disorder were valid, one would expect neurotic and psychotic individuals to have lead exemplary, yea saintly lives—to have been

---

[1] There is, admittedly, an element of circularity in the above argument. If it is maintained that mental illness is caused by unacknowledged and unexpiated sin, or real guilt, then it adds nothing to our knowledge to *define* sin as that which causes mental illness. In fact, there is a sense in which such a definition is not only circular but misleading (see Chapter 13). Obviously, what is needed is an *independent criterion* for identifying sin or guilt—cf. Chapters 10–11 and Mowrer, 1961.

just too good for this world. The fact is, of course, that such individuals typically exhibit lives that have been disorderly and dishonest in extreme degree. In fact, this is so regularly the case [see Chapters 8 and 13] that one cannot but wonder how so contrary a doctrine as that of Freud ever gained credence. Freud spurned The Wish and exalted Reality. What he regarded as Reality may yet prove to have been the biggest piece of wishfulness of all.

Or, it may be asked, how is it if sin and psychic suffering are correlated that not *all* who sin fall into neurosis or psychosis? Here the findings of the Kinsey studies are likely to be cited, showing that, for example, many persons have a history of sexual perversity who are later quite normal. In other words, the argument is that since sin and persistent suffering do not always go hand-in-hand, there is perhaps no relationship at all. The answer to this question is surely obvious. *Some* individuals, alas, simply do not have enough character, or conscience, to be bothered by their sins. These are, of course, the world's psychopaths. Or an individual may have been *caught* in his sin and punished for it. Or it may have weighed so heavily on his conscience that he himself has *confessed* it and made appropriate expiation. Or, quite conceivably, in some instances the individual, without either detection or confession, may have set upon a program of service and good works which has also brought him peace and redemption. In other words, there is, surely, no disposition on the part of anyone to hold that sin, as such, necessarily dooms a person to interminable suffering in the form of neurosis or psychosis. The presumption is rather that sin has this effect only where it is acutely felt but not acknowledged and corrected.

Also, it is sometimes contended that individuals who eventually come to the attention of psychotherapists have, to be sure, been guilty of major errors of conduct; but, it is held, the illness was present first and the misconduct was really just an expression or symptom thereof. If this were true, where then would we draw the line? Is there no such thing as moral responsibility and social accountability at all? Is every mean or vicious thing that you or I, as ordinary individuals, do not sin but rather an expression of "illness"? Who would seriously hold that a society could long endure which consistently subscribed to this flaccid doctrine?

Then there is, of course, the view that, in the final analysis, all psychopathology—or at least its profounder forms—have a constitutional or metabolic basis. One must, I believe, remain open-minded with respect to this possibility—indeed, perhaps even somewhat hopeful with respect to it; for how marvelous it would be if all the world's madness, stupidity, and meanness could be eliminated through biochemistry. But over the years we have seen one approach after another of this kind come into prominence, with much heralding as the long-awaited break-through on the problem of mental disease, only to fade out as manifestly not quite the panacea we had imagined it to be. Some of us may, at this point, even suspect that today the main incentive for keeping the biochemical hypothesis alive is not so much the supporting empirical evidence, which is meager enough, but instead the fact that it at least obliquely justifies the premise that the whole field of mental disorder is the proper and exclusive domain of medicine. Also, and again somewhat obliquely, it excuses the clergy from facing squarely the responsibilities that would devolve among them if neurosis and psychosis should indeed turn out to be essentially *moral* disorders.

The conception of personality disturbance which attaches major etiological significance to moral and inter-personal considerations thus faces formidable resistance, from many sources; but programs of treatment and prevention which have been predicated on these other views have gotten us nowhere, and there is no clear reason to think they ever will. Therefore, in light of the total situation, I see no alternative but to turn again to the old, painful, but also promising possibility that man is pre-eminently a *social* creature and that he lives or dies, psychologically and personally, as a function of the openness, community, relatedness, and integrity which by good action he attains and by evil action destroys.

As long as we could believe that the psychoneurotic's basic problem was not evil but a kind of ignorance, it did not seem too formidable a task to give him the requisite enlightenment or insight. But mental hospitals are now full of people who have had this kind of therapy, in one guise or another, and found it wanting; and if we are thus forced to reconsider the other alternative, the therapeutic or redemptive enterprise, however clear it may be in principle, is by no means simple in practice. If the problem is genuinely one of morality, rather than pseudo-morality, most of us in the secular healing professions, of psychology, psychiatry, or social work, find ourselves reduced to the status of laymen, with no special training or competence for dealing with or even approaching the problem in these terms. We know something, of course, about procedures for getting disturbed persons to talk about themselves, free-associate, "confess"; but the whole aim of this strategy has been insight, not redemption and personal reformation. And clergymen themselves have so often been told, both by their own leaders and by members of the secular healing professions, that they must recognize their own "limitations" and know when to "refer" that they, too, lack the necessary confidence and resources for dealing with these problems adequately [cf. Chapters 11, 12].

Many present-day psychoanalysts will offer no serious objection to the way in which classical Freudian theory and practice have been evaluated in this paper; but they will insist that many "advances" have been made since Freud's time and that these put the whole problem in a very different light. If we ask, "Precisely what *are* these advances?" we are told that they have to do with the new emphasis upon "ego psychology" rather than upon "the unconscious." But what did Emalian Gutheil (1958) tell us at our convention last year in Washington about ego psychology? He said that although analysts now recognize the ego as much more important than formerly, they know next to nothing about the conditions for modifying or strengthening it; and the same position has been voiced earlier by Lawrence Kubie (1956) and in one of his very last papers (1937) even by Freud himself [see also Chapter 13].

Therefore, I do not see how we can avoid the conclusion that at this juncture we are in a real crisis with respect to the whole psychotherapeutic enterprise. But I do not think we are going to remain in this crisis, confused and impotent, indefinitely. There is, I believe, growing realism with regard to the situation on the part of both psychologists and psychiatrists, on the one hand, and ministers, rabbis, and priests, on the other; and I am hopeful and even confident that new and better ways of dealing with the situation are in the making.

What, precisely, these ways will be I do not know; but I venture the impression that Alcoholics Anonymous provides our best present intimation of things to come and that the therapeutic programs of the future, whether under religious or secular auspices, will, like AA, take guilt, confession, and expiation seriously and will involve programs of *action* rather than mere groping for "insight" [cf. Chapters 8 and 12].

4

"Sin," the Lesser of Two Evils*

When the paper which constitutes the preceding chapter was delivered at the symposium for which it was prepared, it created something of a "sensation." There was considerable stir over it at the convention itself; and stories appeared widely in newspapers and national magazines, including Time *(Sept. 14, 1959—"The idea of sin, at least for use in treating the sick psyche, is making a comeback," p. 69),* Newsweek *(Sept. 14, 1959, p. 108), and* America *(Sept. 12, 1960, pp. 686–687).*

Because the symposium paper was, of necessity, brief and left many facets of a complex problem unexplored, it seemed desirable to write a supplementary paper, which is reproduced herewith. In it a number of considerations are touched upon which open the way for more systematic discussion in subsequent chapters.

Following the presentation of a paper on "Constructive Aspects of the Concept of Sin in Psychotherapy" at the 1959 APA convention in Cincinnati, I have repeatedly been asked by psychologists and psychiatrists: "But *why* must you use that awful word 'sin,' instead of some more neutral term such as 'wrongdoing,' 'irresponsibility,' or 'immorality'?" And even a religious layman has reproached me on the grounds that "Sin is such a *strong* word." Its *strength*, surely, is an asset, not a liability; for in the face of failure which has resulted from our erstwhile use of feebler concepts, we have very heavy work for it to do. Besides, sin (in contrast to its more neutral equivalents) is such a handy *little* word that it would be a pity to let it entirely disappear from usage. With Humpty-Dumpty, we ought to expect words to be "well-behaved" and to mean what *we* want them to!

---

* Read at a luncheon meeting of The University Religious Council, Ohio State University, Columbus, March 11, 1959, and published in *The American Psychologist*, 1960, *15*, 301–304.

A few years ago I was invited to teach in the summer session at one of our great Pacific Coast universities; and toward the end of the term, a student in my class on Personality Theory said to me one day: "Did you know that near the beginning of this course you created a kind of scandal on this campus?" Then he explained that I had once used the word "sin" without saying "so-called" or making a joke about it. This, the student said, was virtually unheard-of in a psychology professor and had occasioned considerable dismay and perplexity. I did not even recall the incident; but the more I have thought about the reaction it produced, the more frequently I have found myself using the term—with, I hope, something more than mere perversity.

Traditionally, sin has been thought of as whatever causes one to go to Hell; and since Hell, as a place of otherworldly retribution and torment, has conveniently dropped out of most religious as well as secular thought, the concept of sin might indeed seem antiquated and absurd. But, as I observed in the Cincinnati paper, Hell is still very much with us in those states of mind and being which we call neurosis and psychosis; and I have come increasingly, at least in my own mind, to identify anything that carries us toward these forms of perdition as *sin*. Irresponsibility, wrongdoing, immorality, sin: what do the terms matter if we can thus understand more accurately the nature of psychopathology and gain greater practical control over its ramified forms and manifestations?

But now the fat is in the fire! Have we not been taught on high authority that personality disorder is not one's own "fault," that the neurotic is *not* "responsible" for his suffering, that he has done nothing wrong, committed no "sin"? "Mental illness," according to a poster which was widely circulated a few years ago, "is no disgrace. It might happen to anyone." And behind all this, of course, was the Freudian hypothesis that neurosis stems from a "too severe superego," which is the product of a too strenuous socialization of the individual at the hands of harsh, unloving parents and an irrational society. The trouble lay, supposedly, not in anything wrong or "sinful" which the individual has himself *done*, but in things he merely *wants* to do but cannot, because of *repression*.

The neurotic was thus not sinful but *sick*, the helpless, innocent victim of "the sins of the fathers," and could be rescued only by a specialized, esoteric form of *treatment*. Anna Russell catches the spirit of this doctrine well when she sings, in "Psychiatric Folksong,"

> At three I had a feeling of
>   Ambivalence toward my brothers,
> And so it follows naturally
>   I poisoned all my lovers.
> But now I'm happy; I have learned
>   The lesson this has taught;
> That everything I do that's wrong
>   Is someone else's fault.

Freud saw all this not only as a great scientific discovery but also as a strategic gain for the profession which had thus far treated him so indifferently. It was one may conjecture, a sort of gift, an offering or service which would place medicine in such debt to him that it could no longer ignore or reject him. In his *Autobiography* Freud (1935) puts it thus:

> My medical conscience felt pleased at my having arrived at this conclusion [that neurosis has a sexual basis]. I hoped that I had filled up a gap in medical science, which, in dealing with a function of such great biological importance, had failed to take into account any injuries beyond those caused by infection or by gross anatomical lesions. The medical aspect of the matter was, moreover, supported by the fact that sexuality was not something purely mental. It had a somatic side as well . . . (p. 45).

In his book on *The Problem of Lay Analysis*, Freud (1927) later took a somewhat different position (see also Chapter 9 of the third volume of Jones' biography of Freud, 1957); but by this time his Big Idea had been let loose in the world and was no longer entirely under his control.

Psychologists were, as we know, among the first of the outlying professional groups to "take up" psychoanalysis. By being analyzed, we not only learned—in an intimate, personal way—about this new and revolutionary science; we also (or so we imagined) were qualifying ourselves for the practice of analysis as a form of therapy.

Now we are beginning to see how illusory this all was. We accepted psychoanalytic theory long before it had been adequately tested and thus embraced as "science" a set of presuppositions which we are now painfully having to repudiate. But, more than this, in accepting the premise that the neurotically disturbed person is basically *sick*, we surrendered our professional independence and authenticity. Now, to the extent that we have subscribed to the doctrine of mental *illness* (and tried to take part in its "treatment"), we have laid ourselves open to some really very embarrassing charges from our friends in psychiatry.

In 1954 the American Psychiatric Association, with the approval of the American Medical Association and the American Psychoanalytic Association, published a resolution on "relations between medicine and psychology," which it re-issued (during the supposed "moratorium") in 1957. This document needs no extensive review in these pages; but a few sentences may be quoted to indicate what a powerful fulcrum the sickness conception of neurosis provides for the aggrandizement of medicine.

> For centuries the Western world has placed on the medical profession responsibility for the diagnosis and treatment of illness. Medical practice acts have been designed to protect the public from unqualified practitioners and to define the special responsibilities assumed by those who practice the healing art. . . . Psychiatry is the medical speciality concerned with illness that has chiefly mental symptoms. . . . Psychotherapy is a form of medical treatment and does not form the basis for a separate profession. . . . When members of these [other] professions contribute to the diagnosis and treatment of illness, their professional contributions must be coordinated under medical responsibility (pp. 1–2).

So long as we subscribe to the view that neurosis is a bona fide "illness," without moral implications or dimensions, our position will, of necessity, continue to be an awkward one. And it is here I suggest that, as between the concept of sin (however unsatisfactory it may in some ways be) and that of sickness, sin is indeed the lesser of two evils. We have tried the sickness horn of this dilemma and impaled ourselves upon it. Perhaps, despite our erstwhile protestations, we shall yet find sin more congenial.

We psychologists do not, I believe, object *in principle* to the type of authority which psychiatrists wish to exercise, or to our being subject to other medical controls, if they were truly functional. But authority and power ought to go with demonstrated competence, which medicine clearly has in the physical realm but, equally clearly, does not have in "psychiatry." Despite some pretentious affirmations to the contrary, the fact is that psychoanalysis, on which modern "dynamic" psychiatry is largely based, is in a state of virtual collapse and imminent demise. And the tranquilizers and other forms of so-called chemotherapy are admittedly only ameliorative, not basically curative. So now, to the extent that we have accepted the "illness" postulate and thus been lured under the penumbra of medicine, we are in the ungraceful maneuver of "getting out." [1]

But the question remains: Where do we *go*, what do we *do*, now? Some believe that our best policy is to become frankly agnostic for the time being, to admit that we know next to nothing about either the cause or correction of psychopathology and therefore ought to concentrate on *research*. This is certainly a safe policy, and it may also be the wisest one. But since this matter of man's total adjustment and psychosocial survival does not quickly yield up its innermost secrets to conventional types of scientific inquiry, I believe it will do no harm for us at the same time to be thinking about some frankly ideological matters.

[1] Thoughtful psychiatrists are also beginning to question the legitimacy of the disease concept in this area. In an article entitled "The Myth of Mental Illness" which appeared after this paper went to press, Thomas S. Szasz (1960) is particularly outspoken on this score. He says: ". . . the notion of mental illness has outlived whatever usefulness it might have had and . . . now functions merely as a convenient myth. . . . mental illness is a myth, whose function it is to disguise and thus render more palatable the bitter pill of moral conflicts in human relations" (p. 118). Szasz' entire article deserves careful attention.

For several decades we psychologists looked upon the whole matter of sin and moral accountability as a great incubus and acclaimed our liberation from it as epoch-making. But at length we have discovered that to be "free" in this sense, i.e., to have the excuse of being "sick" rather than *sinful,* is to court the danger of also becoming *lost.* This danger is, I believe, betokened by the widespread interest in Existentialism which we are presently witnessing. In becoming amoral, ethically neutral, and "free," we have cut the very roots of our being; lost our deepest sense of self-hood and identity; and, with neurotics themselves, find ourselves asking: Who *am* I? What is my *destiny?* What does living (existence) *mean?*

In reaction to the state of near-limbo into which we have drifted, we have become suddenly aware, once again, of the problem of *values* and of their centrality in the human enterprise. This trend is clearly apparent in the programs at our recent professional meetings, in journal articles, and, to some extent already, in our elementary textbooks. Something very basic is obviously happening to psychologists and their "self-image."

In this process of moving away from our erstwhile medical "entanglements," it would be a very natural thing for us to form a closer and friendlier relationship than we have previously had with religion and theology. And something of this sort is unquestionably occurring. At the APA Annual Convention in 1956 there was, for the first time in our history I believe, a symposium on religion and mental health; and each ensuing year has seen other clear indications of a developing rapprochement.

However, here too there is a difficulty—of a most surprising kind. At the very time that psychologists are becoming distrustful of the sickness approach to personality disturbance and are beginning to look with more benign interest and respect toward certain moral and religious precepts, religionists themselves are being caught up in and bedazzled by the same preposterous system of thought as that from which we psychologists are just recovering. It would be possible to document this development at length; but reference to such recent "theological" works as Richard V. McCann's *Delinquency—Sickness or Sin?* (1957) and Carl Michalson's *Faith for Personal Crises* (1959, see especially Chapter 3) will suffice.

We have alluded to Anna Russell's "Psychiatric Folksong" and, in addition, should call attention to Katie Lee's 12-inch LP recording "Songs of Couch and Consultation." That entertainment and literary people are broadly rejecting psychoanalytic froth for the more solid substance of moral accountability is indicated by many current novels and plays. It is not without significance that Arthur Miller's *Death of a Salesman*, written in the philosophical vein of Hawthorne's great novel *The Scarlet Letter*, has, for example, been received so well.

How very strange and inverted our present situation therefore is! Traditionally clergymen have worried about the world's entertainments and entertainers and, for a time at least, about psychology and psychologists. Now, ironically, the entertainers and psychologists are *worrying about the clergymen.* Eventually, of course, clergymen will return to a sounder, less fantastic position; but in the meantime, we psychologists can perhaps play a socially useful and, also, scientifically productive role if we pursue, with all seriousness and candor, our discovery of the essentially moral nature of human existence and of that "living death" which we call psychopathology. This, of course, is not the place to go deeply into the substantive aspects of the problem; but one illustration of the fruitfulness of such exploration may be cited.

In reconsidering the possibility that sin must, after all, be taken seriously, many psychologists seem perplexed as to what attitude one should take *toward the sinner.* "Nonjudgmental," "nonpunitive," "nondirective," "warm," "accepting," "ethically neutral": these words have been so very generally used to form the supposedly proper therapeutic imago that reintroduction of the concept of sin throws us badly off balance. *Our* attitudes, as would-be therapists or helping persons, toward the neurotic (sinner) are apparently less important than his attitude *toward himself*; and, as we know, it is usually— in the most general sense—a rejecting one. Therefore, we have reasoned, the way to get the neurotic to accept and love himself is for us to love and accept *him,* an inference which flows equally from the Freudian assumption that the patient is not really guilty or sinful but only fancies himself so and from the view of Rogers that we are all inherently good and are corrupted by our experiences with the external, everyday world.

But what is here generally overlooked, it seems, is that recovery (constructive change, redemption) is most assuredly attained, not by helping a person reject and rise above his sins, but by helping him *accept them*. This is the paradox which we have not at all understood and which is the very crux of the problem. Just so long as a person lives under the shadow of real, unacknowledged, and unexpiated guilt, he *cannot* (if he has any character at all) "accept himself"; and all *our* efforts to reassure and accept him will avail nothing. He will continue to hate himself and to suffer the inevitable consequences of self-hatred. But the moment he (with or without "assistance") begins to accept his guilt and his sinfulness, the possibility of radical reformation opens up; and with this, the individual may legitimately, though not without pain and effort, pass from deep, pervasive self-rejection and self-torture to a new freedom, of self-respect and peace.

Thus we arrive, not only at a new (really very old) conception of the nature of "neurosis" which may change our entire approach to this problem, but also at an understanding of one of the most fundamental fallacies of Freudian psychoanalysis and many kindred efforts at psychotherapy. Freud observed, quite accurately, that the neurotic tortures himself; and he conjectured that this type of suffering arose from the irrationality and over-severity of the superego. But at once there was an empirical as well as logical difficulty which Freud (unlike some of his followers) faithfully acknowledged. In the *New Introductory Lectures on Psychoanalysis* (1933), he said:

> The supergo [paradoxically] seems to have made a one-sided selection [as between the loving and the punitive attitudes of the parents], and to have chosen only the harshness and severity of the parents, their preventive and punitive functions, while their loving care is not taken up and continued by it. If the parents have really ruled with a rod of iron, we easily understand the child developing a severe superego, but, contrary to our expectations, experience shows

that the supergo may reflect the same relentless harshness
even when the up-bringing has been gentle and kind (p. 90).

And then Freud adds, candidly: "We ourselves do not
feel that we have fully understood it." In this we can
fully agree. For the only way to resolve the paradox of
self-hatred and self-punishment is to assume, not that
it represents merely an "introjection" of the attitudes of
others, but that the self-hatred is realistically justified and
will persist until the individual, by radically altered attitude *and action*, honestly and realistically comes to feel
that he now deserves something better. As long as one
remains, in old-fashioned religious phraseology, hard-of-
heart and unrepentant, just so long will one's conscience
hold him in the vise-like grip of "neurotic" rigidity and
suffering. But if, at length, an individual confesses his
past stupidities and errors and makes what poor attempts
he can at restitution, then the superego (like the parents
of an earlier day—and society in general) forgives and
relaxes its stern hold; and the individual once again is
free, "well" [cf. Chapter 2].

But here we too, like Freud, encounter a difficulty.
There is some evidence that human beings do not change
radically unless they first acknowledge their sins; but we
also know how hard it is for one to make such an
acknowledgment unless he has *already changed*. In other
words, the full realization of deep worthlessness is a
severe ego "insult"; and one must have some new source
of strength, it seems, to endure it. This is a mystery (or
is it only a mistaken observation?) which traditional
theology has tried to resolve in various ways—without
complete success. Can we psychologists do better?

5

Judgment and Suffering: Contrasting Views*

It has been argued that if real rather than false (Freudian) guilt is at the root of neurosis and functional psychosis, then therapy should, logically, take the form of "punishment" rather than "treatment." Yet the elimination of punishment ("mistreatment") of the insane has been regarded as a great cultural and humane achievement of the last century or two. Here, obviously, is a complicated issue, which has already been alluded to near the end of the preceding chapter. While it is not certain that punishment from without (e.g., the use of electroconvulsive shock) has no legitimate place in a restorative program, the fact is that the distinguishing feature of most forms of psychopathology is that the individual is punishing himself—or at least trying to. The question is, How should we interpret this tendency, as "crazy" or potentially curative? Other aspects of this intricate but important problem will be considered, from time to time, in later chapters.

In May, 1959, it was my good fortune to participate in a week-long institute held at the University of Saskatchewan under the auspices of the Provincial Government, primarily for psychologists; but there were also three psychiatrists and a clergyman in the group, so that our discussions had a distinctly interdisciplinary flavor. And from these discussions emerged what was for me a new insight concerning contemporary attitudes toward suffering which I believe deserves wider consideration.

During the course of the lectures which it was my privilege to give, I reiterated a point of view concerning the origin and meaning of psychopathology which has been taking shape in my mind over the course of the past 12 or 15 years. *Guilt,* I argued, is the central problem—not just guilt *feelings,* as Freud so beguilingly

* Initially published in *Faculty Forum,* October, 1959, pp. 1–2.

suggested, but real, palpable, indisputable guilt; and here I was at pains to review clinical evidence that disturbed persons are not "disturbed" for nothing. Where neurosis or psychosis is purely functional (as it usually is), the individual, I believe, always has a hidden history of serious misconduct which has not been adequately compensated and "redeemed." And if this be so, then confession, expiation, and "a new life in Christ" (or some equivalent type of conversion) have a practical pertinence which far exceeds the boundaries behind which some theologians have attempted to hold them.

There was, I may say, an immediately positive response to this point of view on the part of many members of the group, including one of the psychiatrists and several of the psychologists. But there was also manifest reservation and resistance on the part of others; so we took some time to hear these persons out and try to understand their misgivings.

Presently it emerged that several of the members of our group felt that this point of view was "punitive" and "rejecting" and "countertherapeutic"; for how could one accept it, they asked, without *blaming* the patient and being disposed to *punish* him? These avowals brought several important issues out into the open. First of all, they permitted other members of the group to point out that no one else needs to blame or punish the mental sufferer: he is blaming and punishing *himself* (or at least *trying* to)—this is the very essence of his condition. Therefore, we can and should show him all the love and charity within our souls, and do not need in the least to play a punitive role. But this is very different from saying that we should dispute or brush aside his assertions of guilt or minimize the reality of his need for deliverance. Several members of the group expressed the conviction that much of our present would-be therapeutic effort is useless and even harmful because we so actively *oppose* the patient's own most substantial psychological realities and his brightest prospects for change and recovery, i.e., his conviction of guilt and sense of sin. Perhaps the patient is not so wrong, not so "crazy" as some of our own *theories* have been!

Then our discussion took a historical turn, and we began to see how widespread and pervasive has been, in recent times, the belief that suffering is never "deserved," never creative and reconstructive. It can hardly be doubted that in many primitive societies the notion of accountability is overworked; and one can point to clear examples of the same sort of thing in the history of Western civilization. For example, not so long ago we held that physical illness and accidents were "God's judgment" rather than the wholly impersonal consequences of germs or other circumstances beyond the individual's control; and we also were inclined, until fairly recently, to suppose that all poverty must reflect sloth or other sins, rather than recognize social injustice and economic exploitation.

But now, in our reaction against this patent overextension of "moral" principle, have we not gone too far in the other direction? There is, as we know, a widespread tendency—sometimes called "scientism"—to assume that human beings cannot be "responsible" for *anything*, that we are all just cogs in a vast cause-and-effect complex and are in no way accountable for anything we do or anything that happens to us. Such a doctrine, aside from its lack of genuine scientific justification, is devastating: no society could long endure which thoroughly accepted it—and neither can an individual human being [cf. Mowrer, 1961].

As we look around us, at mid-twentieth century, two of the most distressing "symptoms" of our times are (a) confusion and apathy in the matter of moral values (witness the "beatnik" movement) and (b) an apparent paralysis with respect to the spectre of mental illness. Can it be that the two conditions are related and that they exist in such acute form *precisely because we have insisted upon separating them*? Perhaps mental *dis-ease* has a meaning and a potential which we fail to recognize.

The whole thrust of medicine is, of course, in the direction of the "alleviation of suffering"; and we are deeply grateful for most medical efforts and accomplishments. But when medicine extends this principle over into the moral realm, as it ostensibly does in its attempt to treat personality disorders, the results are far from reassuring. Psychoanalysis promised to deliver us from neurotic suffering by the bold expedient of reducing the "severity" of our consciences. Unable to make good this promise, analysis is on the wane; and psychiatry is now captivated by the chemical "tranquilizers." Pick up an issue of the *American Journal of Psychiatry* (as I recently did) and what do you find? Nine of the ten full-page or two-page advertisements in the front of the journal reading as follows: "control of emotional turbulence —luminal," "peace of mind—atarax," "calmness, co-operativeness—serpasil," "relief of anxiety—compazine," "valuable in all degrees of psychic disorder—trilafon," "intravenous anesthetic—pentothal," "relieves tension— equanil," "normalizes thinking—pacatal," "produces relaxation—sandril." The other ad was for a portable tape recorder! Combine with this the fact that such a large percentage of other forms of advertising are for those age-old "tranquilizers," alcohol and tobacco, and one sees that the diagnosis of our time as the "Aspirin Age" is a magnificent understatement. What would happen if modern man were forced to confront his guilt and insecurity for just one week without these masks and crutches? Would it destroy us completely or perhaps point the way to a saner and better life?

Historically, the church has been dedicated not to comfort but to *change*, redemption, rebirth. Ultimately its objective, no less than that of medicine, was to relieve suffering—yea, more, to bring salvation and joy. But it did not flinch from holding that sometimes suffering is the absolute and inescapable precondition for our transformation and redemption. What of the modern church? As child-rearing became permissive, religion also became "nonjudgmental" and obligingly eliminated Hell. God is now love and love alone, and judgment is old-fashioned. This past week a student put into my hands a weekly bulletin from one of our local Protestant churches which proclaims that God is "a generous, loving Father" whose "favor toward man is freely given" and takes the Roman Catholics to task for "emphasizing that God is a God of justice"!

Old Testament writers knew that God and parents and conscience can be justifiably angry and that we ignore them at our peril. In denying the moral implications of suffering and seeking to cushion ourselves against it, do we not misperceive and mismanage it in ways which, in the long run, can only spell disaster?

6

The New Challenge to our Churches and Seminaries:

I. A Question of Theory*

In the preceding chapters, attention has been mainly directed to the "crisis" in psychiatry and clinical psychology which has been occasioned by the pervasive acceptance of Freudian psychoanalysis, with its basically biological orientation and emphasis. In this chapter and the immediately succeeding ones, we now look, more explicitly, at the predicament of the churches and seminaries. At first slow to accept Freudianism, they are today displaying an astonishing reluctance to let go of it. This chapter gives some little-known facts about the history of the pastoral counseling movement and shows how, after a promising start in the right direction, it was deflected and distorted by psychoanalytic theory and nondirective counseling techniques.

Initially written, by invitation, for a well known religious periodical, this paper (and its sequel, see Chapter 7) was formally accepted and then mysteriously rejected. Did the latter action reflect defensiveness and reluctance to face up to some unpleasant facts? Or is there something basically inaccurate or perhaps unfair in the present analysis?

Has evangelical religion sold its birthright for a mess of psychological pottage? In attempting to rectify their disastrous early neglect of psychopathology, have the churches and seminaries assimilated a viewpoint and value system more destructive and deadly than the evil they were attempting to eliminate? As a psychologist and churchman, I believe the answer to these questions is in the affirmative. If so, the time is upon us for a searching reappraisal and a new plan of action.

But first let me correct a possible misapprehension.

---

* Published in *Foundations: A Baptist Journal of History and Theology*, October, 1960, 3, 335–347.

There are, I know, some ministers and seminary professors who would be only too happy to have done with the whole "clinical movement." I mean to give them no comfort; for I agree completely with Harry Emerson Fosdick when he says (in a recent article) that earlier in this century there was in Protestant theology and pastoral practice a gaping "vacancy" here which urgently needed to be "filled." The issue I wish to discuss is not the "vacancy"—that has been only too painfully real—but the question of whether the way in which it has been and is being filled is *sound*. I do not ask for less religious concern and effort for troubled persons but for *more*, of a different and, hopefully, *better* kind.

I.

In January of 1926, a then little-known man by the name of Anton T. Boisen published in *Christian Work* an article which has drastically modified theological education and changed church history. It was entitled "The Challenge to Our Seminaries," and its salient thesis was that "in mental disorders we are dealing with a problem which is essentially spiritual" (p. 8). Said Boisen:

> But of any such possibilities the Church is utterly oblivious. She takes no interest in cases of pronounced mental disorder. . . . We have therefore this truly remarkable situation—a Church which has always been interested in the care of the sick, confining her efforts to the types of cases [physical illness] in which religion has least concern and least to contribute, while in those types in which it is impossible to tell where the domain of the medical worker leaves off and that of the religious worker begins, there the Church is doing nothing (p. 9).

Since Fundamentalism preached only a hell to come and liberal theology preached no hell at all, both, argued Boisen, were "blind to the hell which is right before our eyes."

> When we remember that what we know today about the human body has come very largely through the study of disease conditions, is it any wonder that a Church which has so completely ignored the problem of the soul that is sick, is able to speak with so little authority concerning the laws of the spiritual world? (p. 10).

Boisen's plea, therefore, was that the seminaries start sending their students to mental hospitals for an "internship" of a few months or a year.

> For we have here a problem which must be studied from real life and not from books. It is, moreover, absolutely essential to have the co-operation of medical men, for here the provinces of religious and medical workers overlap, and the medical worker is now in possession of the field. The religious worker is a mere beginner, and he must be very careful not to embark on any half-attempt at "soul-healing" (p. 11).

In this way the young minister, upon leaving the seminary, would be able to bring "a new religious psychology" to the people, so that "the Church may once more come into its own and speak no longer as the scribes and Pharisees and interpreters of traditions but with the authority of the knowledge of the laws of the life that is eternal" (p. 12).

II.

The impact of this article and others of a similar nature was such that young theologians soon began going to mental hospitals for the type of internship which Dr. Boisen recommended; and by 1930 the "clinical movement" had gained sufficient momentum to warrant the formation of The Council for Clinical Pastoral Training, to be followed in 1944 by another organization called The Institute for Pastoral Care. Niebuhr, Williams, and Gustafson, in their 1957 book on *The Advancement of Theological Education*, comment upon these developments as follows:

> These two programs have between them initiated and been responsible for a considerable part of the clinical training of pastors for twenty-five years. Many schools have made use of these programs or devised similar ones (p. 123).
> The growth of this program is shown by the following data. In 1943 thirteen seminaries were related to some kind of clinical training program. Nine years later in 1952 there were forty-three schools. Reports made to the present study indicate that about three-fourths of the accredited seminaries, one-third of others, had either developed clinical training programs of their own by 1955 or sent students to the Council or Institute for such training (p. 124).

. . . the close connection between the traditional discipline of "pastoral theology" or "care of soul" and the psychological approach to human personality through first-hand experience of human problems is widely recognized today, and has given rise to one of the most influential movements in theological education, the emphasis on the preparation of the Christian pastor as counselor (p. 122).

There is, of course, no need to document extensively the contrast between the situation in 1926 and now as far as the resurgence of religious interest in personality disturbance is concerned; it is immediately apparent to anyone who has been a church member during this period, and only a little less so to others. However, there are signs of acute unrest and tension in this area, both in the churches and the seminaries; and it will be our objective in the remainder of this article to expose the theoretical issues here involved and, in the sequel to this discussion, to suggest a different practical approach to the whole problem.

III.

Not only did Anton Boisen, in his early articles, show the urgency of renewed religious interest in the mentally ill; he also, in 1936, published a highly readable and perceptive book, *The Exploration of the Inner World*, in which he outlined the theory of psychopathology which he believed most congruent with the great insights of religion and most likely to lead to more effective prevention and treatment. Elsewhere [see Chapter 2] I have reviewed Dr. Boisen's original conceptual scheme in detail. Here a few brief excerpts from his book will catch the tenor of this thinking:

The form of psychotherapy now most in the public eye is psychoanalysis. This in its aims is the exact opposite of faith healing. It has often been compared by its proponents to surgery, and major surgery at that. It is an attempt to lay bare and bring into clear consciousness the disowned sexual desires and cravings which it assumes have become detached from the conscious self and are responsible for the neurotic symptoms. Its aim is to make over the harsh conscience and the rigid ethical standards which have led to the disowning of these sex cravings so as to permit of their incorporation in the personality. To this end the psychoanalyst tries to get his patient to live through again his early experiences. The entire procedure is designed to detach the patient from his early loyalties in order to enable him to build up a new philosophy of life in which the dissociated cravings may be properly assimilated (pp. 243–44).

In all my efforts [as a hospital chaplain and therapist] I rely upon a simple principle derived from my theological training which seems to me far too little understood. I refer to the view that *the real evil in mental disorder is not to be found in the conflict but in the sense of isolation or estrangement.* It is the fear and guilt which result from the presence in one's life of that which one is afraid to tell. For this reason I do not consider it necessary to lower the conscience threshold in order to get rid of the conflict. What is needed is forgiveness and restoration to the fellowship of that social something which we call God (pp. 267–68).

I would furthermore [suggest] that our findings indicate that the sense of guilt, the self-blame and the emotional disturbance which accompany it are not themselves evils but attempts at a cure. The real evil is the failure to attain the level of adjustment called for in some new period of development and the short-circuiting of the vital energies through easy satisfaction (p. 281).

IV.

In retrospect, we now know that the foregoing were prophetic words. But they were not heeded. Instead, the basic assumption of Freudian psychoanalysis—namely, that psychoneurosis arises, not from moral weakness or failure, but from an excessive and irrational severity (or "disease") of the superego or conscience—gradually permeated and possessed the pastoral counseling movement. One of the earliest and most transparent indications of this victory of the Freudian view, as opposed to that advocated by Boisen, was the appearance in 1943 of Harry Emerson Fosdick's book, *On Being a Real Person.* Intended for laymen as well as religious leaders, this book achieved an immediate popularity and widespread influence.

In a chapter entitled "Handling Our Mischievous Consciences," Fosdick made his position clear:

Indiscriminate praise of conscientiousness is psychologically dangerous. Many people worry themselves into complete disintegration over moral trifles, and others have consciences so obtuse that they can get away with anything (p. 133).

Conscience is a tricky function of personal life . . . with equal facility it makes saints, lunatics, and bigots (p. 133).

Following one's conscience can be a distracting experience, and numberless people are torn to pieces by it (p. 134).

We are supposed to sail by conscience and yet we cannot trust it; instead of relying on the compass to keep our course straight, we must keep our compass straight, and that makes nervous sailing (p. 135).

Far from solving the problem of conscience, however, the acceptance of it is often only the beginning of our difficulty. Many do accept their consciences. They are disastrously conscientious. . . . The psychiatrists' offices fill up with people whose consciences are on the warpath, harassing them with worry and remorse over small scrupulosities (p. 143).

The mischief is that conscience can take advantage of its importance and can overbid its hand. . . . No good can come from this plus-activity of conscience, this hang-over of remorse; it spoils the life of the sufferer and darkens the skies of his family and friends. When conscience has fulfilled its function it ought naturally to stop, but commonly it persists, torturing its victim long after the torture has lost all value (p. 147).

Moralism deals with symptoms and condemns results; psychotherapy diagnoses causes and is concerned with cure (p. 152).

Conscience makes multitudes of people miserable to no good effect (p. 153).

That we need more conscientious people is a platitude, common but highly questionable. An immense amount of conscientiousness does more harm than good (p. 157).

Although Dr. Fosdick conceded that behind *some* "morbid conscientiousness" and apparent scrupulosity there may be real guilt, he stoutly maintained—and in so doing capitulated to the primal psychoanalytic premise —that in many other instances conscience is a real monster which complains and tortures the individual without just cause.

v.

In September of 1943, shortly after the publication of *On Being a Real Person*, Dr. Boisen wrote Dr. Fosdick expressing his admiration for and appreciation of many features of the book but deploring its acceptance of the Freudian doctrine of superego over-severity. Said Boisen:

The statement on page 154 that the censorious conscience that can be blighting when used on others can have a similar effect when used on oneself is undoubtedly true; not so, however, the statement on page 152 that self-condemnation is often the most misleading fact that can intrude itself. My observation is that the patient who condemns himself, even to the point of thinking he has committed the unpardonable sin, is likely to get well. It is the patient who blames others who does not get well. The one is a benign reaction, the other a malignant one. Self-blame, even when it leads to severe psychosis, means the recognition that something is wrong and the acceptance of one's responsibility for the difficulty. The emotional disturbance which follows is then analogous to fever or inflammation in the body. It is not an evil but a manifestation of nature's power to heal. . . .

For example, take the hypothetical case you describe on page 150. You refer to the sense of guilt manifested by this young man as a "needless and harmful intruder." If the young man in question were like most of those I have known, the pent-up volume of guilty fears would be instrumental in driving him to the minister's study and the relief he found there would come not so much thru anything the minister said to him as from what he said to the minister about a problem which for him was by no means a minor matter.

I wish that you might have done more toward clarifying the nature and function of conscience. Our psychoanalysts have discovered it and have much to say about it, but from my point of view their theories are far from adequate, while Dewey and Mead and Hocking are not given their rightful due.

In an article entitled "Niebuhr and Fosdick on Sin," which appeared in the *Chicago Seminary Register*, for March, 1944, Boisen repeated and elaborated these concerns. However, he was unable to stem the tide; and the Freudian notion that man sickens, not from sin but from excessive conscientiousness, continued to gain acceptance in theological circles.

VI.

As already noted, there is tension today in our seminaries and churches regarding the Freud-Fosdick position; but this position is clearly in the ascendancy, officially. Millions of ordinary church members have never accepted it, and many individual ministers and seminary teachers likewise deeply distrust it. But it has seemed that "science" was against them, and they have been reluctant to speak out for fear of "contradicting science"; whereas those who believed they were on the side of Psychological Truth have been boldly vocal. Their outspokenness could be illustrated at great length; but two recent examples will suffice. Dr. Carl Michalson, a professor of theology at Drew University, in the chapter on guilt in his *Faith for Personal Crises* (1959), writes as follows:

> Yes, the conscience (popularly conceived) is as ready to condemn us as our most malicious enemy would be. Our conscience is a "prattler," bent less upon our regeneration than upon our destruction. . . . It is our executioner, bent upon our destruction, only confirming our lie about ourselves and hiding from us the truth that we are in God's image, made to be responsible not to our conscience but to Him (p. 59).
> Christians are often scandalized by psychotherapists who seem to relax the moral standard in order to relieve the tension of their client's anxious guilt. The psychotherapist in this instance is a better interpreter of righteousness than many Christians are. . . . Moral flexibility may not in itself be healing but it does less damage than the tightening of the demands which are already cracking one's nature. There are times when aspirin is more healing than action. This is the gospel truth in "the power of positive thinking" (p. 61).

And The Reverend George Christian Anderson, Director of the Academy of Religion and Mental Health, in the first chapter of his book *Man's Right to be Human*, echoes this now familiar refrain. He says:

> Today, psychiatry and the new sciences of behavior compel us once again to examine the precepts by which we live, shocking and enraging those whose houses were built on the foundations of their fathers (p. 15).
> We are now beginning to ask whether our wrongdoing is sin or caused by emotional illness. . . . Health of mind depends on whether we can let these forces ["powerful needs for love, raging hostility," p. 19] come out without feeling excessively guilty or frightened by what erupts from within (p. 17).
> The psychological journey into our inner world [by means of psychoanalysis] helps us to experience our emotions without fear, to admit what we have denied, and to deny what we once believed. Psychiatry obviously must reveal our

morals, and measure the strength of the consequences of our religious faith (p. 18).

VII.

Quite aside from the palpable desertion of traditional Christian ideals and precepts which all such writings represent, there is the additional—and not inconsiderable —complication that secularists and scientists are themselves now busily re-evaluating the whole Freudian *Weldanschauung*.

In the book first published in German in 1938 and subsequently (1950) in English, with the title *Technique of Analytical Psychotherapy*, Wilhelm Stekel, an erstwhile Freudian, wrote:

> I contend that orthodox analysis has reached a crisis which betokens that the end is near, that collapse is approaching (p. xxiv).

And after reviewing many case histories in which it is apparent that real guilt, rather than a mere "guilt complex," was at the basis of the manifest morbidity, Stekel concluded:

> I have had many cases of the kind, but have merely selected a few to show that parapathic [neurotic] disorders may be diseases of the conscience [in a new sense]. The patient suppresses his remorse, tries to drown the voice of conscience, and feigns immunity. Nature takes vengeance (p. 327).

And more than a decade ago, quite unaware of the work of either Boisen or Stekel, the present writer (1950) was forced to take the following position:

> In essence, Freud's theory holds that anxiety comes from evil wishes, from acts which the individual would commit if he dared. The alternative view here proposed is that anxiety comes, not from acts which the individual would commit but dares not, but from acts which he *has* committed but wishes that he *had* not. It is, in other words, a "guilt theory" of anxiety rather than an "impulse theory" (p. 537).

What is the situation, in psychology and psychiatry, today? In another connection [Chapter 1], I have reviewed prevailing psychiatric opinion concerning psychoanalysis, typical of which is the following statement by Dr. Lawrence Kubie (1956):

> We [analysts] have no right to be for or against anything in this field. We have a right only to the most complete humility—humility that says we still know practically nothing about many important elements in the neurotic process or in the psychotherapeutic process (p. 103).

Also in 1957, at its annual convention, the American Psychological Association, for the first time in its history, sponsored a symposium on "Religion and Mental Health"; and in September, 1959, the same organization held a symposium on "The Place of the Concept of Sin in Psychotherapy" which attracted nation-wide attention [Chapter 3].

VIII.

If theologians will take the trouble to examine carefully what is thus happening in the secular professions and sciences on which they have so heavily drawn for their new Psychology, they will find that something like a revolution is in progress, which leaves them clutching Freudian doctrine to their breasts without either biblical or solid scientific support for it. The situation is well summarized in a paper ("Are Psychoanalysis and Religious Counseling Compatible?") which the New York psychologist, Lee R. Steiner, read at a meeting of the Society for the Scientific Study of Religion, held in November, 1958, at Harvard University:

> It is my impression from twenty years of study of where people take their troubles and why they seek out the sources they do,[1] that the ministry makes a tremendous mistake when it swaps what it has for psychoanalytic dressing. Through the ages the ministry has been the force that has at least attempted to keep morality alive. It would be a pity if, in one of the eras of greatest moral crisis, the clergy should suddenly abandon its strength for something that has no validity, no roots, and no value. It is my impression that they would do far better to cling to what they have. Judaism has endured for almost 6,000 years. Christianity for almost 2,000. Where will psychoanalysis be even 25 years from now? . . . I predict that it will take its place along with

[1] See Steiner (1945), *Where Do People Take Their Troubles?*

phrenology and mesmerism. Like them, psychoanalysis was the brain child of a highly inventive scientist, who was completely sincere in his belief that he was opening up a new world. We shall respect Freud for his efforts, as we do Gall and Mesmer. Like them, Freud had the germ of an idea which flared into a way of life for a time, but then vanished.[2]

Today we can no longer honestly accept Freud as the prophet which many theologians have tried to make of him. Instead, he is the Pied Piper who beguiled us into serious misconceptions and practices. In the sequel to this article, I shall try to suggest ways in which the churches and seminaries can recover lost ground in this area and build for a sounder future.

[2] Cf. Dallenbach (1955).

7

The New Challenge to our Churches and Seminaries:
II. The Problem of Action*

Here is a preliminary attempt to go beyond analysis and become action-oriented, to prescribe rather than merely diagnose. Any projected practical program always has to be tempered by circumstances and on-going experience, but the two suggestions made herein are at least promising beginnings. A friend in Educational Administration used to be fond of saying that action in a practical situation is never straight-ahead-according-to-plan. It is always somewhat opportunistic, a slight advance here, an unexpected development or opportunity there. But movement can occur if there is a clear goal and steady pressure towards it.

In 1960 the World Council of Churches announced a conference on ways of revising and revitalizing religious worship—a subject implementing the concerns expressed in the following chapter. In March, 1960, the ministers of the First Community Church of Columbus, Ohio, held the first of a projected series of workshops on new ways to use religion, in conjunction with psychology and social science, to "remove blocks to personal growth." A little later the National Council of Churches held a conference, with several secularists participating, on the place of religion in higher education. These developments are representative of a new "openness" to explore and change, if we can only lay hold of a sound and dependable rationale.

In Chapter 12 we shall go more deeply into some of the suggestions which are made in this chapter (see also Chapter 8).

In Part I of this article [Chapter 6], I have traced the brief history of the pastoral counseling movement and

* Published in *Foundations: A Baptist Journal of History and Theology*, October, 1960, 3, 335–347.

have shown it to have had four stages: (1) that of growing awareness (on the part of Boisen, Fosdick, and
others) of the failure of early 20th-century religion to
speak and minister to man's psychological and emotional
needs; (2) the initiation of the pastoral-counseling, or
"clinical," movement (largely through the work of
Boisen and his students) and Boisen's efforts, epitomized
in his 1936 book, *The Exploration of the Inner World*,
to give this movement a conceptual framework which
would be congruent with the traditional Judeo-Christian
ethic; (3) the blighting of this aim by the intrusion of
the Freudian doctrine that human beings sicken in mind
and soul, not from sin, but from their very excess of
piety (or "moralism"); and (4) current developments
in the sciences and secular professions which are casting
grave doubt upon the validity of the Freudian view and
thus placing many contemporary clergymen and seminarians in the awkward position of having "sold their
birthright."

It now appears that Boisen was right, that psychopathology is a moral problem, through and through, and
that it has gravitated into medical hands by default and
complacency on the part of the Christian ministry and
churches. Recently a church woman in Massachusetts
wrote me a letter which she concluded by saying, "Certainly if these ideas gain general acceptance, psychotherapy would be revolutionized." On the assumption,
substantiated in the earlier article, that these ideas *are*
"gaining acceptance," we shall here explore some of
the implications which follow for courses of action
which our churches and seminaries can pertinently consider and, hopefully, pursue.

I.

In the preceding article, I have called attention to
Dr. Boisen's 1926 article, "The Challenge to Our Seminaries," in which he urged seminary students to do an
internship in a mental hospital in order that they might
bring "a new religious psychology" to the people and
that "the Church may once more come into its own and
speak no longer as the scribes and Pharisees and interpreters of traditions but with authority of the knowledge
of the laws of the life that is eternal" (p. 12). And I
also cited the recent Niebuhr-Williams-Gustafson report

on *The Advancement of Theological Education* to show how widely this admonition is now being followed. But this new "clinical" program has been deflected from the course Dr. Boisen originally conceived for it and has taken on a strongly Freudian and neo-Freudian coloration. This, quite understandably, has created an uneasiness in our seminaries, which, however, has remained muted and is only now beginning to come out into the open. For example, in the report just cited, the authors guardedly say:

> Firsthand experience with persons in trouble is the basic material out of which Christian skill in care of souls must come. . . . Yet in spite of the ease with which this field can lead out and away from its theological center, there is a strong determination in the schools to keep the psychological approach to personality in close relation to the Church and its faith. There is indeed considerable *tension within some schools on the place of this field in the curriculum* (p. 122, italics added).

> Clinical training programs need the schools not only for students and financial support but *also as a source of constructive criticism* (p. 125, italics added).

> The pitfall is that [the student] may begin to "psychologize" everything and try to solve every problem of faith through psychological analysis (p. 127).

II.

The present situation is, I believe, a very serious one and far from what Dr. Boisen originally intended. During the clinical internship and in propaedeutic seminary courses, students are typically schooled in the view that psychopathology is only indirectly a religious concern. They are deeply indoctrinated with the view that neurosis and psychosis arise from too much "morality," rather than too little, and that the minister must carefully recognize his "limitations" in dealing with such problems.

The total impact of this experience has, it seems, not been a good one. Typically, the student returns to seminary either confused, by the manifest contradictions between his religious heritage and psychological and psychiatric doctrines, or with the feeling that here, in psychiatry and psychology, is a redemptive ("therapeutic") power exceeding anything that religion itself can offer. The result is that if and when the seminarian, as parish minister, later undertakes pastoral counseling, it is with the feeling that his "psychological methods" are something apart from his theology and Christian faith and that he can, at best, deal only with persons whose difficulties are relatively superficial. He is carefully instructed, both by members of the secular healing professions and by his own supervisors, on the importance of "knowing when to refer." In his own eyes as well as those of others, he is clearly a second- or third-class operator in this field; and even Niebuhr, Williams, and Gustafson bow to this prevailing state of affairs, when they say:

> We must add the warning that the student needs to learn the kinds of problems which require medical attention and which as pastor he should not try to handle. His ministry is to the person in his religious need (p. 128).

Has this type of program indeed taught our clergy to speak with authority, or as the scribes and Pharisees? [1]

III.

How ingrained the "psychiatric" view has become in the minds of many of our clergymen is reflected, with special clarity, in Anderson's recent book (also cited in the preceding article) entitled *Man's Right to Be Human*, with the equivocal subtitle, *To Have Emotions Without Fear*. Here the stock position is reiterated, that the psychologist, psychiatrist, psychoanalyst, social worker —indeed, almost anyone—is better equipped to deal with serious emotional problems than is the minister. If, as we now have reason to believe, all psychopathology (of the functional varieties) stems from moral *failure*, how fantastic all this is! And yet many ministers have what may be termed a "trained incapacity" and educated reluctance to really come to grips with the problem of mental illness. Instead, they dutifully "refer," as indicated in the following excerpts from the book just cited:

> It was evident that Joe was suffering from a serious neurosis. As soon as Joe was gone I picked up the phone

[1] In an attempt to escape the pall of psychological and medical domination in this area, there is now a tendency on the part of some writers to speak of *Pastoral Theology*, rather than of Pastoral Psychology or Pastoral Psychiatry. But it is doubtful if a *theological* emphasis is so much what is needed as a sounder, more defensible psychological one, although it is realized that a valid absolute distinction here is not possible.

and called a psychiatrist I knew and explained the situation.
He agreed to see Joe the next day. . . . I was able to make
her [Joe's sister, with whom he lived] see that Joe was not
as immoral as he was sick, and that he needed love and understanding, and medical care, too, more than ever (p. 141).

"Most men are beasts; only my Lord in heaven is worthy
of my purity," she continued. I suggested that she come
see me again, but in the meantime I referred her to a
clinical psychologist for some vocational tests. . . . It was
obvious that the young woman was handicapped by a severe
neurosis involving excessive guilt concerning her sexual feelings. Inasmuch as psychotherapy was indicated, the girl was
referred to a psychiatrist who was able to help her accept
her sexuality in a healthy manner (p. 172).

A man came to see me about his wife's growing coolness
toward him. . . . After counseling with both of them individually, I discovered that the wife really loved her husband
very deeply even though she abhorred his sexual claims. I
referred both of them to a psychiatrist for further professional help (p. 176).

This is typical of what is supposed to be "good practice" in the ministry today. And not long ago a young
clergyman who had just come to our community informed
me that he had been advised, in seminary, not only to
be sure to "know when to refer" but also to be very
careful in his sermons not to say anything that would
make anyone "feel guilty." People have too much guilt
already, he had been told; and if you talk about sin and
guilt and moral responsibility from the pulpit, you only
increase the danger of "neurosis." I wonder if this young
man's professors know these lines from page 109 of T. S.
Eliot's play, *The Elder Statesman*:

You think that I suffer from a morbid conscience,
From brooding over faults I might well have forgotten.
You think that I'm sickening, when I'm just recovering!

IV.

What the average theologian and religious worker apparently does not know and is reluctant to recognize is
the extent to which the system of concepts and practices
in which he has been schooled, during his training in
pastoral psychology, is today in a state of deterioration
and impending collapse. From the standpoint of those
of us who know these developments *from the inside*,

it is tragic to see the clergy continue to pay homage to what, in reality, is rapidly becoming a hollow shibboleth. For more than a decade, now, I have been pointing to the logical and empirical incongruities in psychoanalytic theory, on which so much psychiatry and clinical psychology is directly or indirectly founded; and in addition to my already published books and articles in this field, I invite the reader's attention to various reprints and mimeographed papers which will be supplied upon request [now assembled as the chapters of this book].

But in these misgivings concerning psychoanalysis and the sense of untapped potential within the great traditions and insights of religion itself, I am by no means alone, as has been indicated in the preceding article. And to that line of evidence I wish now to add further testimony of failure on the part of that profession in which theologians have placed such supreme faith. Recently I was talking to a supervising psychologist in the Veterans Administration who expressed the most profound disillusionment with prevailing psychotherapeutic methods and referred to VA mental hospitals as "sick institutions." And Dr. H. C. Solomon had this to say in the 1958 presidential address to the American Psychiatric Association:

> Large mental hospitals are antiquated, outmoded, and rapidly becoming obsolete. We can still build them *but we cannot staff them*; and therefore we cannot make true hospitals of them. . . . I do not see how any reasonably objective view of our mental hospitals today can fail to conclude that they are bankrupt beyond remedy. I believe therefore that our large mental hospitals should be liquidated as rapidly as can be done in an orderly and progressive fashion (p. 7).
> If my description is correct and my projections reasonably accurate, a new attack on the "care and custody" of the long-term ill must be attempted. Unpalatable as it may appear, one must face the fact that we are doing little by way of definite treatment of a large number of our chronic hospital population. It is not even the case that we are providing them with first-class environmental care, much less loving and tender care. Therefore, I suggest we take a new look at the problem (p. 8).

Somewhat parenthetically and without elaboration, Dr. Solomon observes:

Our young physicians specializing in psychiatry are not heading toward our large hospitals, nor are the other categories of personnel. In many of our hospitals about the best that can be done is to give a physical examination and make a mental note on each patient once a year, and often there is not even enough staff to do this much (p. 7).

Despite government-sponsored subventions and scholarships, the men and women who are today being trained in psychiatry are not going into state and VA mental hospitals for one major reason. It is not that the need is not great; they can make *more money* in private practice! There are, to be sure, some dedicated and idealistic psychiatrists and clinical psychologists. But the plain fact is that professional psychotherapy is, in general, *a business*; and if it turns out that what the patient secretly hopes to buy (and the therapist implicitly promises to sell) is a cheap form of forgiveness and expiation [cf. Chapter 10], the "therapeutic" transaction is a very dubious business—as Katie Lee slyly implies when she sings (in "Shrinker Man"):

> I've been on one of those "complex" tours;
> I want you to make my problems yours.
> Now gimmie one of them cut-rate cures,
>   Shrinker Man!

Can an enterprise that thus measures in dollars and cents its efforts to minister to sick minds and souls continue indefinitely to command our respect and confidence?

v.

If we have now accurately diagnosed the difficulty, what's to be *done* about it? In the over-all and ultimate sense, I have to say that I do not know. Certainly the total situation calls for courage, social inventiveness, and insights which I do not possess. But I do have two suggestions to make.

I think we now have to recognize that Protestantism has, on the whole, handled the problem of guilt very badly and that the present critical situation is a natural culmination of four centuries of bumbling, indecision, and confusion on this score. As a first step, therefore, toward rectifying our predicament, I believe our churches ought, as Harry Emerson Fosdick argued (somewhat inconsistently) as early as 1927, to return to the practice of confession. We have tried to ignore and by-pass the very notion of guilt and sin; but it won't work. The gospel of sin and salvation (redemption) is not one of bondage but of liberation, hope, and strength; and we must, I believe, return to it in all seriousness.

Pastoral counseling, as presently practiced, is, to be sure, itself a *form* of "confession," but it has two major weaknesses: (1) it is episodic, voluntary, and often belated and therefore lacks the *preventive* function which regular, prescribed confession (when practiced conscientiously and earnestly) has; and (2) "counseling" is now very largely patterned on secular psychotherapy, with its emphasis on "acceptance" and "insight," and does not take sin really seriously. People do not merely "talk" themselves into sin; they *act*. And by the same token, I do not believe anyone ever talks himself *out* of sin. Again there must be action, and this action must involve not only confession, of an ultimately open type, but also "atonement." Confession without a sober program of expiation can be dangerous, in the sense of causing the individual to be overwhelmed with guilt and self-hatred. And this is one of the unrecognized factors that makes many present-day religious counselors so insecure and unconfident. But if we can only understand man's true "condition," ways will be found to overcome the apparent obstacles [see later chapters].

VI.

My other suggestion has to do with a possible change in emphasis in the "missionary" concern of our churches and the problem of staffing our state mental hospitals, which has already been alluded to.

The legal and social climate being what it is at present, clergymen are justifiably afraid to try to go "all the way" with emotionally disturbed persons. Sometimes it is virtually inevitable that an individual pass through a psychotic interlude (for reasons already mentioned) on his way to personal transformation and recovery. It is, of course, not uncommon for psychiatrists themselves to have in treatment patients whom they eventually have to commit to mental hospitals. But if a person is seeing a religious counselor and becomes actively psychotic, the counselor is immediately vulnerable. *He* made the person worse; he should have *referred* the patient; etc., etc.

In an attempt to find a solution to this intolerable situation, a few denominations are experimenting with mental hospitals of their own. Without state support, these are, of course, extremely expensive to operate; and such reports as I presently have indicate that even these institutions rather pride themselves on the fact that they are conducted along "approved psychiatric lines," rather than with any great new insight born of religious precept and conviction.

Alternatively, I would like to see our churches take mental hospitals as *a major object of missionary effort.* Isn't it a little awkward for us to be so concerned about the benighted state of those in foreign lands when the size and condition of our "insane asylums" stand out like great festering sores on the conscience of our own nation? I know a state mental hospital (not atypical) with a population of 4500 patients without a single trained psychiatrist on the staff. Such physicians as there are, are immigrants or have for some other reason commonly failed to obtain a state license for general medical practice. And there is *one* Protestant chaplain and *one* Catholic priest for this "town," where the religious and spiritual needs are surely far greater than in a normal community of comparable size.

So why not let the churches also start at the *other* end of the line, with persons who have already hit bottom; who are in a protected environment, where the only direction they *can* move is up? Here the religious worker can be associated with a person's rise, rather than his fall. And imagine the gratitude, loyalty, and enthusiasm which would be generated in persons who felt that religious insights and practices had saved them from the hell of mental illness!

Elsewhere [Chapter 2] I have argued, with Boisen, that in neurosis and psychosis the afflicted individual is in a moral and spiritual crisis, and that in no other circumstances does the experience of God become such a vivid reality. (See also Frederick West's book, *Light beyond Shadows!*) But the common perception is that so-called mental "illness" really is an illness and has nothing to do with either God or the Devil. Is this progress or one of the greatest popular fallacies of all time? Can it be that we have come to doubt the very existence of God because we do not know where to look for Him and how to recognize His most tangible manifestations? [2] If churches today made a determined effort to come to grips with the problem of mental illness in this country, they could not only perform a great human service; they would also, I predict, discover a new and vitalizing force which will forever elude them at the more superficial levels of religious ritual and observance. As a friend of mine, who is a psychiatrist but also actively religious, recently remarked, "Unless you face the demons, you never hear the angels!"

[2] Cf. Robinson (1928).

8

Psychopathology and the Problem of Guilt, Confession, and Expiation*

If any one chapter is nuclear to this book as a whole, it is the present one. Here we come to grips, empirically, with the question: Does psychopathology involve real *or only "imaginary" guilt? If the psychoneurotic's guilt is not* real, *the whole argument collapses. If it is, then the necessity for a long and complicated series of ideological and institutional changes weighs heavily upon us.*

Some readers, upon completing this chapter, may feel dissatisfied at the absence of any effort to provide a formal definition of "real" guilt, sin, evil. Concern with this problem will come in due course. But what is more immediately important, it seems, is to get some feel for the raw data. Without a strong sense of the pragmatic and factual, definition making can be both tedious and sterile.

The case material and other clinical evidence here cited is not, of course, submitted as definitive "proof" of a universal or absolute principle but only as illustrative of a possibility. Already there is a decided inclination to concede that real guilt can *be determinative in personality disorder. The question is whether it* always is. *The present writer is entirely willing to leave the answer to this question open, pending further research and experience. But even if guilt is real (rather than illusory) in only half or a third of all personality disturbances, it still constitutes an enormous practical problem, with*

---

* In addition to serving as the first of the E. T. Earl Lectures at the 1960 Pastoral Conference sponsored by the Pacific School of Religion, February 23–25, in Berkeley, California, this paper was read before the St. Louis Society of Neurology and Psychiatry, April 1, 1958, and at the Symposium on Current Trends in Psychology held by the University of Pittsburgh, March 12–13, 1959. It has also been published in *Current Trends in Psychology*, X, University of Pittsburgh Press, 1960.

which neither the churches nor secular professions are presently dealing at all adequately. And if it should turn out that real guilt (however disguised or displaced) is the chief etiological factor in all psychopathology, the situation will be still more disconcerting and challenging.

Historically the prevailing view, in literature and non-literate societies alike, has been that man sickens in mind, soul, and perhaps even body because of unconfessed and unatoned real guilt—or, quite simply, from what an earlier era knew as a state of "disgrace" or "sin." However, as a result of complicated historical reasons which have been explored elsewhere [Chapters 9 and 11], this view has, in our time, fallen into disrepute. The church, badly weakened by internal strife and injudicious opposition to science, quietly relinquished its traditional claim to competence in the domain of the sick soul and unprotestingly accepted the emphasis of 19th-Century psychiatry on constitutional and biochemical factors.

It was, therefore, in this remarkable setting that psychoanalysis had its inception and rapid growth. As Freud observed in his autobiography (1935), toward the end of the last century there were, in every large European city, "crowds of neurotics, whose number seemed further multiplied by the manner in which they hurried, with their troubles unsolved, from one physician to another" (p. 27). The church had, in effect, turned a deaf ear to the needs of these people; and the common forms of medical and psychiatric treatment, which were predicated on a somatic conception of personality disorder, were magnificently ineffective. The situation thus called for a boldness which Freud supplied in the form of a clever compromise between the traditional moral view of personality disturbance and medical preconceptions. Guilt, he hypothesized, was indeed a factor in neurosis but it was a false, unrealistic, and crippling guilt which, as a result of a too strict and restricting socialization of the individual, impeded the normal flow of certain instinctual energies, notably those of sex and aggression. So the psychoanalytic physician set out to cure neurotic individuals by championing the rights of the body in opposition to a society and moral order which were presumed to be unduly harsh and arbitrary.

There was, of course, no lack of individuals who were willing to be saved by this plausible-sounding and pleasant philosophy—and who were willing to pay for it, handsomely. Thus, both patients and practitioners of the art were assured. But the day of reckoning is upon us. Our mental hospitals are now, alas, full of persons who have had this new form of treatment and not profited from it; and among them, their erstwhile therapists, and the general public alike there is growing disillusionment and alarm. Once again we are in a period of sober reappraisal; and it is the purpose of this paper to suggest one way of re-thinking the problem which, although in some respects very costly, nevertheless promises a form of redemption more radical and generally applicable than anything we have known in the recent past.

As the title of this paper implies, it will be our plan to consider, first, the possibility that in psychopathology guilt is *real* rather than illusory ("delusional"); then we shall explore the correlative proposition that the aim of communication and self-disclosure in the therapeutic situation is not mere understanding and insight (in the Freudian sense of these terms) but a changed, repentant view of oneself; and finally we shall examine evidence for believing that, however necessary they may be, contrition and confession are not alone enough to restore psychic and moral equilibrium and must be followed by meaningful, active forms of atonement or restitution.

I. HOW REAL IS THE NEUROTIC'S GUILT?—
A QUESTION OF FACT

Freud held that, as a result of a too intensive socialization, some individuals develop so great a fear of their sexual and hostile feelings that, eventually, they even deny these feelings access to consciousness and that it is the alarm which the ego feels when these impulses clamor for recognition and expression (i.e., the danger, as Freud called it, of the "return of the repressed") that generates the characteristic neurotic affects of depression, anxiety, and panic. In 1950 the present writer (see Chapters 18–22) hypothesized that in neurosis it is actually the individual's *conscience* that has been repudiated and "repressed" rather than his "instincts," thus shifting the emphasis from Freud's *impulse* theory of neurosis to a *guilt* theory. Actually, as is now evident, this position had been anticipated by Runestam (1932), Boisen (1936), and Stekel (1938), and it now seems to be steadily gaining in acceptance. However, the doctrine of repression, upon which the difference in opinion here hinges, is a subtle one and not easily amenable to objective verification, so the issue has remained a debatable one [see Chapter 2].

But there is another way of putting the problem which makes it more immediately researchable. According to Freud and his followers, the neurotic is in trouble, not because of anything actually wrong which he has *done*, but merely because of things he would *like* to do but, quite unrealistically, is *afraid* to. By contrast, the other view is that in neurosis (and functional psychosis), the individual has committed tangible misdeeds, which have remained unacknowledged and unredeemed and that his anxieties thus have a realistic social basis and justification.

So conceived, the difference between the two positions can be empirically studied with some precision. According to the Freudian view, the neurotic should have a history of something like saintliness; whereas, according to the other position, he should have a record (albeit a carefully concealed one) of actual and incontestable misconduct and perversity. This issue should by all means be submitted to systematic investigation on a scale corresponding to its significance. But I confess that, for myself, I am already pretty well persuaded what the results would be and will here merely cite a few examples of the kinds of evidence which is already widely available on this score and which I, personally, find convincing.

In the summer of 1956, a manuscript was transmitted to me which has now been published in the *Journal of Abnormal and Social Psychology* (Anonymous, 1958), for which I wrote the following brief introduction. The paper, I should say, is entitled "A New Theory of Schizophrenia."

This remarkable paper was written some two years ago by a then 34-year-old man residing in a closed ward in one of our large VA hospitals with a diagnosis of "paranoid schizophrenia." Soon after the original manuscript came into my hands (through a former student), I had it mimeographed and, in the interim, as occasion arose, have obtained reactions thereto from several clinical psychologists, psychiatrists, and theologians. The evaluations fall into two categories: some hold that the paper is just what it purports to be, an original and highly reasonable *theory* of schizophrenia—while others insist that it is a classical exhibit of the *disease itself*.

The present judgment of the author, now no longer hospitalized, is that his paper, as it stands, is probably valid as far as it goes but needs to be elaborated and extended in certain ways. It is hoped that his further thinking in this connection can be separately published at a later date. In the meantime, readers will be free to form their own opinions as to whether the production presented herewith is an essentially valid, albeit perhaps partial, theory of schizophrenia—or just a "phenomenological perspective." . . .

Here it need only be added that the author of the following essay has a history of personal waywardness and perversion (hence the anonymity) which could easily support his original thesis. He regards the present document as largely an expression of unconscious processes, rather than as something that he carefully reasoned out. It was written, he says, "while I was still following signals and colors; some of it was almost automatic writing." The author gives additional information about himself at the end of the paper.

Before proceeding with a synopsis of the paper proper, it will be well to present the following information, which the author himself gives as his "qualifications" for writing such a paper. He lists them thus:

Nearly four years of psychotherapy.
Nearly two years of living in mental hospitals.
Observation of my mother, who is now hospitalized for the fourth time.
Twelve to fifteen years of self-analysis.
A B.A. degree and one year of graduate work in psychology with philosophy as a minor.
99th percentile on the Graduate Record Examination in psychology.
A nearly life-long desire to contribute to knowledge, especially to solve the problem of mental illness.

But now, to return to the essay itself. Near the outset the author—whom we shall know as Tim Wilkins—says:

I propose that the motive force of schizophrenic reactions is *fear*, just as fear motivates, according to Freud, neurotic mechanisms—but with this difference: in the case of schizophrenia, the chronic fear is more properly called terror, or concealed panic, being of the greatest intensity; and second, as is not the case in neurosis, the fear is conscious; third, the fear itself is concealed from other people, the motive of the concealment being fear. In neurosis a sexual or hostile drive, pointing to the future, is defended against. In schizophrenia, by my view, detection by others of a guilty deed, the detection pointing to the past, is defended against (pp. 2–3).

One of the things that gives this document particular authenticity, for me, is the way in which the author here accepts, without question, the validity of Freud's theory of neurosis but then goes on to report his own very different inductions about schizophrenia. By 1946 or '47, when Wilkins had his last contact with academic psychology, the Freudian theory of neurosis was still very much in vogue; and, writing in 1956, Wilkins seems to have been quite unaware how widely that theory was being replaced by an alternative view quite similar to his own. The fact that Wilkins apparently did not know of these developments, as far as the theory of neurosis was concerned, therefore gives his formulations concerning the schizophrenic psychoses special cogency and independence—and constitutes, perhaps, still another indication of the weakness of the classical Freudian position.

But what, more specifically, *is* Wilkins' theory of schizophrenia? As much as possible it will be presented in Wilkins' own words.

My hypothesis [says Wilkins] may be called the Dick Tracy theory loosely in honor of the familiar fictional, human bloodhound of crime.

Motivated in the very first place by fear, the schizophrenic psychoses originate in a *break with sincerity*, and not in the classically assumed "break with reality." The patient's social appetite (an instinctive drive in primates, I believe), including love and respect for persons and society, is consciously anticathected or forsaken and ultimately repressed with the passage of time, since full satisfaction of sociality entails, more or less, communicative honesty, faith, and intimacy. Also, the tension set up in interpersonal intimacy by the withholding of emotionally important (although perhaps logically irrelevant) information causes unbearable pain. This repression of sociality accounts for the well-known "indifference" of schizophrenics. But if safety can be achieved by means of "perjury" alone without great discomfort, then no further defenses are adopted. Perjury is here defined as avoiding telling the whole truth and nothing but the truth. If, for many possible reasons, perjury is not an adequate and comfortable guarantee of safety, as it usually is not, then "cutting" of social contacts is progressively pursued—all in the interest of safety in respect to avoiding possible punishment. Suppression and repression of the social appetite or instinct is thus central to schizophrenia. I believe that repression of sexual and hostile drive is *not* primary in schizophrenia, although it is secondary, as will be explained further on.

Schizophrenia is the cultivation of a lie. A lie is "proved" to be the "Truth." The real truth is that the schizophrenic is responsibly guilty for some crucial misdeeds. . . .

In my view a large amount of the damage to the schizophrenic's self-esteem results from his contemplation of his own vicious insincerity—which damage is more an effect than a cause of his disease. His unethical defense mechanisms cause him deep shame and fear of loss of others' esteem. In addition, the primary deeds—whose exposure and punishment are avoided by the disease—are shameful. . . .

More broadly speaking, schizophrenia shares with all functional mental illness the ultimate danger of punishment meted out by men, demigods, or gods. Common punishments feared are the being deprived of love of kith or kin, loss of social status, financial security, etc., and especially in the case of schizophrenia the more violent punishments such as being abominated by kith or kin, bodily mutilation, imprisonment, lynching, execution.

This abandonment of social ties and good feeling, in the interest of personal safety, is sometimes starkly simple, as in mutism, but is usually supplemented by the development of "phony" social behavior, that is to say, designedly cryptic or misleading expressions of interests, sentiments, opinions; designedly unfriendly "friendliness;" asking only questions to which the answers are already known; the limitation of conduct to carefully self-criticized, self-rehearsed stratagems, etc. The patient has aggressed, ultimately in self-defense, by means of an undeclared, passive, preventive "war" against his fellow men, and in the interest of preventing defeat (positive victory is soon sensed to be hopeless of attainment) most of his knowledge and sentiments, and indeed his spontaneous behavioral tendencies, have been classified "top secret." Whatever words he actually uses are employed, thus, as self-defensive weapons. My Dick Tracy theory offers the explanation that high reaction time results from "biding time" in the service of caution.[1] Time is needed in order to creatively choose a "phony" (not spontaneous, not honest, not satisfying—except with respect to fear) response that will maximally conceal the patient's mental life and thus insure safety.

A semi-instinctive deceptive stratagem leads schizophrenics, like pursued rabbits, to "zigzag," thus baffling the pursuer's expectations. Unpredictability is the stock-in-trade fetish of schizophrenics. The proximate goal is to avoid being understood. The ultimate goal is to avoid punishment. They "nonwant" punishment (pp. 227–228).

My hypothesis diverges from orthodox theory, I believe, in insisting that a large part of the schizophrenic's fear is not a symptom and is not repressed, but is the main pathogenic force and is accessible to consciousness and even verbalization were the psychotic to violate his more or less conscious policy of dissembling.

There are understandable reasons why others may not have developed this view sooner. The theorist is naturally made to appear somewhat hard-hearted and accusatory [see Chapter 2]. The families and others related to the schizophrenic would naturally resent the implication of crime. . . . [And] it is easy to imagine and believe that physicians and psychologists would not enjoy making a career of being accessories after the fact or having their work open to such interpretation in the sociological "climate" afforded by present-day attitudes. Nor would professional healers in general enjoy arranging for prosecution of patients.

In other words, this theory, even more so than Freud's sexual emphasis, by its very nature would stand to be unpopular all around, both to the patients and the healers and the social group which surrounds them both. In fact, were it not that the truth promises to be practically invaluable in the long run, I would hope that my theory is not true.

As Freud found Shakespeare's Hamlet to be representative of neurosis, I take Shakespeare's Lady Macbeth to typify schizophrenic psychoses. The motto of the schizophrenic might well be, "Out, damned spot!" and that of the therapist working with schizophrenics, "Find the crime!" (p. 228).

---

[1] The author is here alluding to a study of reaction time in schizophrenics with which he was familiar.

There then follow sections with these titles: "Schizophrenia and Criminality Compared," "On Crime and Punishment," "The Theory and Types of Schizophrenia," and "Schizophrenia, A Social Disease," in which further empirical evidence is mobilized in support of the theory and implications drawn which might be tested by further inquiry. And, toward the end of the section last cited, we find this wistful yet trenchant passage:

> My theory makes schizophrenics out, in a sense, to be villains. Yet obviously they would be bungling villains, and the very botching of their lives strongly suggests forceful extenuating circumstances, since without tremendous pressures people seldom, presumptively, destroy what they love as much as all people love themselves originally.
>
> Irrelevantly, it is pleasant to say that human beings are lent dignity (of a rather evil sort, if my theory is true) if one credits the schizophrenics of the human race with being real people who have fallen into disease by having failed to make the right decisions at the right time in regard to problems which even our philosophers and theologians have not solved in the quiet of their studies with the help of the written words of many other minds—while the schizophrenics failed under enormous, frantic pressures, as is typically the case (p. 233).

Then there is a section entitled "Thoughts on Therapy" and, finally, a "Summary," which reads, in part, as follows:

> So what is a schizophrenic? In brief, he is a terrified, conscience-stricken crook, who has repressed his interest in people, unavowedly insincere and uncooperative, struggling against unconscious sexual perversion. He is of no mean Thespian ability. And his favorite Commandment is that which one nowadays facetiously calls the Eleventh Commandment, "Thou shalt not get caught."
>
> Attempts to expose him may only drive him further "underground." But a knowledge of his true nature will surely lead, someday, to somebody's discovering a sure, quick, effective and enduring cure (p. 236).

As already indicated, there are those who insist that the sense of guilt and wrong-doing which the author of this paper stresses is itself pathological; and some would even hold that the misdeeds to which the schizophrenic person points, if real, are an early *expression* of disease, rather than a cause thereof. But this position has the logical defect of making *all* misconduct interpretable in this way and thus obliterates the whole concept of personal and moral responsibility. Moreover, there are now psychiatrists, including some very eminent ones, who feel that this view is unsound even when limited to the most obviously "sick" individuals and that an entirely different orientation is needed. For example, after the publication of Tim Wilkins' paper, Dr. Karl Menninger (1958) wrote as follows:

> I very much liked the article on schizophrenia . . . in the September issue of THE JOURNAL OF ABNORMAL AND SOCIAL PSYCHOLOGY. I wish you would tell [the author] that I think it is fine and that it would be even a little better, in my opinion, if he would not try to distinguish between schizophrenia and other groups of symptoms. Essentially all mental illness must be a reaction to some kind of feeling of rupture with the social environment, and of course it is typical of many patients to identify this with their own aggressive intent or even aggressive acts for which, as [the author] says, they feel guilty and about which they are defensive and evasive and insincere.

Or consider this observation, reported by Hock & Polatin (1949) in connection with their study of a large group of borderline—or what they prefer to call "pseudo-neurotic"—schizophrenics:

> In all the writers' cases, they observed that the patient usually told of a great many sexual preoccupations showing autoerotic, oral, anal, homosexual and heterosexual tendencies, and ideas which sometimes resembled a textbook of *psychopathia sexualis*. These polymorphus perverse manifestations, this chaotic organization of the patient's sexuality, the writers feel, is rather characteristic of these schizophrenic cases. Marked sadistic or sado-masochistic behavior is often linked with this sexual material. This is especially true in patients who rather overtly and without restraint, express incestuous ideas. Many of these patients, especially under sodium amytal, verbalize these ideas freely, or express them freely in drawings (p. 253).

Recently a state hospital conducted an all-day institute for clergymen for which the head of the Social Service Department had prepared a case history of a 33-year-old woman who, it was felt, rather well typified entering patients. For a period of two years, this woman had been having an affair with her brother-in-law; she had on one occasion assaulted her husband with a butcher knife; and on another occasion had thrown a small child over a backyard fence. Finally she became suicidal and had to be hospitalized.

And so might one continue, indefinitely, to mobilize evidence that sin and emotional sickness are no strangers to one another and that it is only by flagrant disregard of the clinical facts that one can imagine that neurotic and functionally psychotic individuals have been too thoroughly socialized and are the victims of an unduly severe, oppressive morality. Therefore, although it is realized that the evidence cited will probably not be sufficient to convince anyone holding a strongly contrary view, it will be accepted here as typical of a much larger body of facts which justify further consideration of the view that mental illness is a social and moral illness and, in the final analysis, capable of remediation only along social and moral lines.

II. GUILT, REMORSE, AND CONFESSION

If it be true that emotionally ill persons are typically guilty persons, i.e., persons with *real* guilt rather than mere guilt *feelings*, the question very naturally arises as to what can be *done* to alleviate such a state of affairs. Everyone apparently has an intuitive compulsion to admit, or confess, his guilt to others; but this is a very painful act and is likely to occur only under great urgency. A dramatic instance of confession, and the conflict it involves, is given in the following paragraphs. They are taken from Standal & Corsini's (1959) book, *Critical Incidents in Psychotherapy*. I may say that the counselor here reporting is not identified, and the client is known only as "Joan." The counselor begins by giving the background facts:

> Joan is a nineteen year old college freshman. She was first seen while she was attending Junior College. The school psychologist had diagnosed her as a Paranoid Schizophrenic on the basis of a Rorschach test and had referred her for

psychotherapy to a counseling center which uses a client-centered approach.

The therapist to whom Joan was assigned (the present author), noted no psychotic symptoms until the sixth interview when she had an hallucination and expressed some bizarre ideas. After this interview, the therapist asked for a consultation with a psychiatrist which was followed by a joint interview with the patient and continuing consultation during the course of treatment.

The critical incident described occurred in the fourteenth interview. Joan had been seen initially for eight interviews, followed by a month and a half of summer vacation, and then five more interviews before she left town to go to a state university. She had been at the university for one week when she called the therapist and said she wanted to come back during the weekend for an appointment. One was set for five o'clock on Saturday.

Joan arrived almost on time, breaking a precedent of coming consistently twenty to thirty minutes late. She said she was quite disturbed and had tried to reach me twice during the afternoon but I wasn't there.

I asked her how much time she would like. (Our previous interviews had all been for whatever was left of fifty minutes after her late arrival.) I opened the possibility of a longer interview in reaction to her apparent degree of disturbance and the inaccessibility of the clinic to her new residence at the university. She asked, "What do you mean?" I said, "I wonder if you would like more than an hour today?" She said, "Yeah, I would." I asked her, "Well, how much time would you like?" She did not try to answer the question so I said, "Suppose we continue until we both get hungry and it's time to go home for supper."

She began then talking about her experience at the university. She described the loneliness that she felt—the isolation. Nobody really loved her. She just felt all alone in the world. Life was so depressing that she couldn't work up interest in anything. She didn't have the push to do anything. If she had the push, she thinks she would commit suicide. If the future were merely an extension of the present, then it would not be worth living for. She was expressing a deep despair when she began to pull herself together again. There would be some hope if she could change herself. She began to feel that maybe she did have the possibility for changing.

During a pause in this working through of feeling, I wondered about the time. Taking out my watch, I discovered that it was six-thirty and that we had been together for an hour and a half. I put my watch on the desk and asked her, "How much more time do you want?" She didn't answer. The watch sounded loud ticking away, so I put it back in my pocket. We went on until about seven, when I began to feel weak and wasn't following her very well. I said this to her and she looked up at me like a scared rabbit. She smiled in a forced way and began putting on her coat as if preparing to leave. I said, "You looked frightened when I suggested it might be time to stop." She nodded. I said, "Almost as if you thought I was rejecting you then." She said, "Yes, that's what it looked like to me." Then she pulled her coat together over her chest. Her hands clenched strongly on the coat and she started to stare at the wall. Her eyes got red but no tears came. She began to tremble. I did not understand what was happening and said, "It seems as if the feelings you have now are making you afraid." She just nodded without looking at me. Her trembling and staring went on for about eight minutes. Then she stood up in front of me. I asked her if she wanted to go home. She looked at me, smiled again in a mechanical fashion and shook her head "no." Then she began wringing her hands, staring at the wall and shaking all over. From time to time her body would lean toward me and then lean away. My heart was beating like a trip hammer. I didn't understand what was happening to her. I was afraid that she might be going into a psychotic break. After about ten minutes of throbbing silence, I said, "It's hard for me to understand what you are feeling." Then she said that she was looking at the lambs on the wall, the faces of the lambs. (There was a flower print on the wall.) "They have two eyes. One is a mean eye and the other is a kind eye. I see the faces of my mother and my grandmother. They are telling me to control myself and I hate them" (pp. 38–40).

When I have previously presented this material orally, I have usually stopped at this point and asked for the impressions of others as to what, precisely, was going on here. Even a group of laymen will come through with a fairly accurate appraisal. They will see, first of all, the thinly veiled seductiveness of the client: her avowed loneliness and vagueness about when she needs to leave. When the therapist tries to force the latter issue, Joan looked frightened, hurt—and he interprets this, probably quite correctly, as indicating a feeling on Joan's part of being "rejected." Clearly the counselor *had* rejected Joan as regards any sexual advances that she may have been making to him. With the situation thus clarified and "restructured," things began to happen. Almost immediately, "she pulled her coat together over her chest. Her hands clenched strongly on the coat and she started to stare at the wall." Presently she stood up in front of the therapist and physically acted-out her conflict by alternatively leaning toward and away from him. Then she hallucinated. *Eyes* are a proverbial symbol of authority and conscience, and Joan reflects her ambivalence toward them by seeing one of the eyes of each lamb's face as good, one bad. Then Joan sees the faces of her mother and grandmother—faces, so to say, which were "behind" conscience. "They are telling me to *control* myself and I *hate* them." The fact that moral authority had here been internalized but not assimilated is thus apparent; and it is noteworthy that such authority is depicted as exclusively female—there is no *fatherly* face here.

Having thus paused the better to grasp this rapidly moving and dramatic scene, we now return to the counselor's narrative.

I told her I was puzzled. Then I said, "I wonder if you are saying—in part you like yourself, in part you don't like yourself." She said, "No. It's other people's reactions to me. They partly like me and partly don't like me." She said that one of the eyes was covered over with wool. I said, "I wonder if you are saying that if people really knew you— could see the real you—that they would not like you." She said, "Yes." [2]

In between these times when we talked together, she was still standing, trembling, wringing her hands and staring at the wall. Then she began to tell me, in a very circuitous way, about her relationship with her father. She started out by saying that when she was thirteen years old, she had seen the divorce papers of her parents. In those papers it said that her father had not wanted her before she was born. Then she went on to describe her father's attitude toward her and after many hints told me about having had incestuous relations with her father. She described this as the experience which has made her dirty, no good, horrible.

She had been standing and shaking for half an hour but having brought out this report of incest, she sat down and

[2] No explicit reference is made here, by either the client or the counselor, to the common expression, "pulling the wool" over another's eyes as a metaphor for deception; but it seems to have been mutually understood and accepted.

relaxed. She looked at me while she talked, really seeing me
for the first time since she had stood up and described how
this experience had affected every part of her life. She had
never told this to anyone before. She felt she could not tell
her mother or her grandmother. Even with her father, she
pretends that it had never happened and he never mentions
it. She no longer has sex relations with him but when she
visits him (her parents are separated) she takes along a
friend to protect herself.

When it was about eight o'clock, I found I was again
beginning to get hungry. I said, "Well, I'm beginning to
get weak again." She said, "You know, I've got a headache
and I'm hungry. I'm just all worn out and I really haven't
much more to say today. But I couldn't tell you. I couldn't
suggest that we stop." It developed that she was afraid that
that would be rejecting me.

Again it takes no special intuitiveness to see what had
occurred here. Joan had come to the interview conflicted
between the possibility of admitting the incestuous relationship with her father and of replicating it, with the
counselor. What she would have actually done had the
counselor gone along with the first possibility we can
only conjecture—first of all because this is not what
happened and secondly because, if it had, there would
have been no record of the case, or at least not one
voluntarily supplied by the counselor! But the mystery
is still not completely solved. Why does Joan have to
single out *this* particular man? Surely there were both
more appropriate and more accessible sex objects in even
her impoverished social environment than this obviously
older, presumably married, and professionally responsible
individual. Actually, the very paradox provides the key.
Joan arranged this Saturday-afternoon tryst with the
counselor, not because she was sexually starved, but
because she was *morally oppressed*; and if she could
have seduced *this* father figure, as she had her original,
biological father, she would have won at least a transitory,
though ultimately bogus, moral victory of considerable
magnitude.[3]

[3] Only those without experience in the psychotherapeutic
situation will regard the sexual interplay here implied as either
unusual or misperceived. The only question is one of interpretation, "dynamics," meaning.

Certainly it was no accident that her father's face was not among those staring out at Joan from the wall—and from the past. As a *father* he was dead—and Joan had helped kill him. Having with Joan's cooperation irreparably disgraced and disqualified himself for this role, *he* could no longer "face" her. But the mother and the grandmother had not been so effectively disposed of; and although Joan *hated* them, they gave her no rest. So on this fateful Saturday afternoon, Joan came not awooing in any usual sense of that term, but rather with confused and mixed intentions of confession and "murder." But her possible victim was this time immune to her devices. When confronted by a hardly mistakable sexual invitation, all he did was to talk about how *weak and hungry* he was feeling! And he was right in perceiving that Joan, or at least a *part* of her, did "feel rejected." This time Joan had met her match; *this* father was incorruptible. And she had the courage and character to make the most of it: to him she then confessed. She had "tried" him, and he had qualified for this different role.

There is only a little more to the counselor's account. He concludes by asking a series of questions:

> What part did the handling of time play in this interview? Did the indecisiveness of the therapist lead to a seductive interplay which aroused transference reactions, helping to precipitate the temporary psychotic break? If so, how should this be evaluated therapeutically? Would a firm initial definition of limits by the therapist have cut off the possibility of the intensive catharsis which occurred during the last hour?
>
> The therapist interpreted the client's hallucinatory thoughts in terms of her attitudes toward her self and her relationships with other people. What would have been the effect of merely reflecting the ideas which she was verbalizing? What would have been the effect of interpreting her behavior in terms of a transference neurosis?

Although the counselor seems to have had a good intuitive grasp of the situation and handled it well, he was so preoccupied, apparently, with questions of "technique" that he was consciously blinded to the deeper significance of what really transpired. After Joan said,

"But I couldn't tell you [and] I couldn't suggest that we stop," his comment is: "It developed that she was afraid that that would be rejecting me." Surely something far more profound was going on here than any such terminology would imply; and it is with precisely this Something More that we are here mainly concerned.

III. IS CONFESSION ENOUGH?

THE PROBLEM OF EXPIATION

Despite the Biblical exhortation that an honest confession is good for the soul, there is reason to doubt that its benefit is unconditional and necessarily enduring; and one wonders how much, in the long run, was really accomplished in the episode we have just reviewed. Immediately thereafter Joan, to be sure, felt vastly relieved; but was she *"cured"*? What guarantee was there, really, that her guilt would be *generally* assuaged—or, indeed, that she would not again resort to the very behavior which had already caused her so much inner discomfort? The author of the Dick Tracy theory puts the problem well by asking in a part of his paper not previously quoted: What good does it do to confess your past errors to someone who is going to be as secretive about them as *you* have been? This, he goes on to say, is *not* the way for a person to achieve social redefinition of personality and true redemption. Just as the offense has been against society—that is, against the laws of man and God—so, one might argue, the confession and forgiveness ("acceptance") must be as broad as the sin itself.

Another one of the "critical incidents" collected by Standal and Corsini bears quite directly upon this question. Here a married woman consults a psychiatrist with complaints of depression and obsessive thoughts that she might injure her young daughter. After desultory talk (during the course of several interviews) had revealed nothing but an exemplary life, the psychiatrist confronted the patient, almost roughly, with the logical incongruity between her symptoms and what she had told him about herself. With great effort, there was then admission of a surprising and particularly degrading perversion; but there was no dramatic therapeutic gain. In fact, the report ends with a comment by the psychiatrist to the effect that the patient is "still in treatment."

One is therefore prompted to wonder what would happen, in situations of this kind, if the confession took a more "public" form. Fortunately we have something of an answer in a case which has been briefly reported by Dr. Anton Boisen (1958). He says:

> The patient in question was a man of thirty-eight years who was brought to the hospital in a severely agitated condition. He thought he had committed the unpardonable sin and that something was going to happen to his wife and children. He would not, therefore, let them out of his sight. He thought a world war was impending and when asked what part he was to have in this war, he replied, "A little child shall lead them." Obviously, he was the little child.
>
> The record of his life was that of a well-meaning, friendly, likeable person who before his marriage, and even afterward, had been sexually promiscuous. What troubled him most was an affair with a woman some ten years older than himself, clearly a mother substitute. There had been two abortions, for which he was responsible. She had died of carcinoma. He blamed himself for her death and the disturbance began shortly thereafter.
>
> The first symptom was heavy drinking. This continued until he lost his job. Following this, he suffered a depression and stopped drinking. Then he developed the idea that the Odd Fellows were out to get him because he had violated the oath he took when he joined them. For several months he was obsessed with ideas of persecution. He reached the point where he went to the police with a request for a permit to carry a gun in order to protect himself from his enemies. He then became finally so disturbed that he confessed to his wife, telling her of his sexual transgressions.
>
> This confession she took in good spirit, but in spite of that fact he became more and more agitated. The idea came that something was going to happen to her and that he had to carry the weight of the world on his small shoulders. Commitment then became necessary. In the hospital he showed intense anxiety. He was sure of only one thing, that things were not what they seemed. He was also deeply aroused religiously. It is not necessary for our purpose to recount his subsequent history beyond reporting that within a couple of months he made an excellent recovery and now, after nearly thirty years, there has been no further trouble.

He is at present a successful contractor and his family is prosperous and happy.

After noting that this man's guilt was real and grievous, Boisen then asks:

Why now the increased agitation following the confession to his wife? Such a question is in order. The answer is clear. The emotional disturbance was not the result but the *pre-condition* of the confession. In his normal state of mind confession would have been impossible. But the profound emotion forced the confession, just as nature's healing power produces a boil or an abscess and then lets the poison matter out. In this case, as in others of the type, the disturbance brought about a certain degree of socialization. It got rid of pretense and hypocrisy and put the sufferer in position to be *accepted for what he really was.* And if it took some time for this powerful emotion to subside, that is hardly to be wondered at" (pp. 5–6, italics added).

All this is eminently reasonable, but does it not over-look another possibility? Voluntary confession of a legal crime may soften the ensuing punishment, but it does not abrogate it. So, may we not assume that confession of an immorality likewise does not end the matter? In Dr. Boisen's case I conjecture that the period of hos-pitalization was *dynamically necessitated by the confes-sion.* This man, probably with human beings generally in like situations, felt that accounts could not be righted until he had, as we often say, "taken his medicine" and *paid* for his past misdeeds. Can it be that we do not properly perceive this function of the mental hospital and hospitalization?

Does mere confession of a legal crime absolve one from all further responsibility or punishment? Suppose that 10 years ago I committed a murder and was never caught or even suspected. But as time passes, my own knowledge of the act becomes increasingly oppressive and I finally go to the local police and say: "You remem-ber a man by the name of Joe Smith who was mys-teriously murdered a few years ago. Well, I thought you might just like to know that I killed him." What would then happen? Would the police say, "How very inter-esting! We often wondered what happened to that fellow. Drop in again sometime." Obviously not! I would be taken into custody, would have to stand trial, and, if formally convicted, would be sentenced to what was deemed appropriate punishment.

Now is the moral law less demanding than the civil and criminal codes? Does conscience have less rectitude than a court? Unless we can answer this question affirmatively, it follows that in the moral realm, no less than in law, confession is not enough and must be accompanied by restitution. This possibility has been generally neglected in our time and may account for widespread confusion and misdirected therapeutic and redemptive effort. Psychologists and psychiatrists have stressed the importance of "insight" rather than personal guilt and repentence; and even the church has preached what Dietrich Bonhoeffer (1948) has called the doctrine of "cheap grace," which he holds is no grace at all [see Chapter 11].

So can it be that, lacking formal (institutional) recognition of the need for atonement following sin, modern men and women commonly make use, unconsciously, of the stigma, *disgrace*, and suffering connected with being "crazy" and hospitalized? Dr. Boisen (1936) has referred to the insane as the *self-condemned*; and to this we might add that they are also the *self-punished*. Depression is manifestly a form of self-inflicted suffering; and it has often been suspected that the reason why electro-convulsive shock "treatment" may speed the recovery of depressed persons is that it aids the work of expiation. Certainly it is not uninstructive that even untreated depression tends to "run its course," that the prospect of recovery from any one "attack" is always good but that recurrences are statistically likely (hence the diagnosis of "cyclothymia"). Therefore, a depression looks very much like an act of "serving time," comparable to what happens in those other places of penance (or penitentiaries) where legally convicted offenders are sent. In both instances, when one has "paid his debt to society," he is again free (of prison in the one case, of depression in the other); and the question of whether an individual will have one or more later depressions or will be "cured" depends (in much the same way as does the reformatory action of prison) upon whether he has really "connected" crime and punishment.

But what of schizophrenia? Here the likelihood of "spontaneous remission" (getting "out," being "free") is not nearly so great; and many students of the problem have been led to suspect a deeper malignancy here— tainted heredity, disordered metabolism, or the like. Can it be that Tim Wilkins is right, that schizophrenia is no less a moral disorder than is depression but that in the one case the individual is still running, hiding, denying, whereas in the other the individual at least unconsciously admits his wrong and accepts the justice of suffering? In the Boisen case—which had such a favorable outcome —we have an individual who showed an admixture of depressive and schizoid reactions; and apparently much depends, with respect to recovery, upon whether one or the other gains the ascendancy. As Dr. Boisen has else-where (1936) pointed out, those persons who react to personality crisis by becoming resentful and bitter and who blame *others* rather than themselves are well on the way to a permanently paranoid adjustment, with a very poor prognosis. But when the individual can blame *him-self* and see his predicament as one for which *he* is largely responsible and which *he* can do something toward changing, the prospects of recovery—and personal trans-formation—are much brighter [see Chapter 13].

Toward which of these courses is would-be therapeutic endeavor usually directed? How often we have tried to get the neurotic or psychotic (sinful?) individual to see his difficulties as stemming from sources outside his own ego or self—from a too strict superego, from unreason-able, tyrannical parents, or from a "sick society"! And how often we have perhaps thus unwittingly pushed the individual in the very direction that leads to destruction rather than salvation!

At mid-twentieth century, perhaps secular psycho-therapy has already rediscovered one ancient religious truth and is on the verge of discovering another. Perhaps one of the reasons why classical psychoanalysis, with its cardinal emphasis upon "free association," so often makes a painful and productive start and then tails off into years of dull and unprofitable talk is that it does not help the analysand move from free association (confession) on to atonement, except to the extent that the financial sacrifice which analysis usually entails provides it in at least temporary or "symptomatic" form. Perhaps the *next* half century will be well spent if we do nothing more than learn how, once again, to make use of meaningful and effective restitution as a regular and expected concomitant of confession (cf. the book of Leviticus in the Old Testament). Perhaps there are both individually and socially more constructive forms of self-punishment and atonement than incarceration in a mental hospital.[4]

[4] Since the above was written, the author has learned of a book now in preparation, under the editorship of Dr. Albert Eglash, which will bear the title, *Creative Restitution: Guidance and Rehabilitation of Offenders*. Although concerned mainly with the reclamation of legally defined criminals, this book may have important implications for the mentally ill as well—if they, too, *are* "offenders." The fact that, in the case of criminals, confession or at least "conviction" has already occurred might seem to make the total task of rehabilitation easier here than with the mentally ill; but, being *self*-condemned, the latter may, for this reason, have potentialities which at least the criminal psychopath is commonly supposed to lack. Also, as an emendation to what has been said in this paper, it should be added that there is no intimation here that the particular "crimes" to which the mentally ill confess have necessarily occurred. As Tim Wilkins observes (in a part of his paper which is not reproduced here), a trivial or even nonexistent act may be reported and stressed to "cover" the *real* misdeed (cf. Stafford, 1950; Mowrer, 1953; Fliess, 1957). Some psychiatrists are of the opinion that it is a mistake to encourage (or even permit) a psychotic individual to talk about the evil acts he has committed, on the assumption that even though he may start with valid reports he will soon progress to imaginary "crimes" and thus become increasingly delusional and disoriented. Two considerations are pertinent here: (a) If a therapist took the patient's *first* report of wrong-doing seriously and immediately started thinking with the patient about a plan of restitution (instead of dismissing it as unimportant), perhaps the patient would not need to compound his real sins with fabricated ones; and (b) if a patient *starts* with a fabrication, might it not be profitable to suggest that he try to return to a less dramatic but more tangible and real action that may have generated guilt?

9

Psychotherapy and the Problem of Values in Historical Perspective
or,
The Devil and Psychopathology*

One of the reasons for caution in accepting the hypothesis that mental illness has a moral basis is the ubiquity of the contrary view, that it is indeed an illness and unrelated to anything for which the individual so afflicted might be held accountable. Either the illness interpretation is essentially sound or else, if erroneous, it must be examined and explained as one of those remarkable anomalies of which the history of culture is not, alas, without precedent. Here we extend the effort already begun, in Chapter 6, to plumb the historical depths of the problem and in this way, hopefully, discover circumstances which will shed new and much-needed light on certain present-day perplexities.

This inquiry also brings us back, once again, to the question of the nature of The Unconscious; and on the surmise that it is benevolent, rather than evil (as Freudian theory would have it), the possibility opens up for a new synthesis of depth psychology and religion: namely, that The Unconscious, thus reconceived, is akin to what has otherwise been known as The Holy Spirit. This perception of the situation is congruent with and a development of the general position adumbrated in Chapter 2. Such a re-evaluation and re-interpretation of The Unconscious may go far, not only to achieve such a rapprochement, but also to dispel the pessimism and impotence which have long beset the whole domain of psychopathology.

* Initially prepared for a symposium on "Psychotherapy and Values" held at Ohio State University, May 28–29, 1959, this paper was also presented at the University of Minnesota, April 16, under the auspices of the Department of Psychology, and later served as the second of the 1960 Earl Lectures, on "Psychoanalysis and the Judeo-Christian Ethic."

In a related paper [Chapter 8] the writer has suggested that we have seriously erred in interpreting guilt, clinically, as mere guilt *feeling* rather than as a reality-based state stemming from palpable, incontestable misconduct. In support of this view, a paper entitled "A New Theory of Schizophrenia" by an anonymous author (1958) is cited in which the position is taken that schizophrenia is typically a condition in which a person is driven by a sort of progressive terror lest his sins find him out. Then, in an account of a dramatic interview with a young woman known as Joan (Standal & Corsini, 1959), we see how great the pressure may be, in some schizoid individuals, to disclose their misconduct and thus, hopefully, find peace and reconciliation. But confession, as we know, may bring transitory relief without, however, effecting a permanent cure. This consideration is exemplified in a case history recently published by Boisen (1958), in which a man becomes emotionally disturbed and confesses infidelity and other serious breaches of morality to his wife; but, far from finding an honest confession good for his soul, this man becomes even more disturbed and has to be hospitalized. Boisen's interpretation of this course of events goes as follows.

> The emotional disturbance was not the result but the precondition of the confession. In his normal state of mind confession would have been impossible. But the profound emotion forced the confession, just as nature's healing power produces a boil or an abscess and then lets the poison matter out. . . . And if it took some time for this powerful emotion to subside, that is hardly to be wondered at (pp. 5–6).

In other words, the view here set forth by Boisen is that by the time an internal crisis reaches a point where it is powerful enough to prompt a confession, it may have gained so much *momentum* that it "carries" the person past the functional objective, which is confession and the attainment of openness. In the paper first cited, I have suggested the alternative possibility that disturbance often continues beyond the point of confession (and thus makes confession seem useless and even harmful) for the reason that confession is not, of itself, dynamically sufficient and must, in many instances, be accompanied by some form of atonement or expiation. Where this demand is consciously recognized, the individual may make a profound resolution or "vow" which will alter the entire course of his life and thus "save" him; but where the needs of the situation are not so well understood, it is as if the unconscious forces drive the individual into manifest insanity (and hospitalization—or worse) as the punishment, suffering, and humiliaton he must endure before he can again (if ever) comfortably face himself and others.

If, in the neurotic or psychotic individual, guilt is *real* rather than fancied, the whole logic and strategy of secular psychotherapy has to be reconsidered. I say *if* the guilt is real. This is a question of fact which has been answered to my own satisfaction but is, of course, open to further investigation by others. However, granting that the psychoneurotic individual *is* responsibly guilty and not just a victim of false scruples, an even more basic question arises as to *why* Western civilization ever came to doubt or deny the relationship between guilt, *real* guilt, and psychopathology. This question can, I believe, be answered only in the light of certain broad historical developments, which we shall explore in the pages that follow.

I. THE REFORMATION AND THE RISE OF SECULAR PSYCHOTHERAPY

Prior to the Protestant Reformation, no one (relatively speaking) doubted the reality of guilt. It did not matter whether you *felt* guilty or not; if you had *acted* in certain ways, *done* certain things, you took it for granted that you must confess and obtain forgiveness. Otherwise, your soul was in mortal danger.

Martin Luther and the other Reformers, of course, changed all this. There had, it seems, been widespread abuses and corruption, of a kind not without historical precedent. For some time prior to the Reformation, redemption from guilt required not only that the individual confess and do ordinary penance but that, in addition, he buy special "indulgences," for himself and also for others dear to him who might now or at some future time be in Purgatory (Bainton, 1950). Here one can hardly escape being reminded of the scene in the Temple where Christ scourged the moneychangers for their traffic in forgiveness. This outburst, probably more than any other single act or combination of acts in the life of Christ, turned the entrenched forces of orthodox Judaism against him and led to his execution. Only by the most improbable combination of circumstances did Luther survive the fury which *his* criticisms and insubordination released; and if one holds that the revolution which followed was less momentous than the Christian "reformation," who can say what would have happened if Luther, too, had been martyred?

As the Protestant Reformation became consolidated, it was, of course, inevitable that sweeping changes would be instigated with respect to confession and penance. Milder changes were readily imaginable; but both practices were, in effect, abolished. Grace, it was argued, is not dependent upon other men but comes from God alone. Therefore, you were to take your case to God, in prayer, and ask for his forgiveness directly, without priestly intervention. This arrangement was regarded as a great stroke of genius. And I can remember my own father telling me, as a child, a "joke" which went as follows. For some time a small boy had been given a dollar every month and told to go to the priest for confession. Finally, the boy became curious and asked his parents who confessed the priest. The answer was, the Bishop. Who then, he asked, confessed the Bishop? The Cardinal, came the reply. Who confessed the Cardinal? The Pope. And who confessed the Pope? No one confessed the Pope, the boy's parents told him; he took *his* sins to God. To which the boy, with a flash of inspiration, exclaimed: "I think I'll do as the Pope does; I, too, will take my sins directly to God and *save* my dollar!"

This new provision for a short-cut to God and absolution was supposedly a great innovation, liberation, and triumph. But history may yet show that it was instead a grim and costly error. There can surely be no denying that, on the whole, Protestantism has handled the problem of guilt very badly. It has left its followers in a state which perhaps made them "creative" and "ambitious" in a feverish, unhealthy way; but it has also disposed us to the mass neurosis and pervasive anxiety which are so much a part of the modern scene.[1]

Gradually Protestantism is recognizing this ambiguity in its doctrines and practices and is today in the process of reinstituting confession. If this assertion seems rash, I would cite the development of "confession to a Christian brother," as advocated by Deitrich Bonhoeffer (1954), in his book, *Life Together*, and now practiced in the German Lutheran Church. But, even more pertinently, I would call attention to the pervasive recourse to "pastoral counseling" in this and other countries, which, although it has the trappings of secular psychotherapy, is surely but a disguised return of the confessional (see especially Meehl *et al.*, 1958, pp. 68–69). [See also Chapters 11 and 12.]

However, since pastoral counseling has been so largely inspired by and patterned upon secular psychotherapy, it is not surprising that it, too, has important shortcomings. Secular psychotherapy, we must remember, does not really believe in guilt, only guilt feelings (or a "guilt sense"; White, 1956); and the aim of the type of "confession" which it encourages, *i.e.*, free association, is "insight" rather than repentance and restitution. Moreover, as Bonhoeffer (1948) in his book, *The Cost of Discipleship*, argues, Protestantism has itself really abandoned

[1] In a footnote Fromm (1955) says: "All figures show that Protestant countries have a much higher suicide rate than Catholic countries. This may be due to a number of factors inherent in the difference between the Catholic and Protestant religions, such as the greater influence which the Catholic religion has on the life of its adherents, the more adequate means to deal with a sense of guilt employed by the Catholic Church, etc. But it must also be taken into account that the Protestant countries are the ones in which the capitalistic mode of production is developed further, and has molded the character of the population more completely than in the Catholic countries, so that the difference between Protestant and Catholic countries is also largely the difference between various stages in the development of modern Capitalism" (p. 151). Therefore, the little story related above is doubly illuminating: it shows not only the reduced capacity of Protestantism for handling individual guilt but also its encouragement of thrift and material prosperity.

the strategy of confession and atonement in favor of what he calls the doctrine of "cheap grace."

> Cheap grace is the preaching of forgiveness without requiring repentance, baptism without Church discipline, Communion without confession, absolution without contrition. Cheap grace is grace without discipleship, grace without the Cross, grace without Jesus Christ, living and incarnate. . . .
> Costly grace is the gospel which must be *sought* again and again, the gift which must be *asked* for, the door at which a man must *knock*.
> Such grace is *costly* because it calls us to follow, and it is grace because it calls us to follow *Jesus Christ*. It is costly because it costs a man his life; and it is grace because it gives a man the only true life. It is costly because it condemns sin, and grace because it justifies the sinner (pp. 38–39).

Most pastoral counseling, as we know it today, therefore falls short, as does secular psychotherapy, of the crucial and ultimate step in the quest for salvation and personal wholeness. If one takes the neurotic's guilt seriously, that is, if (as now seems likely) "neurosis" is just a medical euphemism for a "state of sin" and social alienation, therapy must obviously go beyond mere "counseling," to self-disclosure, not just to a therapist or counselor, but to the "significant others" in one's life, and *then* on to active redemption in the sense of the patient's making every effort within his power to undo the evil for which he has previously been responsible.[2]

[2] The Catholic Church has, of course, always taken guilt seriously to the extent of holding to the necessity of contrition, confession, and satisfaction or penance (*Catholic Almanac*, 1959 p. 277). And so the question is sometimes asked, Why are Catholics not more protected than they are from personality disturbance, if the management of guilt and mental health are related? The answer seems to be: (a) many Catholics do indeed enjoy unusually good mental health; (b) some Catholics—and indeed their confessors—are perfunctory about confession and penance, i.e., the punishment often does not fit the crime, psychologically; and (c) the Catholic Church identifies contrition, confession, and penance as a *sacrament*, whose central aim is other-worldly salvation rather than mental health or adjustment in this life. Therefore, Catholicism provides no clear test, either in practice or in theory, of what confession and penance can do in a more naturalistic way.

At this juncture it is, of course, easy to get involved in a tedious theological debate as to whether salvation is by "good works" or by "grace alone." For myself, I have no desire to argue the point but will merely state that I, personally, take my stand with the Apostle James and Deitrich Bonhoeffer, against the Apostle Paul and Martin Luther, or at least against the extreme interpretations sometimes put upon their teachings. Be it granted that it ill becomes a man to proclaim his own righteousness—this, surely, is a judgment for *others* to render. But to assume that grace or redemption or change comes only as a result of divine *election* or *selection* is, to my way of thinking, to cast a hopeless blight on the whole problem [see Chapter 11; also Mowrer, 1961].

No other therapeutic or "redemptive" movement, within the church or without, has in recent times been so successful as Alcoholics Anonymous. Here guilt is seen as basic and real; and its open admission is regarded as an indispensable first step, to be followed by a definite program of good works and restitution. Sometimes, when the accomplishments of Alcoholics Anonymous are alluded to, it is asked: But why was the Oxford Group not also a success? Up to a point the Oxford Group *was* a success (see Clark, 1951); and that point was that it encouraged confession and openness but had no provision for taking its members on from there. If it did nothing more, the movement deserves credit for having inspired the formation of AA, where the weakness of pure Buchmanism is offset by a clearly specified program of "missions" and mercy.

The trial which AA has blazed is the only one down which I can at present gaze and see anything that looks like the road to the future. How AA principles can be adapted or modified to meet the needs of other kinds of confused and suffering people is not fully clear to me. But I am as sure as I can be of anything that no therapy will be radically and broadly successful which does not take the neurotic's guilt seriously and does not help him

---

For a quite remarkable, and unusual, attempt to deal with the naturalistic (psychological) implications of confession in the Catholic context, see Wilson (1954) [see also Chapters 11 and 12].

admit his errors openly and find ways to work in dead earnest to rectify and compensate for them.

As an active churchman, I believe that the concept of God is vital and meaningful and that the so-called "vertical dimension," between God and man, is vital and meaningful; but I do not believe that this relationship can be *either* vital or meaningful if it is not complemented and, indeed, often *preceded* by serious concern on the part of the individual with the *horizontal* dimension, namely, the relation of man to man. The total situation has well been termed "triangular," with God, the individual, and one's fellowmen at the three corners. The nature of the relationship is also well described by the following lines:

> I sought my soul and sought My God,
> But neither could I see;
> And then I sought my neighbor,
> And then I found all three.

Intrepid and bold as the Protestant Reformation undoubtedly was in many ways, one can hardly avoid the judgment, at this vantage point in history, that it was also crucially incomplete (cf. Section VI; also Tillich, 1948). If, for the third time in the past two thousand years, there is again widespread mercenary traffic in forgiveness, perhaps this scandal, no less than the former ones, will prompt changes of a radical and "redemptive" kind.

II. THE HISTORICAL SITUATION
AND FREUDIAN PSYCHOANALYSIS

In his *Autobiography*, Freud (1935)—writing with his usual plausibility and charm—speaks of the circumstances, both personal and cultural, which prompted the development of that remarkable body of theory and practice which was to be known as psychoanalysis. By the end of the 19th Century, the church, as we have seen, had largely abandoned its interest and claim to competence in the area of psychopathology; and medicine had an essentially organic conception of the problem, with the result that there were, as Freud observed, "crowds of neurotics, whose numbers seemed further multiplied by the manner in which they hurried, with their troubles unsolved, from one physician to another" (p. 27).

Being a Jew in a nominally Christian country, Freud experienced one disappointment and frustration after another in his original hope of securing an academic position; and finding himself thus, as he said, "forced into the Opposition" (p. 24), the outcast Jewish doctor eventually began, understandably enough, to direct his professional attention to what we may also call the "outcasts" among patients. The superabundance of neurotic individuals who were seeking Something and not finding it and the accident of Freud's finding himself now aligned with "the Opposition" provided the sour soil in which psychoanalysis germinated and began its growth. "My therapeutic arsenal [in the beginning]," Freud said, "contained only two weapons, electrotherapy and hypnotism, for prescribing a visit to a hydropathic establishment after a single consultation was an inadequate source of income" (p. 25). And when, at length, Freud became disgusted with both electrotherapy and hypnotism, he simply began listening to his patient *talk*. From this seemingly inauspicious beginning came the now well-known analytic technique.

As we shall presently see, the solution which Freud ultimately offered to the emotionally, morally, and spiritually troubled person is very far from a religious solution; and we are now beginning to supect that it is also very far from a soundly scientific one. Yet the fact is that Freud, and the disciples whom he soon attracted, at least walked in the Valley of the Shadow *with* these unhappy, distraught individuals, in a way which neither the ordinary physician nor the typical clergyman of the time had been willing to do. Surely it is not without deep significance that a theologian recently remarked: "Regardless of whether Freud was right or wrong in his theory, he at least *tried* to minister to a class of sufferers on whom the church, Protestant and Catholic alike, had turned its back. This is to our inescapable and enduring shame!" (De Wire, 1958).

The end of the 19th Century found the Catholic Church still licking its wounds from the Reformation and smarting from the memory of its folly in dealing with Galileo. And, in the decades just past, the credibility of the Church had, of course, been further challenged by Darwinian evolution. While Protestantism had perhaps not shown the same degree of opposition to science, it too was in a precarious state because, among other reasons, of its ineffective handling of the problem of guilt. Therefore, when Freud, in the name of science, began to proclaim discoveries in the realm of mind as revolutionary as those of Copernicus and Galileo in astronomy and of Darwin in biology, there was little religious vitality to oppose him.

Although Freud thus spoke in the name of Science, and eschewed all theological considerations, it is no accident that he was a Jew and that psychoanalysis, as ideology and as therapy, developed as it did. Having suffered repeated rebuffs and disappointments at the hands of what he referred to as the "compact majority," Freud had no reason to be anything but gratified by the embarrassment and failures of organized religion; and he let no opportunity pass for striking at what was not only a personal affront but also, as he conceived it, the enemy of all mankind (cf. Freud, 1928). Having been excluded, or at least so he imagined, from the opportunities and privileges which would have perhaps been open to him as a Christian, he gave up trying to function within conventional boundaries and developed what he himself, with magnificent understatement, termed "a certain degree of independence of judgment" (p. 11).

III. FREUD AND THE KABBALISTIC TRADITION

Just how great was Freud's disaffection from conventional streams of thought and values becomes clear when we discover that not only was he alienated with respect to Christianity but also from the main currents of Judaism. In a remarkable book by David Bakan (1958a) which will be considered more fully in the next section, we learn that Freud's family, together with many other Viennese Jews, had migrated from Galicia, which, says Bakan, "had been saturated with Jewish mysticism" (p. 80), of the Kabbalistic variety. This sect, or splinter group, differed from traditional rabbinical Judaism in a number of ways which, as Bakan ingeniously shows, strikingly anticipate important and distinguishing features of psychoanalysis. The following excerpts capture some of the salient features of Kabbala and suggest a probably more than coincidental relationship to psychoanalysis.

One of the meanings of the word Kabbala is *tradition* in a way which connotes oral transmission. Another meaning is *acceptance* as the mystics are accepted before God. A third meaning of the term is *that which is received*, suggesting its revelatory character. The Kabbala is something referred to as the Secret Wisdom to indicate that it is comprehensible only to the initiated. . . .

Kabbala has always had about it an aura of danger, perhaps for good reason. In the light of the later psychoanalytic developments, this danger may be best understood as that associated with bringing repressed material into consciousness (p. 70).

Recalling our earlier discussion of the friendship between Freud and Fliess, Kabbalistic tradition provides a further hint concerning the nature of the relationship. In his psychoanalytic work, which we maintain is Kabbalistic, Freud needed an "associate," because the burden of the Kabbalistic thought is too difficult for anyone to bear in independent study. . . .

The tradition is one pervaded by a sense of secrecy. . . .
The Kabbalists were endowed with mystery and power (p. 71).

As will become increasingly evident in what follows, a theory of repression and the role of the ego in repression are already germinal here. Abulafia [a 13th-Century Spanish Kabbalist] has essentially two methods of meditation in order to achieve the desired release of the soul. The first of these is an interpretative method based on taking liberties with the letters of the alphabet (p. 76).

The second important method for which the first is but a preparation is called "jumping and skipping" [which Bakan identifies as a forerunner of the method of free association] (p. 77).

Associated with such meditation is an intellectual ecstasy identifiable with psychoanalytic insight (p. 79).

Furthermore, Abulafia regards the Kabbalistic teacher as extremely important, a harbinger of the idea of the transference (p. 80).

That Freud would have had contact with Kabbalistic thought and practice is insured by the circumstances already cited, to which can also be added the fact that during the latter half of the 19th Century Adolf Jellinek, who was a close student of Kabbala, was, Bakan reports, "the most popular Jewish preacher in the city of Vienna in his day. It is said that when Jellinek spoke on the week end the Jews of Vienna would discuss what he said for the whole succeeding week" (p. 81).

Hence we arrive at the conclusion that Freud not only stood apart from Christianity but that he had little affinity even for orthodox Judaism. He was, however, very probably influenced, consciously or unconsciously, by a singular and indeed somewhat sinister variety of Jewish mysticism. In his expressed allegiance to science and in yet other ways, Freud revealed also a sympathy with and admiration for classical Greek culture, a fact which is well known. But the knowledge of his affiliation with Kabbalism, as brought out by Bakan, is new and puts psychoanalysis into a surprising context, which will be further considered in the next section.

IV. DID FREUD "PLAY THE DEVIL"?

It is remarkable how slow we sometimes are to perceive realities which we do not expect, or wish, to be true. It is more than thirty years now since the writer first became interested in psychoanalysis and resorted to it, as a form of psychotherapy and, hopefully, also as a new way of life. For the better part of two decades he tried to make it "work" but to no avail; and so, little by little, he became critical of psychoanalysis and returned to more conventional views and values. And this experience is today by no means uncommon. Yet it is with a real sense of surprise and even shock that one reads the evidence which Bakan, in his book *Freud and the Jewish Mystical Tradition* (1958a), has assembled for believing that Freud not only repudiated Mosaic and Christian conceptions of God but, in addition, *identified himself with the Devil.*

That Freud, as Bakan maintains, felt himself in mortal conflict with Moses, the Law Giver, is not, of itself, surprising. Perhaps the most basic tenet of psychoanalysis is that neurosis is due to too great severity of the superego; and Freud may be said to have "invented" psychoanalysis for the avowed purpose of combatting conscience, the superego, the Law, and, by implication, the Law Giver. Then, reasons Bakan (1958b):

> If Freud conceives of himself as the new Lawgiver, . . . he must at one and the same time be like unto Moses, the previous Lawgiver, whose place he must preempt, and must be destructive of Moses. The new Lawgiver must revoke the older Law. The identification with Moses turns into its opposite, the destruction of Moses" (pp. 323–24).

The Talmud and the other Rabbinical writings constitute an elaboration of dicta of the Mosaic code, which the Orthodox Jew takes upon himself to guide his life at every moment and in connection with every action. In a word, Moses is representative of the superego, the force generated within the individual to keep him from "instinctual gratification." The force which maintains renunciation of instinctual gratification is the fear of punishment. In the allegory of the discussion of a statue [of Moses, by Michelangelo] Freud is saying that the feared punishment will never eventuate. The superego is restrained (p. 324).

Freud's repeated affirmation of his Jewish identity becomes illuminated through *Moses and Monotheism*. If it is the Jew who carries the burden of the historical superego, then it is only a Jew who can really remove the sense of sin. We recall in this connection Freud's assertion that psychoanalysis could only have been created by a Jew; in a letter to his Swiss friend Oskar Pfister he wrote, ". . . by the way, how comes it that none of the godly ever devised psychoanalysis and that one had to wait for a godless Jew?" If the Jews represent the authority of the Law, only a Jew can declare that the Law is dead. Psychoanalysis, in this larger cultural sense, may be viewed as a fundamental effort to modify the classical image of the Jew. . . . Thus Freud plays the role of a new Moses who comes down with a new Law dedicated to personal psychological liberty (p. 329).

For Freud and psychoanalysis the task of treating neurotic individuals thus became at one with the liberation of mankind from the Mosaic Law, a task which Bakan (1958a) characterizes as "Messianic." He says:

> One of the critical features of Messianism is its goal of leading people out of slavery and oppression. Thus Freud's whole effort at the creation of psychoanalysis may be viewed as Messianic in this respect (p. 170).

But since the oppressor was none other than the mighty Moses and since his traditional adversary was the

Devil himself, it is logical—though none the less astonishing—that Freud should have consciously identified himself with the Devil. At the end of Chapter 22 Bakan quotes Freud as having once remarked to colleagues:

> Do you not know that I am the Devil? All my life I have had to play the Devil, in order that others would be able to build the most beautiful cathedrals with the materials that I produced (p. 181).

There then follow the five chapters which comprise Part IV of the Bakan book, entitled "The Devil as Suspended Superego." In 1923 Freud published a remarkable paper on "A Neurosis of Demoniacal Possession in the Seventeenth Century," in which he relates the story of the painter Christoph Haitzmann, who in a period of discouragement and depression had contracted with the Devil to be his, body and soul, at the end of nine years in return for success in his art and surcease from sadness. As the time approached for the contract to be consummated, Haitzmann became increasingly agitated (showing symptoms which would today probably be regarded as schizophrenic—see Macalpine & Hunter, 1956) and successfully sought priestly intervention and protection.

In *Freud and the Jewish Mystical Tradition*, Bakan develops and convincingly documents the thesis that, at least metaphorically, Freud himself had, some twenty-five years earlier, entered into a "Satanic Pact" and that psychoanalysis was the result thereof. For a period prior to the publication of *Die Traumbeutüng* in 1900 (which he always regarded as his masterpiece), Freud had been in a state of unproductivity, discouragement, and depression (as is now known from the Fliess correspondence; see Bakan, 1958a, p. 221 and p. 224). But then some sort of personal change or rearrangement of his emotions and mental powers took place; and we get more than a hint of what this change was from the motto in Latin which appears on the title page of this book. The quotation is taken from a passage of Virgil's *Aeneid* and, when translated in its entirety, reads:

> Well, if my powers are not great enough, I shall not hesitate—that is sure—to ask help wherever help may be found. If the gods above are no use to me, then I'll move all hell.

And here Bakan comments, insightfully:

> If God is identified with the superego, then the corresponding antagonistic image is the Devil, who dwells in hell. As we have indicated earlier, in the psychoanalytic relationship the analyst is at one and the same time the representative of the superego as well as a tolerant, understanding father figure. Now what is the Devil, psychologically? The answer is eminently simple, on one level. *The Devil is the suspended superego.* He is the permissive superego. The Devil is that part of the person which permits him to violate the precepts of the superego (p. 211).

In summarizing Chapter 27, Bakan says:

> In our discussion of hypnosis, cocaine, and the transference, indications of suspension of the superego were suggested. Our introduction of the Devil idea into this discussion rounds out the great drama which was taking place in Freud's mind in his creation of psychoanalysis . . . (pp. 212–213).

And finally, toward the end of Chapter 30, we read:

> The Devil is then a cure for despair. He is called upon as an assertive act when all hope is gone. And in this sense also, the Devil is always the Tempter. The essential message of the Tempter is that the anticipated rewards associated with resistance to temptation will not be forthcoming, that *faith* is groundless. The Devil presents the new hope, and supports this promise by *immediate* tokens of his favor. But since these tokens themselves bring so much relief, one permits oneself, in his relationship to the Devil, to be thus taken in (by the Devil), since he feels that he has already been taken in (by God).
>
> In more secular terms, Freud suffered from acute depressions. His self-analysis, and his development of psychoanalysis, were the cure for his depression. His practice had already provided him with ample evidence that diseases which other people were suffering from, for which there was no other hope, could be cured by such means. In his despair over making a living, and in his despair over anti-Semitism, he had "little or nothing to lose" by his "audacity." Furthermore, this new set of methods which he was producing held out the promise of bringing patients to him and so solving at least the problem of making a living (p. 236).

Thus does Bakan develop and document his contention that Freud, at least metaphorically, "played the Devil"—but that he did so in a good cause. However, as we know, "playing the Devil" also carries the implication of eventually *causing disaster!* It is this aspect of the situation to which we now turn our attention.

V. THE ROLE OF THE PSYCHOANALYST— THERAPIST OR TEMPTER?

Today no one, of course, "believes" in the Devil in the sense in which he was conceived in the Middle Ages. Instead, we have come to "believe" in Freud and psychoanalysis. But now we are confronted by the astonishing possibility that Freud and his works are the 20th-Century equivalent of the Devil, thinly disguised. And this possibility is rendered all the more palpable by the fact that Bakan, who has so vividly brought this possibility to our attention, is himself an admirer and defender of Freud. The logic by which Bakan reconciles this apparent contradiction and justifies *his* "audacity" cannot be reproduced here, partly because it is intricate and partly because I am not sure I fully understand it. But we can and should note one or two additional bits of evidence which Bakan (1958a) adduces in support of his remarkable thesis:

> The question of the *seriousness* of Freud's entry into the Satanic Pact may well be raised. Freud was a modern man who did not believe in supernatural beings (p. 215).
>
> Perhaps precisely because Freud did not accept the supernatural reality of the Devil, he could permit himself the full exploitation of the metaphor. We may imagine that at times the sense of possession became quite strong; and it is this feeling of possession that Freud is analyzing in his paper [ostensibly dealing with the 17th-Century painter, Christoph Haitzmann] (219).

According to Bakan, both Freud and Haitzmann had sought the help of the Devil in their struggle against depression, which is a work of the superego. Therefore, metaphorically at least, the powers of the Devil might be thought of as generally useful in the campaign *against* the superego, a campaign which is supposed by psychoanalysis to be so essential to the treatment of all neurosis. Says Bakan:

> Throughout the Middle Ages the Devil was a star in the great spiritual drama which was then taking place. As Freud

had so aptly pointed out, even though the Devil is perhaps no longer a personage in the same sense as in the Middle Ages, the psychological phenomena associated with his image are still current and important. We have already indicated the psychological significance of the Devil image as an ally against the superego, or better, as its suspension (p. 231).

More prosaically this can be stated as follows: The disease of the neurotic is his guilt. This guilt is, in itself, an evil and its removal is good. . . . If God is the guilt-producing image, then the Devil is the counterforce. . . .

As Freud said in discussing Anatole France's *Revolt of the Angels*, "War will produce war and victory defeat. God defeated becomes Satan and Satan victorious will become God" (p. 233).

But enough of conjecture and finely spun inferences! What, in actual practice, is the strategy and goal of psychoanalysis? Analysts have been a little hesitant about publishing verbatim accounts of what, in fact, transpires in analysis. And when, on occasion, this reluctance has been overcome and verbatim transcripts have appeared, one understands why analysis, like a Witches' Sabbath, prospers best in an atmosphere of secrecy and darkness. The following excerpts, quoted by de Grazia (1952) from a psychoanalytic transcription, illustrate the point:

PATIENT: Not only is there this fear of being in an intimate relationship with a woman, but I am also obsessed with the fear concerning that blasphemous thought. The reason for this seems to be that I had sold myself to the devil, merely by thinking this thought to myself. It is a fear of being possessed by the devil. I know it is rather absurd and based on the old theology. The devil seems to represent all that is evil or bad.

The fear of selling myself to the devil takes my thoughts back to a dream I had at the age of 5 or 6 years. I was sleeping with my mother at the time. I woke up trembling very violently. I thought I saw a phantom fly across the room. It was like a flame, and yet it was like an imp grinning at me. It flew across the room and out of the window. I was scared to death.

THERAPIST: What is the flame you would get if you were sleeping with your mother?

PATIENT: Love of my mother, I suppose.

THERAPIST: What is the flame you would get if you were sleeping with a young lady?

PATIENT: Passion.

THERAPIST: Would you?

PATIENT: No, I expect I should be scared to death, and trembling violently, like I was in the dream.

. . . Now my main concern is this idea or obsession that I am possessed by the devil.

THERAPIST: Suppose you are?

PATIENT: That would mean that one would lose control of one's will.

THERAPIST: What is natural?

PATIENT: Do you mean that what I am afraid of is my own natural urge to live a normal natural life . . . ?

And during the next session:

PATIENT: Perhaps I am scared of a girl because I am terrified that my sexual feelings might run away with me, and I might not act rationally.

THERAPIST: What might you do?

PATIENT: I might love her too much.

THERAPIST: What would that lead to?

PATIENT: My desire would be to put my arms around her, and tell her I love her. But I was scared.

THERAPIST: Does that seem so terrifying?

PATIENT: Well, I might have sexual intercourse with her: that would be going too far.

THERAPIST: Would it?

PATIENT: Well, perhaps not as far as sexual intercourse. If that is the devil, perhaps he is quite a harmless devil. Perhaps the sooner I went to the devil the better.

THERAPIST: If that is all there is to it, why is there all this scare?

PATIENT: Apparently all this time I have been afraid of being possessed by my own nature. The thing I want more than anything else is to lead a normal natural life. Since coming to you I have understood that this fear of being sold to the devil is nothing more or less than fear of my own nature on the one hand, and on the other hand a preference for it, which I have thought was a preference for the devil.

The whole amazing thing has become quite plain to me. It is amazing how the obsession left me last night after that talk with you (pp. 100–102) [cf. Berg, 1948, pp. 78–80].

A playwrite could not have produced a better script for a modern re-enactment of the temptation and fall of man as it supposedly occurred in the Garden of Eden. Here Adam and Eve were attracted by the possibility of eating of the fruit of the Tree of Knowledge but were restrained by God's contrary commandment (superego). But, step by step, the Devil showed them how pleasant, natural, and harmless eating the fruit would be. The Devil succeeded, and Adam and Eve were "cured" of their apple-eating inhibition. But the cure ultimately proved, of course, to be worse than the "disease"; and this seems also to hold for the fruits of psychoanalysis. In one of the last papers he ever wrote, Freud (1937) looked back upon the therapeutic accomplishments of psychoanalysis and did not find them reassuring. Typically, Freud said, patients give the appearance of making a good recovery and leave analysis; but then, sooner or later, they are likely to experience a recurrence of their old difficulties or the outbreak of new ones.

> In studying various developments and changes we focus our attention entirely on the result and we readily overlook the fact that such processes are usually more or less incomplete, that is to say, the changes that take place are really only partial. A shrewd satirist of the old Austria, Johann Nestroy, once said: "Every advance is only half as great as it looks at first." One is tempted to think that this malicious dictum is universally valid (p. 330).

And two decades later, an eminent American analyst (Kubie, 1956) was prompted to confess:

> In this connection I recall Edward Glover's statement [personal communication] that analysts sometimes seem to achieve their greatest successes when they are beginners. Even if Glover's statement was in part an ironic and rueful jest, it indicates a mood of healthy reserve about our right to claim therapeutic omnipotence or omniscience. . . . My own observations of analytic defeats have convinced me that basic gaps remain in our knowledge of the dynamic processes both of illness and of therapy. . . .
> Only a few years ago (although it seems a long time in my life as an analyst) I harbored the comforting expectation that increasing analytic sophistication and experience would yield a higher percentage of therapeutic successes. . . . My reluctant impression is that this hope has not been realized (p. 87).

From testimony now available from both the friends and the foes of analysis, it is clear that, at best, analysis casts a spell but does not cure. By aligning himself with the patient's id, the analyst ("Devil"?) may indeed succeed, as Bakan puts it, in *suspending* the superego; but the superego (or conscience), more commonly than we might wish to believe, is a reflection of enduring social realities; and the advantage we gain by overcoming it in analysis is dearly paid for later, many times over. Man's salvation must surely come, not from his looking and moving *downward*, but from an *upward* reach, toward reconciliation and community, made by means of confession and manifest restitution.

VI. THE END OF AN ERA—AND AN ALTERNATIVE

Even though Freud today stands indicted of having "played the Devil," there are many modern-minded men and women who will not greatly blame him. By their narrowness, bigotry, arrogance, sanctimony, false piety, irrealism, supernaturalism, and hypocrisy, several generations of theologians and laymen have given organized religion an exceedingly negative imprint and reputation; and if there have been those who said, "Let the Devil take them," it can hardly be wondered at. Galileo and Darwin were primarily scientists, and all they asked was to be let alone to do their work. Because of their particular subject matter, they were not greatly interested in religious issues, and became so mainly to the end of trying to protect themselves and their scientific activities from unwarranted interference. But with Freud the situation was different. His subject matter was inherently closer to that of religion; and if he was not to go along with religion (as he obviously had no intention of doing), then he had to go *away from* and *against* it, in as emphatic and militant a way as possible. Hence, as we have seen, he played *the Devil*.

But, much as we may sympathize with both the personal and the historical situation which, as we may say, *produced* a Freud, we cannot at this point in time, regard his total effort as anything but a failure. In fact, this surely is the hallmark of Evil: ultimate disaster after what appears to be great accomplishment and gain. It is the long haul that provides the test of rightness and righteousness; and already, barely two decades after

Freud's death, the signs of confusion and disintegration in the movement he launched are rampant.

During the same two decades there has been a remarkable upswing in church attendance and general religiosity. But can we be sure that these developments have as yet a clear ideology and rationale? There is still a babble of tongues in respect to the genesis and treatment of those profound and, alas, prevalent disturbances of the human spirit which we doggedly dub mental *illness*. And the contradictions between science and religion seem in many ways as basic and irreconcilable as ever. But there is upon the horizon a ray of hope which comes from as unlikely a direction and is as altogether extraordinary as any of the other developments which have been considered in this paper.

As a result of a succession of personal and professional experiences whose narration will have to wait for another occasion, I have become increasingly convinced, during the last ten or fifteen years, of the basic unsoundness of Freud's major premises and have, literally, read myself back into a position which can be at least loosely identified as Judeo-Christian. However, it was only recently that a book came into my hands which says, and says very clearly and confidently, something which is wanting in most contemporary religious literature and preaching. I refer to Henry P. Van Dusen's book, *Spirit, Son, and Father* (1958). I wish there were time to develop the reasons why I feel such great excitement over this small volume. Instead we must be content with the merest intimation of what Dr. Van Dusen is saying. But first let me state, what is of course well known to many, that Henry Pitney Van Dusen is no upstart theologian or fly-by-night scholar. He is currently President of Union Theological Seminary, in New York City, a member of numerous important boards and foundations, and the author or editor of some 18 other thoughtful books. And now he comes forth with an argument which is absolutely revolutionary and yet is as obvious and plausible as something one has known all his life!

The gist of this argument is that in our interpretation of the Christian Trinity, we have erred and confused ourselves by making the order: God the Father, the Son, and the Holy Spirit. Van Dusen, paradoxically and yet shrewdly, insists that the aspect of this trilogy which has been least emphasized and understood is, in reality, the most important and most immediately knowable. "Something is lacking, and that which is lacking is what is most important" (p. 11), he says with eloquent simplicity. Dr. Van Dusen quickly gains the reader's confidence and interest by acknowledging that he, along with most laymen, had long regarded the concept of the Holy Spirit, or Holy Ghost, as extremely vague and at least mildly repulsive and unsavory. And yet, argues Van Dusen, there are strong historical and Christian grounds for believing that it is through the idea, indeed the *experience*, of the Holy Spirit that all other religious phenomena and practices are inspired and validated. Then, after citing a growing number of other writers who are today also taking this point of view, he asks: "Is not this the true message of 'Christian Hope' for which our generation longs?" (p. 11).[3]

With such phrases as "omnipresence of the Divine influence," "immediately present and supernormally powerful," "the moral consciousness," "the very principle of personal religion," "the Transcendent God in action," "the Immanent God in residence" and by reference to the "inner light" of the Quakers, Buchman's "guidance of the Spirit," and Kant's "categorical imperative of duty," Dr. Van Dusen conveys something of the general connotation which he would have us attach to the notion of the Holy Spirit. He properly notes that it is at this level of thought and experience that the "ecumenical movement" on the part of various Christian denominations finds its soundest and most meaningful justification —and to this he adds, even more broadly:

> Here, then, is the elemental meeting-point of all religion and the proper starting-point for a comparative study of the faiths of mankind (p. 99).

A major, not to say insurmountable, stumbling block to the acceptance of Christian orthodoxy for many con-

[3] In correspondence, Dr. Van Dusen has called attention to two other pertinent studies. They are Lindsey Dewar's *The Holy Spirit in Modern Thought* (1959) and A. B. Come's *Human Spirit and Holy Spirit* (1959).

temporary men and women is the not uncommon insistence upon the uniqueness and particularity of Christ and of the Divine Revelation through Him. For the scientifically trained mind, order, regularity, and uniformity pervade the Universe; and suspension of natural law is as unthinkable as is the episodic intervention of supernatural powers and agencies. Hence, what the scientist looks for in the realm of religion, if he looks for anything, is a set of principles and concepts which are universally and eternally applicable and operative. In Van Dusen's book, what has previously been seen as perhaps *least* promising in the Holy Trinity becomes actually the *most* promising as the basis of a science-religion reconciliation. And the significance and workability of this rapprochement becomes especially pointed when one examines, specifically, the domain of psychopathology.

VII. THE HOLY SPIRIT, PSYCHOPATHOLOGY, AND THE UNCONSCIOUS

As is of course well known, Freudian doctrine holds that the impulses which are bottled up in the neurotic's unconscious and there provide the wellsprings of psychopathology are essentially "evil," i.e., they are, characteristically, the impulses of hostility and lust.[4] Granted this premise, the objective of analytic therapy is, logically enough, to release these impulses from repressive control —to let the evil *out*; and this is why therapy has been conceived at least metaphorically, as the Devil's work. In the neurotic individual, concern over virtue and rightness of conduct has, presumably, done its work only too well and has to be counteracted.

[4] This supposition is so widely known that it hardly needs documentation; but since reference has already been made to Freud's paper, "A Neurosis of Demoniacal Possession in the Seventeenth Century," we may note the particular phrasing which Freud there gives to it: "What in those days were thought to be evil spirits to us are base and evil wishes, the derivatives of impulses which have been rejected and repressed. In one respect only do we not subscribe to the explanation of these phenomena current in mediaeval times; we have abandoned the projection of them into the outer world, attributing their origin instead to the inner life of the patient in whom they manifest themselves" (p. 437).

But now we are having to reconsider all this, and the most likely alternative position is that neurosis is not a result of blocked and outraged biological forces but is rather an expression and consequence of "evil" in a very different sense. The Freudians, of course, recognize that guilt is central to neurosis, but it is always a guilt of the *future*. It is not what the person has *done* that makes him "ill" but rather what he *wishes* to do but dares not. In contrast, the emerging alternative—or, more accurately, the *re*-emerging one—is that the so-called neurotic is a *bona fide* sinner, that his guilt is from the past and real, and that his difficulties arise not from *inhibitions* but from *actions* which are clearly proscribed, socially and morally, and which have been kept carefully concealed, unconfessed, and unredeemed. Freud's assumption, consistent with the position just ascribed to him, was that man is basically an animal, that his most fundamental nature is biologically ("instinctively") given, and that it is cultural and moral interference with "things of the flesh" which make him emotionally sick. From many quarters now comes reaffirmation of the view that man is preeminently a *social being* and that for him the supreme anguish comes, not from bodily deprivation or pain, but from the rupturing of his sociality which we broadly denote by the word sin or alienation. For example, Dr. Karl Menninger (1958), after reading "A New Theory of Schizophrenia," which has already been cited at the outset of this paper, wrote to say:

> I very much liked the article. . . . I wish you would tell [the author] that I think it is fine and that it would be even a little better, in my opinion, if he would not try to distinguish between schizophrenia and other groups of symptoms. Essentially all mental illness must be a reaction to some kind of feeling of rupture with the social environment . . . (personal communication).[5]

Clear adumbrations of this point of view can be traced back nearly a quarter of a century. In 1936 Anton T. Boisen published his epochal *Exploration of the Inner World*, in which he postulated an outraged conscience (rather than id) as the basis of neurosis and suggested

[5] For more extended statements of this point of view, see, among others, Anderson (1959) and Jourard (1958).

that there is something potentially constructive and growth-producing in such a state of mind. Two years later, the erstwhile Freudian analyst, Wilhelm Stekel, published a similar point of view in a book which did not, however, become available in English and generally known in this country until 1950. And in 1947–48 the present writer, then unaware of the views of either Boisen or Stekel, began the publication of a series of articles (see Mowrer, 1950, 1953) in which repudiation and repression of conscience, rather than id, was likewise stressed. Now, again apparently independently of the sources just cited, Bishop Arvid Runestam, of Sweden, in 1958, published a book entitled *Psychoanalysis and Christianity*,[6] in which he writes:

> The psychoanalytic theory about repression, and the widespread neuroses based thereon, . . . give the impression of a strong rancor on the part of psychoanalysis toward the needlessly strict censure of the life drive by contemporary morality. . . . Psychoanalysis stands forth both in theory and practice, by and large, as a potent promoter of the right of the spontaneous instinct-guided life to make itself effective. It is not as if it means that all morality is evil per se. But morality presents itself more as a necessary evil than as a positive good. Conscience and the "superego" receive the role of operating purely negatively and restrictively on that which alone appears to possess the right to life, "the life stream" itself (p. 37).

> However, there are two objections to the psychoanalytical doctrine of repression. These, by the way, finally unite into one. With reference to the notion that it is primarily the sex instinct and the emotional energy it involves, which the analysts imply have been unduly restrained, one may ask: As one looks at the present situation and the contemporary moral condition, is there anything that seems to indicate that this drive has really suffered such terrible damage? On the contrary, is it not at least plausible that the repression leading to neurosis is caused by the repressing of other, usually considered higher, instincts? Have the religious and moral instincts—or, if we do not like to call them "instincts," those factual, inherited or acquired religious and moral forces, emotions, imaginings, needs—been treated more mercifully by contemporary ruling powers than the lower

[6] This book is a revision and translation of a much earlier Swedish edition, which appeared in 1932. For its day, the original version was prophetic indeed!

instincts have? May it not be that these *higher* instincts, needs, and forces, religious and moral, have suffered damage, and that repression and neuroses have their bases just in this? (pp. 41–42).

Would it be too large a leap to equate or at least liken The Unconscious, as reinterpreted by the writers just cited, to the Holy Spirit, as Van Dusen conceives of it? If such an identification (or even a partial one) can be granted, a new and powerful basis is at hand for the integration of psychology and religion. Here is a force in human personality and in the Universe whose manifestation and functioning can be scientifically studied and which, at the same time (according to Van Dusen; see also Boisen's reference to "that social something called God") is the heart and essence of religious experience.

How very different this conception is from the classical Freudian one is indicated by the fact that where Freud expected to find—and, with the aid of "diabolical" strategies, release—Evil, we now believe the Holy Spirit to reside! This changing view of the unconscious has been more fully developed elsewhere [Chapters 2 and 8] and cannot be elaborated here. But enough has already been said to show how revolutionary all this is from a theoretical standpoint; and it is not at all inconceivable that corresponding reforms will follow in practice, in both religious and psychological circles. Freud, as we have seen, did not take guilt seriously; it was instead instinctual deprivation and frustration that concerned and interested him. One is little short of dazzled by the possibilities that seem to lie before us if, for a change, we were to take guilt seriously and at the same time worked out ways of dealing with it which are more realistic and effective than those which have characterized Protestantism and even Catholicism in its least vital forms.

In his book, *Spirit, Son and Father*, Van Dusen cites a "bold prophecy" made some years ago by F. D. Maurice to this effect:

"I cannot but think that the reformation in our day, which I expect to be more deep and searching than that of the sixteenth century, will turn upon the Spirit's presence and life, as that did upon the Justification by the Son" (p. 15).

And a few pages later Van Dusen himself remarks:

Time and again, the Holy Spirit has dropped from the center of attention because it has been lost from the heart of experience; theological crystallization and controversy have preoccupied men's minds reliance upon creed and cult, upon form and structure, has displaced expectation of new disclosures, sometimes with determinative influence and often with baneful effect upon man's conception of the Holy Spirit. Always, perhaps at long last, the Holy Spirit has returned, first as an experience and secondarily as a doctrine, to revive men's souls and banish their defeat and despair, and then to reanimate the dead skeletons of ecclesiastical organization and redeem the dry rot of dogma (pp. 27–28).

If psychology and religion can join forces, both conceptually and practically, it is not beyond imagining that we shall *yet* live to see men's souls revived and their defeat and despair vanquished.

10

Psychology, Theology, and the Social Self *

Certainly the commonest and, in some ways, the most serious objection to the notion that sin or real guilt is the root cause of personality disturbances is that such a state or condition cannot be objectively, scientifically defined. What are the criteria, *it is asked, according to which we decide what is good or bad, virtue or evil? And by implication, if a phenomenon can't be precisely, operationally defined, it doesn't exist. Many of us have very much wanted to get rid of moral values, to believe that reality is ethically neutral, and that experience or action is good or bad only insofar as it is followed by pleasure (lust) or displeasure (unlust). But gradually we are rediscovering that there is more to human existence than mere biology and that social systems (and, indeed, personality itself) cannot exist without prescribed and proscribed patterns of feeling and conduct (cf. Chapter 3).*

After some preliminary considerations, we come to grips in this chapter with at least one way of thinking about the problem of ethics, operationally and objectively, and of dispelling some of the wishful doubting in which we have previously engaged. Here we also touch upon the currently much-debated issue of conformity and nonconformity. The charge that values and ethics are unscientific concepts (and therefore not to be taken seriously) seems to be giving way to the view that no conception of personality and of society can be truly scientific which ignores *these considerations.*

---

* The third of three lectures, on the general subject of "Psychoanalysis and the Judeo-Christian Ethic," presented February 23–25, 1960, under the auspices of the E. T. Earl Lectureship Foundation and the Pastoral Conference of the Pacific School of Religion, Berkeley, California.

In the first lecture in this series, I tried to show that man is pre-eminently a *social* creature—or, in theological phrase, a Child of God—and that his greatest anguish comes, not from bodily discomfort or instinctual frustration, but from violation of his sociality, from estrangement, from unacknowledged and unatoned real guilt. And in the second lecture we examined some of the historical reasons—or should we say, vagaries?—which caused us to abandon this ancient and empirically-based position and drift into the style of life epitomized by the term "Freudianism." It is now clear that, despite his explicit disavowal of philosophical intent and his insistence that he was merely a scientist and physician, Sigmund Freud actually conceived of himself as having a messianic mission in the world and was aiming at nothing less than a cultural and moral revolution.

But there are now widespread and growing indications that the premises upon which this reformation was to be founded are unsound and that Freud's aims and motivations were not messianic but demonic. We have good reason to believe that psychopathology, instead of stemming from unexpressed sex and hostility, comes rather from an outraged conscience and violated sense of human decency and responsibility. This radically revised perception of the basis and nature of mental illness suggests an affinity with both classical and contemporary conceptions of the Holy Spirit and points the way to a new synthesis of religion and contemporary psychological and social science.

How, then, shall we proceed in this, the third and final lecture? Since the first two lectures were written some months ago, I propose, first of all, that we briefly examine and evaluate intervening developments and then decide upon the direction of our ensuing discussion.

I. FURTHER SIGNS OF THE COLLAPSE
OF FREUDIANISM

Although it is not particularly recent, I want to begin by citing an invited address delivered to the American Psychiatric Association in 1956, by Dr. Percival Bailey. Dr. Bailey is Director of the Illinois State Psychopathic

Institute; and his address, which has just come to my attention, is entitled "The Great Psychiatric Revolution." Here Dr. Bailey reluctantly expresses the opinion that the so-called "psychiatric revolution" which was produced by Freudian psychoanalysis has come to naught. He says:

> The great revolution in psychiatry has solved few problems. . . . I understand now why, in the last years, I have a recurrent dream that I am wandering through a dense pathless forest but never arrive anywhere before I finally wake. Lately I have another recurrent dream: A vine, seeking in vain a support on which to climb to higher things, twines around its own base (p. 402).

More specifically, Dr. Bailey says:

> It has become a habit, in beginning a psychiatric lecture, to pay tribute to Freud's genius. Thus Montague (1955), in his dinner address to this Association, remarked: "This general [pessimistic] viewpoint has received what is perhaps its most striking reinforcement from a source which undoubtedly represents the most insightful contribution to our understanding of human nature in the history of humanity. I refer to the psychoanalytic theories of Sigmund Freud." He [Montague] then proceeds to demolish the viewpoint. This is an old procedure; Freud (Wortis, 1954) complained bitterly of it. Still, his teachings continue to arise like a phoenix from its ashes. Lately a psychologist was overheard at the Chicago State Hospital expounding for the delectation of the affiliate nursing students, on whom we spend thousands of dollars every year to bring them to our hospitals, the discredited theory of infantile parental incest in all its pristine naivete. When one remembers how the teaching of Franz Josef Gall still colors all our neurological thinking one wonders how long the hoary errors of Freud will continue to plague psychiatry (p. 395).

And Dr. Camilla Anderson, staff psychiatrist at Salem (Oregon) State Hospital (and author of a 1957 book entitled, *Beyond Freud*) has, in like vein, remarked in a recent letter: "I cannot help but feel that the equation of Freud with the devil [in the second lecture in this series] is clinically sound and also socially. I believe that we shall not soon overcome his pernicious influence."

Writing in the *Reader's Digest* for January, 1960, Dr. H. J. Eysenck, Director of the Psychological Laboratories of the Institute of Psychiatry at the University of London, in an article entitled, "What's the Truth about Psychoanalysis?" points out that psychoanalysis is no more effective in the cure of personality disorders than the mere passage of an equivalent period of time would be. Like Dr. Bailey, Eysenck also refers to the revolution which analytic theory and practice supposedly brought about in psychiatry and then observes laconically:

> The success of the Freudian revolution seemed complete. Only one thing went wrong: *the patients did not get any better* (p. 40).[1]

Many of you will also have seen the 21-page spread in *Look Magazine* (for February 2, 1960) entitled "Psychiatry—The Troubled Science." And particularly significant was the appearance, last year, of a book by Professor Richard LaPiere, of the Department of Sociology of Stanford University, entitled *The Freudian Ethic*. The *Saturday Review*, for August 1, 1959, ran a six-page synopsis of this book, entitled "The Apathetic Ethic." There are many arresting and quotable passages in this synopsis (as in the book itself), but the following catches the general tenor and flavor:

> As a code of conduct the Freudian ethic, as it will be termed hereafter, is entirely negative. It is composed of sentiments and attitudes regarding man's capabilities which, if literally applied, would keep him from attempting anything positive, to say nothing of attempting to devise anything new. Some appreciation of this state of mind can, perhaps, be gained from the terminology used by those who subscribe to it. In their discourse there is recurrent reference to guilt feelings, personal insecurity, instability, frustration, trauma, and "tensions." Such terms are used in reference not only to recognizably abnormal individuals but to everyone. Still more revealing is the total absence in the Freudian

[1] Analysts were always frank to admit their lack of success with paranoid personalities and the addictions, including alcoholism. What conditions did this leave in which to achieve their so-called "triumphs"? Basically, anxiety states and depressions, which tend to be naturally self-limiting and transitory (though often recurrent). Thus, if a person is in analysis two or three years, it is not unlikely that he will find himself feeling a good deal better. But there is serious question as to how much credit analysis can take for it. The chances are the person would have improved anyway. (Cf. Freud, 1937).

discourse of such terms as self-confidence, personal integrity, self-reliance, responsibility, or such an earthy term as "guts" (p. 40).

Also pertinent to our purposes is the following passage:

It is the thesis of this study that many of the changes that have been of late years occurring in our society are malfunctional and that they will, if they continue uncorrected, constitute our unrecognized road to disaster. These changes are being wrought by men of many kinds and various functions—by psychiatrists and child psychologists of the Freudian persuasion, by permissive parents and progressive teachers, by welfare workers and impressionable judges, by managers of business and industry and leaders of labor and academic life, and by politicians and political administrators of many sorts. Moreover, they are being demanded or welcomed, or at least passively accepted, by almost everyone (p. 44).[2]

Here I would suggest one or two not unimportant emendations of Professor LaPiere's statement. By some odd coincidence, he fails to mention that professional group which, just at present, is probably doing more than any other to perpetuate what he calls the Freudian Ethic. At a time when psychiatrists and psychologists are rather generally abandoning psychoanalytic theory and practice, ministers and theologians are, as a group, subtly or stridently advocating it. I realize, of course, that there are many clergymen who are outstanding exceptions to this observation; but as a profession, theologians are at the moment, it seems, more heavily under the sway of Freudian ideology than any other comparable group, including psychologists and, quite possibly, even psychiatrists [Chapters 4, 6, and 9].

The churches and the seminaries are, I believe, actually in process of house cleaning and will presently recover from this aberration. Recently, I had the privilege of hearing a tape recording of the keynote address delivered, in August of 1959, by Harvey Cox at the opening session of the annual meeting of The National Student Councils

[2] See also a series of three lectures entitled "Rake's Progress in Religion" delivered by Dean R. E. Fitch during the 1960 Pastoral Conference of the Pacific School of Religion, Berkeley, California.

of the YMCA and YWCA. Allow me to quote an excerpt from this tape. Having cited the Columbia sociologist, C. Wright Mills, on the distinction between "troubles" and "issues," to which we shall return presently, Cox says:

> As a student YM and YW, I think we have been smitten by a hasty love affair with depth psychology, with troubles, with symptoms. Think of all the ink spilled over discovering myself, of unmasking and revealing each other's true and undisguised egos. I think we've had about enough of the Who-am-I? bit. Think of the countless programs we've had trying to answer this somewhat misleading question. And then think just how far this is from Biblical radicalism.

A member of the Salvation Army also recently gave me a quite remarkable piece of information. The "Army," it appears, keeps "statistics." And what do they show? Some years ago this organization, along with religious denominations generally, decided that it was losing out on a good thing and that it, too, should go in for the "depth psychology" alluded to by Mr. Cox. And what is the result? A steady decline in the effectiveness of this organization in salvaging lost, disorganized men and women. A directive has therefore gone out from the Commissioner, at the Salvation Army's Headquarters in Chicago, to its schools and training centers to abandon the "depth" approach and revert to its more traditional methods.[3]

There are, I believe, many similar trends in our more conventional religious denominations. But a confusing complication exists here, namely, the unprecedented recent upsurge in church attendance and membership. I personally do not doubt that this "return to religion" is somewhat related to the renewed interest on the part of clergymen in personal problems—to the resurgence, that is, of personal counseling, and of the impact of this interest upon the pulpit ministry. But I would ask you also to consider the alternative interpretation offered by Harvey Cox. He says:

> For myself, the return to religion is only evidence on the wrong side. I think most of it is simply a speed-up in the

[3] Cf. *God at the Scrap Heaps* by H. F. Milans (1945) and S. L. Brengle's *Helps to Holiness* (1948).

anxious effort to cling to a 19th-century style of life which has on it the mark of futility.

And the fact that a person of my own persuasions has been invited to give these lectures, here at the Pacific School of Religion and the 38th Annual Pastoral Conference, this year is, it would seem, yet another indication of the willingness of churchmen at least to entertain the possibility that they have been, literally, mis-taken in this area and need to reconsider their own great traditions and indigenous potentialities. This is not, by any means, to say that all we need is simply to return to pre-Freudian theology and doctrine. As I tried to indicate in the second lecture, psychoanalysis came as a judgment upon 19th-century religious ideology and practice. But we must not take the judgment, the indictment, the curse itself as the cure—which, as I see it, is substantially what many theologians have been disposed to do.

In short, what I have just suggested is that on-going developments indicate, with every increasing clarity, the steady deterioration of what Professor LaPiere has aptly called the Freudian Ethic and that we have no choice but to get about the business, at once, of finding something more suitable and substantial to take its place. Conant's dictum that, in science, a theory is never overthrown by contradictory facts, only by another, *better* theory, is well known. Surely empirical evidence tending to refute Freud's basic assumptions has been lying profusely about all the time. But 19th-century theology had manoeuvred itself into so many metaphysical absurdities that when Freud came along with his brazen and brilliantly formulated heresies, the Church was no match for him. Now we see Freud in a truer light, not as Messiah but as Deceiver, and the Church will continue to pay homage to him at its peril.

II. WHAT, THEN, SHALL WE DO TO BE SAVED?

For several years now, during the Summer Session at the University of Illinois, I have taught a course in our College of Education entitled "Mental Hygiene for Teachers"; and when we get about half or two-thirds through this course (which covers much of the same ground we have explored in these lectures, although more systematically), students regularly begin asking: So what can we *do* about the situation? As the diagnosis of our predicament becomes clear, they begin asking about the prognosis, the prescription for corrective action. In the past I have been compelled to say that I did not know the answer. But the situation is, I believe, gradually becoming clarified. As I have already indicated [Chapter 7], it would appear that the Church must become concerned, in a new and more vital way, with the problem of mental illness. No longer should it take a position of subservience to a profession which, by its own admission, has failed to solve this problem [see, for example, Chapter 4]; instead, it must approach the problem indigenously, that is, in terms of religion's own great insights and authority. And if its present precepts and principles are not sufficient to this task, they must be modified and revised until they are.

As part of such a program, it seems clear that we are moving toward a reinstitution of regular confession in the various Protestant denominations. "Pastoral counseling" is merely a euphemism for a voluntary, nonprescriptive form of confession; and this, if handled rightly, can unquestionably be helpful—far more so, I believe, than it ordinarily is at present. But we also need to move on from the prevailing medical notion that one goes for "help" or "treatment" only after one is *in* trouble, i.e., already "sick," to an active program of prevention; and it is here that the obligatory aspect of confession takes on special urgency. There is at present considerable receptivity to this idea; and I should not be surprised to see it effectively implemented in the near future, particularly in Lutheran and Episcopal circles.

I realize, of course, that these statements, without the full context from which they derive, may sound arbitrary and, to some, perhaps even heretical; but in the Nyvall Lectures this spring, I hope to develop this train of thought in a fully documented and more persuasive manner [see Chapters 11 and 12].

What remains, then, for us to consider this evening? I believe that in order to round out the argument and analysis launched in the first two lectures in this series we should employ the remainder of our time together along the following lines. For some decades now, we have been in the habit, whenever a person was deeply troubled and disturbed, of saying: He (or she) "needs therapy." At last we are waking up to the fact that the "therapy" we have been so blandly prescribing for others (and ourselves) is fundamentally worthless—a "therapy" which does not heal and which, as a general social philosophy and guide to life, is downright pernicious. Now we are beginning to realize that the commodity which practitioners of this dubious art have been selling for $25 to $50 an hour, or whatever the market will bear, is a snare and delusion and that a radically different approach is called for. Now, instead of talking just about "sick" individuals, we are beginning to talk about a sick *society*; and I submit that an important aspect of this generalized sickness is the very fact that we speak of our individual and collective difficulties *as* "sickness," rather than as sin or evil. As Professor LaPiere has pointed out, sickness is a stultifying and enervating concept; by contrast, there is something salutory and vitalizing about the notion of evil. It gives us, by implied antithesis, a new vision of the good and something to work *for*, something positive and substantial on which Dr. Bailey's "vine" can cling and grow.

In short, then, it seems that what we have been calling "therapy" itself *needs* "therapy," and when this becomes the case, the nature of the problem shifts into a whole new register, a different universe of discourse. Some years ago, Rollo May (1953) pointed out that whenever there is widespread need for individual psychotherapy in a society, there is an institutional and structural crisis in that society. And Harvey Cox, in the address already alluded to, develops this thought even more explicitly. Having cited C. Wright Mills for the distinction between *troubles* and *issues*, he says:

> Troubles are personal, singular, and individual. Issues are structural, general, pervasive. When one man can't get a job, that's trouble; when six million men are out of work, that's an issue. When an occasional couple can't make a marriage work, that's trouble—maybe very serious trouble. When the divorce rate climbs to a failure of one out of three marriages, that's an issue.

Now I submit that in the psychiatry-religion area, we are today confronted, not just by troubles—i.e., individual failures to function within an essentially sound institutional and ideological framework—but by *issues*, deep, pervasive questions of such urgency that, as Professor LaPiere suggests, our collective as well as individual survival may well depend upon the way in which we respond to them. Therefore, in the time that remains this evening, I propose that we continue our quest for clarification of these issues, on the assumption that this is a necessary prelude to, or at least concomitant of, practical reconstruction and reform.

In thus stressing the importance of intellectual analysis, I realize the danger of being taken in something of a contradiction. On other occasions [see, for example, Chapter 3], I have argued against the therapeutic importance of "insight" and sheer theoretical "understanding" in favor of concrete modifications of behavior. Informally, I have often cited an aphorism by E. Stanley Jones to the effect that it is easier to *act* yourself into a new way of thinking than to *think* yourself into a new way of acting. And Lloyd Douglas commonly has characters in his novels admonish others to seek the "understanding" that comes, not from mere thought and talk, but from actually *trying out* another life style and interpersonal strategy. "Make an investment, perform an experiment," is Douglas' terse way of putting it.

Now Jones, and Douglas, and Cox are not, I believe, in the least disparaging the normal interplay of thought and action. Rather are they rebelling against the interminable rumination and "free association" that goes on in psychoanalysis and related procedures, with an explicit ban on experimentation with new types of action, new patterns of conduct and life style. During a classical Freudian analysis, the patient is expressly forbidden to make any major decisions or changes, in his life, on the grounds that while the treatment is in process he will not be competent to do so and might make serious mistakes. The patient, while in treatment, *may* be encouraged to "reality test" in the matter of greater expression of sex and aggression; but anything so radical as turning over a new leaf and trying to put one's moral house in order is strenuously discouraged.

One of the many paradoxes that have beset psychoanalysis is that while maintaining the essential irrational-

ity of man, it put its supreme trust in *verbal* operations
and neglected the power of what G. H. Mead has called
the concrete *social act*. Small wonder, therefore, that
analysis often stretches out interminably and in the end
—if there *is* an end—leaves the analysand in an intellectual and emotional morass. Somewhat parenthetically,
yet with all seriousness, I want to suggest that the comfortable and well-to-do classes in our society have been
trying to buy forms of personal redemption not nearly as
potent as those cures or "therapies" to which the poor
have always been limited. I am thinking not only of Alcoholics Anonymous, but also of the dramatic transformations of men and women which the Salvation Army frequently achieves; and there is even evidence—see for
example Boisen's book, *Churches of Crisis and Custom*
—that certain practices in the so-called sect churches are
drastic but potently restorative.[4] In other words, I am
suggesting that the time has come when we must recognize that, in our efforts to purchase a form of salvation
which is supposedly better and less crude than anything
which the poor can afford, we have been, in effect, wast-
ing our money. There is no clear evidence of the efficacy
of professional psychotherapy—certainly nothing to compare with the manifest transformations achieved by AA
and the Salvation Army; and I have often wondered if,
when we find we "need therapy," we would not be better
off if, instead of getting a so-called therapist and paying
him a generous fee, we gave the same amount of money
each week to some really good cause.

A Swedish psychoanalyst, Dr. Nils Haak, who has written
extensively on the importance of high fees, says the belief

[4] I am thinking, for example, of a story which a minister
of one of the so-called sect or "fringe" denominations told
me recently of the way in which confession before his congregation, demanded by the authorities of his group when he was
apprehended in homosexual practices, *cured* him of this perversion, then and there, and laid the basis for successful marriage and parenthood. In secular psychotherapy, by contrast,
we are ordinarily content with much smaller changes or "movement." Some years ago a dramatic critic, in commenting on the
performance of Katharine Hepburn in a play, remarked that
she had run the emotional gamut "from A to B." A similar
characterization is in order with respect to the results of psychotherapy.

that what is cheap is of little value is deeply rooted in the human mind. He argues that by demanding a high fee, the analyst appears to the patient as a forthright individual who dares to be honest about money. This makes the analyst a fine person for the patient to emulate. A high fee, Haak says, also prevents the patient from feeling infantile and becoming dependent upon his analyst. For the neurotic patient who likes to hurt himself, the making of large payments to the analyst, according to the Swedish doctor, is an excellent outlet for neurotic feelings. If the analyst were to allow the patient to pay only a small fee, it might give him a humiliating sense of gratitude that would interfere with his therapy. There is also the attitude of the analyst to consider, according to Dr. Haak. If he charges a low fee, the analyst may begin to doubt his own motives for doing so. He might wonder whether he is in love with his patient, or if he really hates the patient and is trying to cover up by being kind. This sort of thing can seriously interfere with the analyst's ability to help (p. 45).

Some of you will no doubt recognize the foregoing quotation as a part of R. H. Berg's recent article in *Look Magazine* to which I made reference earlier. Another argument which is sometimes advanced is that what the analyst offers the patient is primarily his close attention as the patient talks and that if he, the analyst, has any financial worries he is likely to be distracted by his own problems.

Dr. Haak conjectures that anything that comes cheap is likely to be perceived as being of little value. More pertinent to the situation would be the observation that a commodity, such as psychoanalysis, can cost a lot and still be worthless, except, as he implies, for the masochistic or symptomatic relief it involves. I submit that if we need to make a sacrifice, there are morally and socially more relevant ways of doing this than supporting a psychoanalyst in a penthouse.

But this is something of a digression. The point I want to make is this. Mere thinking, talking, analyzing will not save us; our final redemption can only be found in a radically changed life style. The capacity to make such a change is often dependent, at least to some extent, upon new visions, new conceptions which we acquire intellectually; and it is upon this assumption that I suggest we continue our attempt to clarify certain matters which currently seem to be the source of considerable confusion.

III. THE PROBLEM OF EVIL
EMPIRICALLY IDENTIFIED

If a significant aspect of our great sickness as a people and as a society is that we *speak* of sickness rather than of sin, and guilt, and evil, then it follows that we must reconsider these concepts. This, however, is not easy for us. We are unaccustomed to thinking in these terms and find them quite uncongenial. At the opening meeting of a graduate seminar this semester, the very first question raised by the students was: But what *is* guilt? Psychologists and psychiatrists, along with many religious leaders and the general laity, have been taught to think in terms of guilt *feelings*, that is to say, a *sense* of guilt which is unrealistic and nonfunctional and which you can get rid of only if you can find, and afford, a really "good" therapist. The notion that guilt is *real* and not to be banished by mere talk or "counseling" or "analysis" is quite beyond our common comprehension.

Historians of the future may be able to discern more clearly than we do today the circumstances which caused us, as a people, to drift into this remarkable condition. No doubt the true and complete explanation is complex; but a prominent factor in the situation which I believe we can already see with some clarity is that the traditional guardians of our moral and spiritual values have insisted upon speaking of these matters in terms and in a context which are no longer very meaningful to the mentality and thought forms of modern man. One of the reasons, I believe, for the current popularity of Paul Tillich as a theologian is that he has had the courage and discernment to be so *non*theological in the conventional sense of that term. Recently I met with a group of ministers who quickly identified me, in their minds, as an unregenerate naturalist and not at all to their theological taste; and a few hours later I met with a university faculty group, in the same community, who perceived my position as morally reactionary, unscientific, and, as far as they were concerned, theological and supernaturalistic. More than anything that has happened in a long time, this experience brought home to me the extent of our diversity and confusion and our egregious lack of unity in this area. This is not, I believe we would all agree, a healthy state of affairs. There is, in our time, no social, moral, and ethical solidarity and confidence. The difficulty with the position of traditional theology is that its logic and thought forms are foreign to the modern mind; and the problem for the individual who is imbued with what he believes to be a thoroughly scientific and objective world view is that he may be unable to find therein any place for moral values, standards, and ethics. Traditional theology was the original thesis (if we may use the familiar Hegelian paradigm); scientific naturalism has been the strident antithesis; and from this clash must come, I believe, a *new synthesis* of some kind (Mowrer, 1959). I, personally, cannot envision this new ethical frame of reference with great clarity; but there is one facet of the picture which seems to me perfectly definite.

There is, in our time, a widespread distrust of moral injunctions and values which is at least rationalized by the following argument. To be good, it is argued, is to *conform* to existing rules and social prescriptions; and these, it is pointed out, may be either outmoded or otherwise nonfunctional; and if we obey them, then we perpetuate them and so are not being good but, in reality, stupid and evil.

Some years ago I recall a young married woman who came to me in considerable distress because her husband, with whom she was very much in love, "played around," as she put it, with other women when they went to social parties. The husband, who also valued the marriage and by no means wished to lose his wife, later agreed to come in for a talk; and it soon came out that he justified his philandering at parties on the grounds that he aspired to be a writer and felt that he needed a little extra titillation and romance in order to be "creative."

In a sort of microcosm, this marital situation symbolizes at least a part of our larger problem: we pretend to be afraid of convention and morality and social regulation and order on the grounds that it will stifle so-called progress, invention, discovery, creativeness. One immediately sees, of course, how easily such a formula can be used to justify and excuse the most blatant instances of immaturity, selfishness, and moral laxity. There is, however, a legitimate side to this argument which must be faced. Leaving aside those who are obviously exploiting this dilemma in a personal way, there are many contemporary men and women who are sincerely wondering how one can be good, in the sense of conforming to an established social code or system, without also losing that spontaneity and creativity which we so greatly value today and regard as essential to meeting the unpredictable needs of our changing civilization. Here, surely, is the essence of our dilemma: on the one hand we seem to find that the penalty for disregarding the rules of society is mental illness and that, on the other hand, we must preserve our freedom to change and try *new* ways of life.

Actually, I do not believe this paradox is half so difficult as we sometimes try to persuade ourselves, and so suggest the following way of looking at it. Let us imagine a man (which is not hard to do) who does not like to pay his income tax. He has, as I see it, four alternatives:

1. He can pay his tax, accurately and honestly, and say nothing about his disgruntlement. He may feel that, given the present state of world affairs, there is not much he can do about the problem and that he is, in any event, more interested in other things. Now despite the widespread presumption (stemming from Freudian theory) that it's bad for us not to express our annoyance, there is not the slightest evidence that this sort of restraint ever made anyone emotionally ill or destroyed his character. It may not be the most "creative" way imaginable of meeting situations of this kind, but it is at least a perfectly respectable and safe one.

2. Or, a man, faced by the tax dilemma, can again pay his taxes, accurately and honestly, but then make whatever protest he feels is in order. In this particular instance, he is likely to discover, rather quickly, that just grumbling accomplishes little or nothing and that he must look for the conditions and causes behind the present tax situation. He may, as a result, become a staunch supporter of the United Nations, as a vehicle for promoting greater international law and order, thus lessening the threat of war and the necessity for ruinously costly competition in the arms race. The point is that

just because one scrupulously obeys a law or regulation does not in the least mean that one cannot work—openly, honorably, and effectively—for its modification.

3. Or, our hypothetical individual can pay none or only a part of his income tax as an open and avowed *protest*. He may be sent to prison for his pains; but we must not forget that the method is an honest one and *can* be extremely powerful. In modern times one of the most dramatic examples of its effectiveness was the campaign of nonviolent resistance to British rule which Gandhi and his followers mobilized in India. The Indians were oppressed, to mention only one example, by the price of salt, which was a government monopoly, and were forbidden (by what were known as the odious Salt Laws) to make salt for themselves from the seawater which was freely available to them. So Gandhi announced that he was going to walk a distance of some hundred and twenty miles to the sea and openly make salt in defiance of the regulations of the British government; and he invited others to join him, which they did by the hundreds. "When attacked, beaten, or imprisoned by the officials, do not resist, do not flee, do not fight back," Gandhi urged. "Our oppressors will soon have no heart for beating us further, and the Salt Laws will be revoked." As a result of this heroic March to the Sea, as it is now called, the Salt Laws *were* revoked; and eventually application of the same powerful strategy—of open, nonviolent resistance—completely broke British rule and resulted in a Free India. Here, surely, was a power, a *moral* power, more effective than club, sword, gun, or bomb. Limited nonconformity with openness, integrity, and courage is available to us all, at all times; and it can be as mighty as the mustard seed alluded to by Christ in the parable.

I say *limited* nonconformity. Why limited? Because, in the example given, Gandhi and his followers were, in fact, scrupulously observing a higher law than the one they were violating: they kept their honor, their openness, their integrity—and the world respected and will not soon forget them. This observation now leads us, by contrast, to the fourth way in which one may try to deal with a rule or regulation which one finds inconvenient or otherwise objectionable.

4. Let us return to the income-tax example. Here the individual again does not pay his tax or pays it only partially, but then implies or claims that he has paid it *in full*. His legal crime is thus compounded by deceit, hypocrisy, and dishonor. And far from making a man strong, as Gandhi's Salt March did for those who took part in it, *this* strategy destroys personality. In our time two seemingly unrelated things have happened: on the one hand, mental illness has defied our best efforts to understand and control it; and, on the other hand, we have developed a widespread distrust of moral law and principle. Only recently, within the last few years, have we come to realize that there may here be a very vital and important connection. Some of us now suspect hidden guilt as being the central problem in all psychopathology. Integrity and integration, we note, come from the same root: and it now appears that we cannot have one without the other. Cheating and chiseling erode character as they devitalize society. If we accept the benefits and privileges of a given social system, then we are honor-bound to observe the regulations and rules of that system, *unless* we are willing to defy the system *openly* and take the consequences thereof.

Obviously one can think of abnormal conditions such as when a country is over-run by an enemy or such as the Jews encountered in Nazi Germany in which all manner of ethical dilemmas arise. But the circumstances under which most of our crack-ups occur involve no unusual or extenuating circumstances. Of course, we hear much today about how our society as a whole is "sick" and that one can survive only if one *defies*— rather than obeys—it. This, again, seems to me to overlook a very elementary distinction, namely, that between personal sin and corporate sin. Vance Packard is entirely correct when he points out that whereas we once looked upon waste and conspicuous consumption as an evil, we now are openly encouraged in it as an aid to an "expanding economy." I believe that in our world the doctrine of an "expanding economy" is an evil, but it is a *corporate* evil. By its very nature it is public, and we are all more or less involved in it. The time will come, I predict, when we are going to repent it bitterly; but I don't think it's going to make anyone go crazy. The very fact that

PSYCHOLOGY, THEOLOGY, AND SOCIAL SELF   147

we are all in it *together* means that there is no loss of sociality, no estrangement from the significant others, and so no madness.

By contrast, *personal* sins are those which the community does not condone, may in fact severely censure, and which the individual, if he commits them at all, commits privately, secretly. Blind and unwise as our society may be in its current economic presuppositions, it is still pretty well consolidated, it seems, with respect to a lot of things; and it is in the areas in which virtually everyone is at least overtly agreed that personal sin, secrecy, and psychopathology follow in that order.[6] Recently I heard a state hospital psychiatrist comment on how frequently incest figures in the background of the patients whom she sees. Does anyone really think that incest is a fine thing and ought to be generally practiced? I doubt it. Yet it does occur, and I do not believe anyone can long bind his guilt with respect to it by talking about the moral absurdities and ambiguities "of society." Besides, as I have tried to show, there is a perfectly straightforward way of fighting corporate sin without in the least compromising oneself, i.e., falling into *personal* sin. Personal sin occurs, as I see it, and sows the seed of psychological destruction when and only when the individual violates a social injunction or regulation but *pretends that he has not.*

I wish to conclude this section with a moving and prophetic quotation from Dietrich Bonhoeffer. In his book, *Life Together,* he says:

> In confession the break-through to community takes place. Sin demands to have a man by himself. It withdraws him from the community. The more isolated a person is, the more destructive will be the power of sin over him, and the more deeply he becomes involved in it, the more disastrous is his isolation. Sin wants to remain unknown. It shuns the

[6] Occasionally I have been invited to expatiate on the concept of Original Sin. If I allowed myself to do so, I would really lay myself open to the charge from theologians of practicing their profession without a license. But, for whatever it may be worth, my untutored layman's opinion is that this doctrine is nonsense, as is that of the Substitutionary Atonement, and has done much harm in the world [cf. Chapters 11 and 12].

light. In the darkness of the unexpressed it poisons the whole being of a person (p. 112).

And Eric Fromm, in his book *The Art of Loving*, says without equivocation, that the loss of relatedness and community is the ground of anxiety and the beginning of insanity (see also Kirkendall, 1960).

IV. A NATURALISTIC PARAPHRASE
OF PERDITION AND REDEMPTION

If the foregoing analysis is sound, the condition which we currently refer to as neurosis or psychosis is the same as that which an earlier era knew as a state of sin or disgrace; and the defining characteristic of both is the presence in one's life of shameful secrets. When Havelock Ellis was once asked what he thought of Freud's ideas, he dismissed the question by saying that, in his opinion, personality difficulties are due, not to the unconscious, but to *the unuttered*. Freud's theory has, however, had a diabolical fascination for us; and it is only now that we are beginning to realize how thoroughly misleading and destructive it is.

If it is indeed the untold rather than the unknown that devastates us as persons and robs our lives of joy and meaning, how can this view of the matter be given a theoretical formulation approaching in elegance and plausibility that of psychoanalysis? In a moment I shall have a suggestion to make in this connection, but first a collateral observation. When a neurotic (sinful?) person is asked, "What *makes* you so anxious, so depressed, so distraught?" he is likely to reply that he does not know. And the Freudian rejoinder is then, typically, "Yes, that is true. You *don't* know the causes of your troubles. They are repressed, unconscious, and thus beyond your *unaided* capacity to deal with. How fortunate, therefore, that psychoanalysis is available to you as a method of making the unconscious conscious and thus helping you discover the real origin of your difficulties and making you then able to deal rationally with them."

I remember hearing John Dollard some years ago, when we were both on the staff of the Yale Institute of Human Relations, once remark that whatever Freud's scientific contributions might be, he had certainly started a *big business*. Now, more clearly than before, we can see the nature of that business. Certainly no one is going to get rich telling others that their emotional turmoil comes from unconfessed and unexpiated sin. That road to redemption is too rough, and we shun even the thought of it if we possibly can. The Freudian doctrine is, of course, very different—far more pleasant sounding and appealing. According to it, we are *not* "to blame" for our suffering; but—and here is the joker—by the same token neither can we do anything about our condition *by ourselves*. Only the psychoanalyst can save us; and this he is very willing to do, he says, provided we can pay him sufficiently well for his efforts. For the poor, as the Hollingshead-Redlich New Haven study has shown, psychoanalysis has never been a live option; and it is no accident that it is among them that we find other, simpler, and more radically effective methods of salvation at work. Also, as Bonhoeffer in his book, *The Cost of Discipleship*, has indicated, many Christian churches have similarly tried to provide, for those who can afford it, a doctrine of salvation through forgiveness uncomplicated by personal embarrassment, genuine contrition, and meaningful restitution. This, Bonhoeffer has called "the doctrine of cheap grace"; and because it *is* cheap, in personal involvement, sacrifice, and change, it is no grace at all. Despite its exorbitant fees, psychoanalysis also preaches a doctrine of cheap, easy grace. If you can only pay for it, buy it, someone else will do the real work of curing you, while you lie comfortably on a couch.

One of the crying needs of our time, surely, is for a therapeutic (redemptive) alternative which is available to the well-to-do, without carrying the illusion that we can purchase it with mere money instead of at the personal cost which the poor have always had to accept. Jesus Christ, we need to remind ourselves, was a poor man. He and his disciples moved about on foot, preached and taught in the open, without benefit of costly church or temple, and their appeal was to the poor. I. A. Richards once observed, ironically, that every profession is a conspiracy against the laity. The truth of this statement as regards psychoanalysis needs no elaboration. In a slightly more benign way, the same charge can, I believe, also be directed against theologians and clergymen. In the Catholic Church, they openly claim to derive their unique power to forgive sins as a result of the so-called direct apostolic succession. And while making no such claim in this area, Protestant theologians surround Christianity with *other* mysteries which only they can presumably interpret. I take it as suggestive, again, that the most radically redemptive enterprises which we today know, notably the Salvation Army and Alcoholics Anonymous, are *lay* movements with their "leaders" coming, not from our universities and seminaries, but from the ranks of their own converted and transformed personnel. Here the Priesthood of All Believers is more than a high-sounding Reformation slogan; it is a living reality.

But to return, now, to the attempt to schematize the strategy of deception and personal fraudulence which, we conjecture, is the uniform precondition of emotional or, as we might better say, *moral* disturbance. Freud thought in vivid, graphic similes and communicated his ideas, abhorrent though they were, in a clear and memorable way. Only the parables of Christ himself compare perhaps in trenchancy and heuristic aptness and are actually inferior, at least by modern standards, as a conceptual scheme. Hence, the task of formally systematizing the alternative to Freudianism which seems to be emerging—or, rather, re-emerging—remains for the future. The sociologist, George Herbert Mead, made some notable steps in this direction, as did Harry Stack Sullivan within the psychiatric framework and also Martin Buber, as a theologian.[7] Here I shall make no attempt to review or synthesize their respective contributions but will instead suggest a heuristic device which I have found effective on other occasions.

In class one day I found myself drawing a straight line across the blackboard, from left to right, as a means of depicting normal, upright day-to-day human living. A morally and emotionally healthy person, in common parlance, is said to be on the up-and-up, predictable, consistent, a *straight* shooter. This is not, of course, to

[7] Of special interest in this connection is a book by P. E. Pfuetze which systematically relates and compares the writings of Mead and Buber. This book, significantly, is entitled *The Social Self*. [See, also, Chapter 11.]

say that such a person is *perfect*. From time to time, even the best of men and women "stumble," "slip," or momentarily "fall." But they know how to correct their errors, how to pick themselves up, redeem themselves. I once heard a colored attendant in a mental hospital remark to a patient: "The Good Book says, when you *down*, don't wallow!" And the psychiatrist, David Levy,

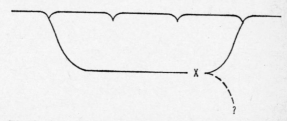

Fig. 1. A *crude attempt to diagram normal and abnormal life styles. The top horizontal line, with its occasional imperfections or "dips" but essentially straight course (from left to right), represents ongoing existence in a normal, emotionally and morally healthy individual. When such a person makes a mistake, he corrects it and "goes on." But some individuals, while pretending to be "on the level," allow themselves to "sink in sin," as shown by the descending, lower line. Because of the danger, strain, and self-revulsion involved in such a "double life," the individual eventually experiences a crisis (at X); his sins "catch up" with him and he is overwhelmed by guilt and anxiety. Now his option is a slow, painful "come-back" (ascending line) or further withdrawal from the whole human enterprise (descending broken line), in the form of suicide, chronic paranoia, or general deterioration. The diagram could perhaps be usefully elaborated to show how some persons, as a result of crisis experience, also rise to "new heights." But, as it stands, the diagram illustrates the most essential features of the present analysis.*

voices the same thought when he says that one of the hallmarks of good character and emotional health is resiliency, bounce. Therefore, I would modify the straight line, as shown in the accompanying figure, so as to provide for periodic dips and recoveries, imperfections, dents, but not nose dives.

However, not everyone has the strength of character or wisdom to correct his mistakes, promptly and fully, which means that when he slips he takes a real plunge, as shown by the lower line in the figure. Let me suggest an illustration. A bank employee needs a little extra money for a few weeks. He has access to stacks of currency which he knows will not otherwise be used during this period so decides to "borrow" some of it, with the full intention of replacing it. But his affairs do not move as he had hoped, and he is unable to replace the money and, in fact, soon finds himself in need of another "loan." And each time he thus illegally helps himself, it becomes easier to do so again, the thought of restitution becomes more and more remote—and our friend is soon a confirmed embezzler.[8]

Now for a time things may go smoothly with this fellow, and he may even regret his not having adopted such a procedure earlier. But he is, of course, in constant jeopardy, as indicated by the discrepancy between the top line, which is what he pretends to be (namely, an honest bank employee), and the bottom line, which represents the level to which he himself knows he has sunk. Eventually, of course, something nearly always happens, and our embezzler "gets caught"; that is to say, there is a *crisis*, which is represented by the large X in the diagram. Now the choice, if he *has* one, is between slow, painful repayment or "restitution" (see the ascending line) and criminal proceedings, imprisonment, disgrace, and, not inconceivably, suicide (descending line).

Here the crime is a financial and legal one but it nevertheless provides a good model for *moral* defection and *human* "bankruptcy." Mistakes or sins of an interpersonal character which are unacknowledged and unredeemed also involve delinquency and deception; and although things may seemingly go nicely for a time, something likewise eventually happens which precipitates a crisis, but now within the individual's own mind or "soul"—and So-and-So, we say, has had a "nervous

---

[8] In a recent study, Cressey (1953) points out that a part of the embezzler's "problem" is that it is "unsharable." This state of affairs, it seems, characterizes many other situations which get human beings into emotional or legal difficulties. It is an essential feature of the present argument that no one ever goes to prison or to a mental hospital who has (or *had*) nothing "to hide."

breakdown." The fact is, he probably has been *down* for some time, so that we could speak more properly of an *attack* or *outbreak of conscience*. We say that the individual has become mentally ill, emotionally sick, and needs "treatment." But it is probably more discerning to say that he has been "sick" for quite some time and that what we now perceive as manifest "illness" is really an inner revulsion against a duplicitous and disgraceful life style and an attempt, as Boisen would say, at correction and cure.[9] I believe it is not inaccurate to posit that virtually all of our contemporary efforts to deal with the psychoneuroses are aimed at symptoms, and do not get to the real root of the matter, and so remain ineffective. Note how often we speak of *restoring* the individual to his *former* self, when not restoration but *reformation* is what is needed.

As if at last awakening to the absurdity of this approach, we are beginning to ask again the question: What is the true and ultimate nature of man? We were willing, for a time, to accept Freud's dictum that man is pre-eminently an animal, an organism, whose ultimate destiny and fulfillment rests in his instinctual life. This view we now distrust, and are rediscovering man's inveterate sociality and morality. Freud said that the alienation which is involved in personality disturbance is between man's conscious mind and his body or,

[9] It goes without saying that a person does not necessarily risk mental illness when he abandons one set of social and ethical standards and drops down to a "lower" level of functioning. If a person makes this sort of transition *openly*, we may say that he is a "black sheep" or (in sociological jargon) *downward mobile*; but since his defection is a matter of public knowledge and carries its own natural and immediate consequences, such a person's mental health is not in jeopardy. It is the person who continues to lay claim to full membership in a group whose standards he is secretly disregarding who is prey to "bad conscience" and "mental illness." Also, we should note that "recovery" from such a state of affairs is *never* easy. As the diagram illustrates, it is a decidedly "up-hill" business; and it is totally unrealistic to encourage such persons, either in the context of secular psychotherapy or religious conversion, to believe that their "salvation" can be simple and easy. Salvation is, nonetheless, *possible*; and it is our obligation to see and delineate that possibility clearly and accurately.

in terms of the title of one of his theoretically most significant books, between *The Ego and the Id*. Our perception is now changing and we see that the battleground lies, rather, between the individual and, again to quote Boisen, "that social something we call God."

Over the main entrance to Emerson Hall, which used to house psychology and philosophy at Harvard, is engraved the Old Testament query or, more properly, awe-inspired exclamation: "What is man that Thou art mindful of him?" For a time it looked as if God had forgotten us, as we had abandoned and turned away from Him. But if it is indeed the Holy Spirit that is working in us when we are "disturbed" and "emotionally sick" [see Chapter 9], then God is very much with us, indeed, and it behooves us to seek Him out on friendlier terms, that we may be spared knowing Him only in His Wrath and Vengeance.[10]

I hope that none of you will feel that in these lectures I am purporting to say anything new or original, except in a very superficial and transitory way. One of Harry Emerson Fosdick's published sermons is entitled "Redigging Old Wells." And here Fosdick describes the great watering places which the patriarch, Abraham, planned and provided at strategic points in Palestine. When the Philistines pillaged the land, these wells were despoiled and filled; and Abraham's son, Isaac, made it his business to re-open the well-springs of his father. Just because something is old is no reason to think it is necessarily unsound or inferior. Although I hold no brief for the metaphysical baggage which the Judeo-Christian Ethic has accumulated in the course of 2,000 years, I do maintain that this Ethic embodies some perduring verities which we can today ignore only at our deadly peril. Surely the author of the 139th Psalm glimpsed the eternal when he wrote:

[10] It has become unfashionable (see also Chapter 5 to talk about the *wrath* of God. I am indebted to Dr. Elmer Million for calling to my attention the statement (by an unidentified author) to the effect that the "wrath of God" is the way in which those who oppose His will experience His love. The implications of this way of viewing the matter for child-parent relationships and practices are clear and illuminating.

Whither shall I go from thy spirit? or whither shall I
flee from thy presence?

If I ascend up into heaven, thou art there: if I make
my bed in hell, behold, thou art there.

If I take the wings of the morning, and dwell in the
uttermost parts of the sea;

Even there shall thy hand lead me, and thy right hand
shall hold me.

If I say, surely the darkness shall cover me; even the
night shall be light about me.

Yea, the darkness hidest not from thee; but the night
shineth as the day: the darkness and the light are both
alike to thee. . . .

Search me, O God, and know my heart: try me, and
know my thoughts;

And see if there be any wicked way in me, and lead me
in the way everlasting.

And Francis Thompson, in the first stanza of his great
religious poem, "The Hound of Heaven," puts the same
thought no less majestically and with peculiar cogency
for our time, when he says:

> I fled Him, down the nights and down the days;
>   I fled Him, down the arches of the years;
> I fled Him down the labyrinthine ways
>   Of my own mind; and in the mist of tears
> I hid from Him, and under running laughter.
>   Up vistaed hopes I sped;
>   And shot, precipited,
> Adown Titanic glooms of chasmèd fears,
> From those strong Feet that followed, followed after.
>   But with unhurrying chase,
>   And umperturbèd pace,
> Deliberate speed, majestic instancy,
>   They beat—and a Voice beat
>   More instant than the Feet—
> "All things betray thee, who betrayest Me."

II

Protestant Christianity:
I. Ambiguity and Disaster*

The title of Section II of this paper is "The Strange Affinity of Protestant Christianity and Freudian Psychoanalysis," which might well serve as a subtitle for the paper as a whole. Certainly the traditional precepts of Christianity are not such as to lead one to expect a ready assimilation of Freudian principles; yet such an assimilation, astonishingly enough, has occurred—or, perhaps more accurately, is being widely promoted. The situation is thus extremely perplexing and problematic. Here, in the present chapter, an effort is made to understand this situation in terms of historical and cultural developments which date back at least to the Protestant Reformation. It may, in fact, not be too bold to conjecture that the Reformation, by its deficiencies and anomalies, actually produced psychoanalysis. If so, it can be argued with some cogency that the only way to extricate ourselves from the dead end of Freudianism (see Chapter 10) is to continue the Reformation. As we shall see in the last section of this chapter, there is actually widespread and growing support for such a program, which will be more fully elaborated in Chapter 12.

I. INTRODUCTION

There can, I believe, be no reasonable doubt that in that area denoted by the terms Psychiatry and Religion, we are today in a state of crisis. For the past several decades we have been in the habit of saying to anyone

---

* Delivered at North Park College and Seminary on May 2 as the first of the David Nyvall Lectures for 1960; also presented, earlier, at a meeting held in Los Angeles, April 21, 1960, under the auspices of the Department of Pastoral Care of the Hospital of the Good Samaritan and later, in September as a Geehns Lecture at the Southern Baptist Theological Seminary, in Louisville, Kentucky.

who is in emotional difficulties, "You need therapy." But now we are realizing that our so-called therapy is itself sick and needs "therapy" (cf. Chapter 10). As long as we continue to believe that all is well in this area and that all we need is more of the same, just so long will we continue to spiral downward in a vicious circle which, as Richard LaPiere (1959), Huston Smith (1960), and others are suggesting, is bringing our very civilization and established way of life into jeopardy.

Personality disorder of sufficient severity to require hospitalization is today commonly acknowledged as the nation's number-one "health problem"; and the prevalence of divorce, delinquency, suicide, perversion, and addiction of various kinds—including the habitual use of alcohol, tobacco, and various other tranquilizers—bespeaks the widespread tensions and poor personality integration in the populace at large.

Religion, to which we have traditionally looked for redemption from evil and guidance in the good life has all but abandoned its claim to competence in these matters. To be sure, in recent decades there has been an attempt, in the guise of the pastoral counseling movement, to regain lost ground; but here the dominant ideas have been essentially secular; and when clergymen themselves have serious personality problems, they almost invariably seek a secular therapist rather than depend upon inspiration and direction from within their own profession. On several occasions I have made the statement that contemporary Protestantism has handled the problem of personal guilt very poorly; and it is, I think, no accident that this assertion has not been seriously challenged. For as long as Protestant clergymen preach the Christian gospel on Sundays and then, on weekdays, have recourse to secular psychotherapists for help in the management of their own lives, their message will have little force or effect in stemming the tide of personal and social disorganization in our time. As Anton T. Boisen observed more than 30 years ago, most Protestant religious leaders have allowed themselves to drift into a position from which they can speak only as the scribes and Pharisees, not with authenticity and authority (see Chapter 6). They proclaim certain tenets of Protestant doctrine, particularly of a Calvinist stripe, from their pulpits, but seem completely unimpressed that this doctrine is not saving *them*, much less the persons to whom they ostensibly minister. They preach justification by faith and roundly condemn "good works," and seemingly take no account of how poorly this doctrine itself works, in the lives of modern men and women.

In August, 1956, a story appeared in *Life Magazine* on "Why More and More Ministers Crack Up," in which the author maintained that the trouble lies simply in overwork. Modern churches, he argued, make excessive demands of their ministers; and the solution suggested was for all churches of more than 500 members to have two or more ministers, with a clearly defined division of labor. While this is no doubt a good practical suggestion, it does not, I believe, get to the root of the difficulty. The trouble basically is that the modern clergyman is in an ambiguous and agonizing situation: pretending to minister the Bread of Life to others and having no deep trust in it himself.

Here the inconsistency of the clergy is equalled only by the audacity of the secular therapists to whom they turn, not only for personal guidance but also for intellectual inspiration and enlightenment. Although it has been evident for at least 20 years that classical Freudian psychoanalysis is a therapeutic fiasco, yet the assumptions concerning the nature of man from which this form of treatment was derived continue to be acclaimed as if one could move the world with them. I don't know how often, when I have criticized psychoanalysis, the protest has come back: "But isn't it true that the super-ego *is* overly severe in the neurotic individual and needs to be softened, made less harsh and demanding?" It is true that this is what Freud *said*, and a lot of people have tried to believe and apply this doctrine. But it is public knowledge that both therapy and prevention which are based on this premise lead only to the most dismal consequences; and one might suppose it was time that we stopped, for purely pragmatic reasons, accepting the premise itself. If it doesn't *work*, what is there to make us think it is *true*, especially when it contradicts some of the most basic principles of the Judeo-Christian ethic?

II. THE STRANGE AFFINITY
OF PROTESTANT CHRISTIANITY
AND FREUDIAN PSYCHOANALYSIS

For a long time it was a mystery to me why Protestantism and Freudian psychoanalysis have hit it off so well. In many ways they are very strange bedfellows indeed. The New Testament, to say nothing of the Old, seems fairly to cry out in opposition to everything which psychoanalysis stands for; and Freud, in his book, *The Future of an Illusion*, made his opposition to and contempt for religion crystal clear [cf. Chapter 9]. Yet present-day Protestantism and Freudian analysis are so blended and interdigitated that it is hard to tell where one ends and the other begins.

The total explanation of this astonishing state of affairs is, I am sure, complicated. But do we not find food for thought in the fact that both Protestantism, insofar as it is Calvinistic, and the secular psychotherapeutic enterprise, insofar as it is Freudian, equally stress *the helplessness of man?* Calvin saddled us with the doctrine of predestination and divine election; and Freud spoke of psychic determinism and the tyranny of the unconscious. Both would have us believe that we are totally incapable of helping ourselves; and they differ principally in the extent to which they hold us accountable for the distressing predicaments in which we commonly find ourselves.

Protestantism has been curiously one-sided in its argument on this score. While holding that when we behave badly it is by our own volition and choice, it then insists, paradoxically, that when we behave well this is by the grace of God, for which we deserve no credit. In other words, the doctrine is that when we are confronted by an apparent option of good and evil, we can *choose* only the evil, and are fully accountable for having done so; but if we do *the good* rather than the evil, this is because of God's will and direction. In short, man can willfully and deliberately act and work himself into a state of perdition; but he cannot, by the reverse strategy, save or redeem himself. Salvation comes, if it comes at all, only by the grace and unpredictable favor of God.

Small wonder, then, that such a doctrine leads to the condition of uncertainty and "despair" about which Soren Kierkegaard has written so poignantly in his *Sickness unto Death* and *Attack upon Christendom*. And it is, I submit, this same despair that fostered the development and growth of Freudian psychoanalysis; for psychoanalysis takes the further step of making man irresponsible and unaccountable, not only for his salvation, but also for his sins as well.

According to Freud the neurotic individual is helpless because certain of his problems have been relegated to and lost within the Unconscious Mind. But Freud was at least more consistent and, in one sense, more benign. Unlike Calvin, he held the individual accountable neither for his salvation nor for his sin. As a child, the individual who is destined to be neurotic as an adult, has supposedly been so harshly and unreasonably treated by his parents that he has no alternative but to repress certain impulses, certain instincts; and it is this act of repression or dissociation which lays the basis, according to Freud, for that special misery called neurosis. Thus psychoanalysis goes Protestant theology one better and makes us not only unable to help ourselves in the matter of "recovery" but also blameless, and unaccountable, for having gotten ourselves into our "neurotic predicament" in the first place.

It is, therefore, not surprising that so many Protestant clergymen, as well as the members of their congregations, have flocked to secular psychotherapists for "help." The analyst not only gives a more definite promise of salvation; he also holds us less "to blame" for our difficulties. Calvinist Protestantism has said to us: "You are responsible for your sins, but you are incapable of being equally responsible for your redemption. God condemns you for your evil, but He will pay no attention to your own efforts to redeem yourself and will Himself save you or not, according to His inscrutable pleasure." This, I submit, is a psychological and human absurdity and a Christian deviation and perversity. But instead of rectifying this perversity, we have compounded it by plunging into psychoanalysis, which extends the heresy to its logical limits and takes away our responsibility, choice, and freedom not only with respect to our salvation but also for our sin as well.

III. THE NEO-ORTHODOXY OF THE NEO-FREUDIANS

On other occasions I have documented the statement that there is not a shred of evidence that psychoanalyzed individuals permanently benefit from the experience [Chapters 1, 9, and 14]; and there are equally clear indications that psychoanalysis, as a common philosophy of life, is not only nontherapeutic but actively pernicious. Here I shall not attempt to review the objective evidence but will speak instead about the reactions of a psychiatrist with whom I recently had considerable contact at a small, intensive three-day conference. His position was, in effect, this. Yes, he agreed that psychoanalysis is unsatisfactory. He had been trained in it, had applied it, and could not make it work successfully and so had abandoned it for a different form of practice, for which he had higher hopes. He could not, he admitted, prove as yet that his approach was superior to that of Freud; but, he said, "people keep coming to you and you have to do something." And what precisely was this something which he was doing?

It turned out that his deviation from Freud consists largely in the fact that he does not require his patients to lie on a couch and does not observe certain other so-called "technical rules" of analysis; but he is still advocating the basic Freudian premise that in neurosis (which I hold is just a medical euphemism for a state of unacknowledged and unredeemed real guilt), the individual is blaming and punishing himself *quite unnecessarily*. As we grow up, this psychiatrist said, "we become our own parents," which was his way of paraphrasing the Freudian notion that the conscience or superego is an incorporation or introjection of our parents' standards and values. And then he added, "We know the injustices to which we were subjected back there in our family. We know what the atmosphere in our home was like. And yet we insist upon treating ourselves, as adults, in the same harsh and unreasonable way our parents treated us as children."

In insisting that our children develop a sense of guilt and the capacity to blame themselves, we pave the way for neurosis, according to this psychiatrist. And by supporting this kind of child training, the churches, he said, "are propagating a most vicious kind of mental ill health. The churches create this type of attitude in people, and I get the sweepings from it. I'm tired of seeing religious parents and the churches teach children to tramp on themselves and would like to see this group take an official stand against such practices." We are "divine," the psychiatrist argued, and we have no right to treat ourselves in this way. And he blamed religious institutions for teaching a doctrine of sin, and guilt, and self-condemnation instead of a doctrine of self-love, self-forgiveness, and self-acceptance.

How unrealistic can we get? Conscience, that is to say the capacity for self-blame and self-punishment, is a marvelous human and social invention, which has the highly adaptive function of causing us to "tramp on ourselves" in order that others don't have to do this for us. I know not a single reputable sociologist or anthropologist who would seriously maintain that we can have a society which does not internalize, as they would say, the norms of the culture (Mowrer, 1961). Otherwise we have, not a society, not an organized, disciplined, orderly group, but an aggregate of psychopaths or, more accurately, sociopaths. And this is precisely the direction in which classical psychoanalytic theory and treatment and the so-called psychotherapeutic enterprise in general have been pushing us and the direction in which we are actually *moving*. Was it not the very fact that the individuals involved in the 1959 television quiz-show scandals did *not* "tramp on themselves" that permitted them to act as they did? This is only one of dozens of similar illustrations of what happens when human beings refuse to "be their own parents" and to act as responsibly in their adult life as their parents tried to teach them to act as children.

As indicated in the preceding section of this paper, Calvinist Protestantism took the first major step toward that brand of personal irresponsibility which is sociopathy, by making us supposedly powerless to do anything constructive about our guilt and sin; and then psychoanalysis came along and took us the rest of the way by insisting that not only can we not help ourselves move toward recovery; we are wrong to blame or punish ourselves in the first place. We should love and accept and respect ourselves so perfectly and so completely and so unconditionally that we refuse to condemn, punish, "tramp on" ourselves, no matter what! This, I submit, is *not* self-respect. This is the ultimate in self-contempt and rejection! For it requires us to regard ourselves, not as human beings, but as a variety of organism not basically different from the beasts of field and jungle, with no morality, no standards, no character, no spirit. Who *wants* to lose his capacity to condemn and punish himself if he really behaves badly. This, surely, is the Pearl of Great Price; and a so-called "therapist" who would take it from us does not respect us but despises us, himself, and the whole human enterprise. It is true, of course, that if we did not have the capacity for self-condemnation and self-punishment, we would never be neurotic or functionally psychotic, but neither can we be human without such capacity. As Boisen (1936) has observed, susceptibility to this anguish is the price we pay, the risk we take, for our efforts to be something more than vegetables and beasts. This is why I have said on other occasions [Chapters 9 and 14] that psychoanalysis is not messianic but demonic, not salvation but slavery and bondage of the worst kind.

IV. GUILT IS THE GREATEST EVIL

Following a lecture which I gave recently at the University of California at Los Angeles [March 7, 1960], Dr. D. P. Boder made some extemporaneous comments which I found extremely illuminating and which I believe I can reproduce almost verbatim. He said:

The Freudian theory of emotional sickness and its treatment is a direct outgrowth of the writings of the 19th-Century German nihilistic philosophers. Nietzsche, particularly in his book *The Genealogy of Morals*, repeatedly affirms that guilt is a weakness. And the poet Schiller, in his play, *The Bride of Massina*, has the chorus end the play by speaking these lines:

Life may not be the highest possession,
But guilt is the greatest evil.

Since Protestant Christianity instills in us the capacity to experience guilt but with no personal resource or reliable possibility for alleviating it, we can see why men of intelligence and vitality began to think and utter such outrageous ideas. And Freud, far from saving us from this rebellion and despair, perfected and systematized it. Today we are paying the price for having accepted this ideology.

You will, I hope, realize that here I am speaking in a highly generalized way. There are, perhaps, a few psychotherapists here and there who are practicing their profession along lines radically different from those laid down by Freud. But they have not as yet become very articulate in the professional literature and it is hard to identify them. There are, of course, plenty of therapists who are purportedly non-Freudian; but the majority of these, I fear, are like the psychiatrist whom I cited earlier: because they have abandoned classical Freudian technique or some minor aspect of the theory, they *call* themselves non-Freudian, or neo-Freudian, or perhaps even anti-Freudian while continuing to accept the major premises of Freud's philosophy and thought.

The nondirective or client-centered type of therapy which is associated with the name of Carl Rogers will, of course, be immediately thought of by many as "non-Freudian." But as I am here using the term, I would say that Roger's approach is deeply "Freudian" (cf. Youngs, 1960). Like classical psychoanalysis, it begins by not holding the individual personally responsible for his difficulties and gives him no prescription for dealing with them on his own initiative. Rogers views the individual as inherently good and holds that he is corrupted and diverted from his indigenous growth tendencies along normal and healthy lines by the untoward actions and attitudes of those around him. Here the encouragement of self-pitying and hostile tendencies within the client is hardly less direct than it is in psychoanalysis. And although Rogers (1951) has seemed not to accept Freud's doctrine of repression, he speaks of the "denial of experience" which, operationally, is not easily differen-

tiated from dissociation or repression, thus re-affirming
the doctrine of the Unconscious and the individual's
essential helplessness with respect to it. I understand
from others who have recently worked with Dr. Rogers
that his views are in process of being revised; but as of
his best known and most recent public utterances, I
believe this appraisal is a reasonable and accurate one.

It can, of course, be objected that my strictures against
Protestantism are likewise not universally applicable. And
here the argument may take either of two directions.
Some will insist that I do not understand what Calvin
"really meant." Although I think I have a fair conception of what Calvin stood for (cf. Gilkey, 1960), I must
confess that I am not greatly concerned about the understanding of Calvin himself. What is important for our
purpose is the widespread *popular conception* of what he
meant; and I am therefore using "Calvinism" in much
the same way as I am "Freudianism." I can myself quote
excerpts from Freud's writings which seem categorically
to contradict the general position here (and popularly)
attributed to him. But the important thing is the main
thrust and impact of the thought of these men; and if
this does not in all details correspond to precisely what
they said (especially toward the latter periods of their
lives, when they had had a chance to reconsider a bit),
this does not particularly matter. We are concerned here
with cultural forces, and the very fact that I have chosen
to deal with both Freudianism and Calvinism as they are
popularly understood is consistent with this aim and goal.

The second of the two types of objection referred to
a moment ago is this, namely, there are certain Fundamentalist or "sect" groups within the Protestant spectrum
who have *not* "fallen" for Freudianism to the extent that
liberal Protestantism has. This I readily grant; but at
once we have to make a distinction between those groups
which are explicitly Calvinistic and those which are
decidedly not. The Calvinistic sect groups are in much
the same position as was Protestantism in general before
the advent of liberalism and the infiltration of Freudianism. They leave man with his guilt and do not attempt
to deliver him from his "despair" by the Freudian formula of making him not only helpless but also blameless.
They are thus, in one sense at least, in a sounder posi-

tion than are the liberal Protestant groups and have, one may say, less to repent. But they are still on the horns of the dilemma which Calvinism itself poses and do not offer a satisfactory resting place.

In contrast, there are some so-called sect groups which preach and practice a form of Christian doctrine which seems to me remarkably close to primitive Christianity and which has been remarkably little affected by the more dubious aspects of the Reformation. Later we shall have occasion to look again, more closely, at these groups, at the same time that we also consider the place of Roman Catholicism and Judaism in the modern world [Chapter 12]. First, however, it will be necessary to review certain other considerations of a somewhat different nature.

V. SECULARIZATION AND CRISIS

Before one can have anything like an adequate understanding of the present crisis in psychiatry and religion, one must, I believe, carefully note the extent to which numerous functions which prior to the Reformation were regarded as the proper concern of the Church have today been *secularized*. The Reformation was a valiant effort to free mankind from the oppressive control and domination previously exercised by the Church Universal. And separation of Church and State, in as many areas as possible, was seen as basic to this enterprise.

Separation of Church and State in the area of politics was, of course, a prime objective of the Reformation; and we still have a strong feeling that religious groups should "stay out" of politics, at least in the formal sense of the term. *Education* has likewise been extensively secularized. Our public schools are testimony to the success of this movement, even though there is still resistance in some quarters, both in theory and practice. The trend toward secularization has also been marked in the area of *charity*. Here we note the widespread development of public relief, as well as numerous welfare agencies of a private but, again, largely secular nature. The introduction of insurance of various kinds has had a similar effect in this connection: now, instead of giving directly to persons who have suffered physical calamity, such as loss of home by fire or flood, or incapacitating illness or death in their family, we pay regular "premiums" to a company which carries out these functions, quite automatically and impersonally, for us.

In these areas, then—of politics, education, and charity —it looks as if separation of church and state, in some degree at least, is here to stay. We shall later [Chapter 12] have occasion to examine some of the less fortunate consequences of the secularization of charity; and there are also those who point to evils that arise in public education. But, by and large, the gains seem to exceed the losses—at least this is the way the situation is popularly perceived; and there is no strong inclination for our society as a whole to revert to the earlier condition of church control in these areas.

There is, however, another area in which secularization has occurred, with results which are far from satisfactory or reassuring. I refer to the management of the problem of *personal guilt*. Traditionally the solution to this problem has rested very largely in the hands of the church; and although Protestant and Catholic leaders alike continue to lay claim to interest and competence in this area, the fact is that those persons who are most deeply burdened and broken by guilt and moral failure are now quite regularly turned over by the churches to the state for "care and treatment." This statement, to be sure, involves an assumption, namely, that in so-called mental illness or psychopathology the central problem *is* guilt, unconfessed and unatoned *real guilt*; but elsewhere [Chapters 3, 4, 5, 7, 8, 10, 14] I have assembled so much evidence for believing this assumption to be justified that here I propose to take it for granted. On other occasions [Chapters 9 and 10] I have also cited extensive evidence for the assertion that the state mental hospital, as a therapeutic agency, is a failure and that the time is upon us for re-thinking the whole attempt to help guilt-ridden persons in a secular, medically controlled setting.

The phenomenon of *legal* guilt is manifestly a state responsibility and probably should remain so, at least insofar as the determination of responsibility for specific acts is concerned. But here again there is question as to the success of the state's efforts at treatment and rehabilitation. Legally, retribution is the principal instrument of "justice," and as a deterrent to crime on the part of others, it may be quite essential; but there is widespread disillusionment regarding its redemptive powers, and such writers as Albert Eglash (1958, 1959) are now suggesting that prison programs ought to proceed much more along lines of *restitution* rather than retribution.

It appears, then, that secular, state-directed efforts to rehabilitate guilty people—both those who have been legally adjudged guilty (i.e., criminals) and those who (as Boisen has said) are *self*-condemned (i.e., the insane) —leave much to be desired. In both areas there has been a widespread attempt, particularly under medical aegis, to eliminate the whole notion of moral involvement and to treat both groups as if they were *sick*. The result is that we are now beginning to talk about our whole society being "sick," and I have elsewhere suggested [Chapter 10] that the essence of this "sickness" is the undue extension into these areas of the sickness concept itself.

But there is another side of this problem which is quite as important as the one we have just been considering. Religion, as an institution, can very possibly survive *without* having a direct role in politics, or in education, or perhaps even in charity in the material sense of that term; but there is grave question as to whether religion can survive, i.e., remain vital and meaningful, if it similarly relinquishes its responsibility for ministering to those who are devastated by personal guilt. I have previously argued [Chapters 6, 7, 8], as Anton Boisen has done for the past thirty-five years, that the church loses its very excuse for existence and cuts itself off from essential sources of inspiration and validation as soon as it refuses to go "all the way" with the person who is in that emotional and moral crisis which we call neurosis and psychosis. As soon as the church turns such a person over to some other agency or profession to deal with, it signs and seals its own death warrant.

This view of the situation was brought home to me with special cogency and force recently when I heard a young minister use a *purely hypothetical* human situation to illustrate a point in theology, in a group where a psychiatrist who was present was promptly able to cite a real, flesh-and-blood "case" to the contrary. Boisen has long pleaded with ministers and theologians to put their books away for a season and to study those "human documents" one finds in what he also colorfully calls "the wilderness of the lost." This is not a great innovation or departure for Judeo-Christianity; instead it is a challenge to the churches to return to a *depth* of ministry which they have generally abandoned. In the parable of the lost sheep, Christ tells of the good shepherd leaving the ninety and nine that are safely in the fold and going to look for the one that has gone astray (Matt. 18:10). Is it not the very fact that the modern church has become indifferent to *lost souls* that has reduced its vitality and authenticity almost to the vanishing point? As long as ministers, priests, and rabbis are impelled and compelled to "refer" and defer to psychologists and psychiatrists when members of their congregations meet severe personal crises, just so long will they find themselves in the predicaments described earlier in this paper.

Recently a college student, in a group where this matter was under discussion, epitomized the situation admirably as follows. She said: "Because the church has refused to go after the *one* lost sheep, we now find that we are *all* 'lost,' confused, neurotic."

VI. SHADOW OR SUBSTANCE?

I cannot claim to be at all fully informed regarding contemporary trends in Protestant theology, but my casual impression here is of a land of shifting sands. Vogues and fashions there are in abundance, but I fail to see anything that looks much like the bedrock of perduring human realities. One writer, by unusual eloquence, force, or novelty, will gain a following, only to be superseded by someone else who outdoes him at his own tricks. Just at the moment Professor Paul Tillich is in the limelight. I am not competent to judge much of what he has written; but in the one area where I have some claim to specialized knowledge I find him thoroughly ambiguous. Take, for example, this passage from a recent sermon entitled "The Good I Will, I Do Not":

> In pulpits, Sunday schools and families, Christians have called sinful the natural strivings of the living, growing and self-propagating body. They concentrate in an inordinate,

purely pagan way on the sexual differentiation of all life and its possible distortions. Certainly, these distortions are as real as the distortions of our spiritual life, for instance, pride and indifference. But it is itself a distortion if the power of Sin is seen in the sexual power of life as such. In this way, such preaching completely misses the image of Sin as Paul depicted it. What is worse, it produces in countless persons a distorted guilt feeling which drives from doubt to anxiety, and from anxiety to despair, and from despair to the escape into mental illness and the desire to destroy oneself (p. 22).

What, precisely, is Tillich saying here? As is so typical of many of his writings, this passage contains a number of vague allusions and obscurities. But what Tillich *seems* to be saying here, and over and over again in many other places, is this: The Protestant church has given us an acute capacity to *feel* guilt, quite unrealistically, with no adequate means of resolving it. Therefore, with the Freudians, he is suggesting that we reject guilt *at its source* and thus not *have* to deal with it. Guilt, much of it religiously inspired, he says, with Kierkegaard, Neitzsche, Schiller, and Freud, *is* our sickness. In a recent letter to a mutual friend, another distinguished seminary professor takes a very different point of view. He says: "In so far as Christians have fallen for the notion that guilt is a sickness they have made theological donkeys of themselves. Much as I love and respect [Harry Emerson] Fosdick, I suspect he and others of his persuasion got themselves quite mixed up about 'sin.'"

Here, surely, is a hopeful note, but it is not in the ascendancy today. It is not the vogue of the moment. Today there are literally thousands of ministers who are under the spell of Tillich, Fosdick, and the other Freudian apologists. And what is the basis on which ministers accept the leadership of such men? Is it because psychoanalysis has been empirically validated? Not in the least. It is rather because theology, by becoming bookish and unredemptive, has lost its true center of gravity, its contact with basic human realities, and its leaders bob about like loose corks in a choppy sea. They turn to Freud because they have lost their own integrity and anchorage. If religious leaders had been deeply involved in the care and redemption of seriously disturbed persons for the past century, instead of systematically "referring" such persons, there would have been no Freud and no necessity for a Tillich or a Fosdick to try to legitimize him!

Recently, at the conference to which I have previously alluded, I heard seminar professors and distinguished parish ministers make statements such as these: "Today pulpit theology is a bunch of words." "Theology comes between us and people." "The minister has trouble getting his person and his profession together." "The church must find a new form for its message."

I submit that the prime reason for this distressing state of affairs is the fact that theology, i.e., the science and art in which many of our ministers are trained, is undisciplined verbiage. By what *operations* is it validated, tested, refined, clarified? What are the *canons of evidence* which a minister uses for deciding what to preach or write about? What are the rules according to which he decides what is truth and what is error? Granted that this is at best a difficult area in which to be wise, the minister who merely reads, preaches, and perhaps does a little pastoral counseling with carefully selected cases can hardly be expected to have deep insights and to inspire great confidence.

Challenge a parish minister or seminary professor to *stay with*, rather than "refer," a person suffering from a severe personality crisis, and what is the typical rejoinder: "But I'm not *qualified* for that sort of thing!" The fact is, such a minister is not qualified. Because the church does not concern itself with the one genuinely lost sheep, the whole congregation is eventually lost; and the minister himself goes into "therapy" with the same would-be secular healers to whom he has been referring others. Today's clergyman can, I maintain, save himself only by the radical expedient of returning to the full-fledged business of saving, rescuing, redeeming others. And when he does this, pulpit "theology" will recover the substance and stability which are today so conspicuously lacking. Here is one function which *cannot* be secularized, without calamity to all concerned.

VII. THE REFORMATION MUST GO ON

Ladies and Gentlemen, I must acknowledge at this juncture the surprise and, indeed, embarrassment I feel at finding myself, as a psychologist, playing the role of theological and religious analyst and critic. The presumption thus involved is, of course, enormous; and I venture upon such a course only after having become persuaded that the contemporary psychotherapeutic enterprise, and its vagaries, cannot be understood without examining the theological situation, in both its contemporary and historical dimensions. Even so, if there were absolutely no precedent among more competent scholars for the type of reservations and concerns I am expressing, I might still lack the necessary audacity to enter into such a discussion. But the fact is, one finds considerable support for this sort of thinking in the works of some of the most distinguished theological writers of this generation.

In February of 1960, it was my privilege to hear the lectures, on "The Christian Faith and Historical Thinking," which Dr. Wilhelm Pauck, Professor of Church History at Union Theological Seminary, gave at the Pastoral Conference sponsored by the Pacific School of Religion, in Berkeley, California. Here Dr. Pauck reminded his audience that the leaders of the Reformation were of a decidedly medieval stamp of mind, and that their insights and truths are not necessarily pertinent or applicable in our time. He pointed out that as a result of this hiatus, "Christianity has become a minority movement" in the modern world and stoutly maintained that "The Reformation *must* go on."

Almost immediately afterward, in the *Christian Century* for March 2, Professor H. Richard Niebuhr, of the Yale Divinity School, published an article entitled, "Reformation: Continuing Imperative." The first part of this paper is largely autobiographical and not particularly pertinent to our interests; but the later part is highly so and will be quoted at some length.

> My primary purpose today is not to protest. It is still that of the reformation of the church. I still believe that reformation is a permanent movement, that *metanoia* is the continuous demand made on us in historical life. The immediate reformation of the church that I pray for, look for and want to work for in the time that may remain to me is its reformation not now by separation from the world but by a new entrance into it without conformity to it. I believe our separation has gone far enough and that now we must

find new ways of doing what we were created to do. One side of the situation is that represented by the "world" today, at least the Western world. It seems to me that in that world men have become deeply disillusioned about themselves and are becoming disillusioned about their idols—the nations, the spirit of technological civilization and so on. They no longer expect the powers in them or around them to save them from destruction (whether through holocaust or boredom) or from the trivialization of an existence that might as well not have been. The so-called underdeveloped nations —including Russia—do not yet know that there is no hope and no glory and no joy in the multiplications of our powers over nature, and we have no way of saving them from going through the experience through which we have passed or are passing. But in the West the most sensitive, if not yet most, men are living in a great religious void; their half-gods have gone and the gods have not arrived. The religious revival we are said to have had in recent years has been, so far as I can see, less a revival of faith in God and of the hope of glory than a revival of desire for faith and of a hope for hope. And it further seems to me that our churches have been filled (our seminaries too) with men and women who are experiencing that emptiness; further, that there is in the society at large a host of similarly minded persons who have not even considered the church as possibly ministering to their need. I am haunted in the presence of that situation by the phrase: "the hungry sheep look up and are not fed" (p. 250).

Professor Niebuhr then calls for a "resymbolization of the message and the life of faith in the One God" and concludes by saying:

> I do not know how this resymbolization in pregnant words and in symbolic deeds (like the new words of the Reformation and the Puritan movement and the Great Awakening, like the symbolic deeds of the Franciscans and the social gospelers) will come about. I do count on the Holy Spirit and I believe that the words and the deeds will come about. I also believe, with both the prophets and, of all men, Karl Marx, that the reformation of religion is the fundamental reformation of society. And I believe that nothing very important for mankind will happen as a result of our "conquest" of space or as a result of the cessation of the cold war unless the human spirit is revived within itself (p. 251).

Such statements as those just quoted from Niebuhr and Pauck not only underscore the general shakiness of contemporary theology; they are also an open invitation to rethink our most fundamental presuppositions. But they do not give us any very confident or clear indication of the direction such thinking should take. Turning to Tillich's book, *The Protestant Era*, a collection of essays first issued in 1948 and reissued, in abridged form, in 1957, one finds little help in the earlier chapters; but the book ends with a paper, initially published in 1939 in the *American Journal of Sociology* and entitled, "The End of the Protestant Era?" which is hard-hitting, direct, and—up to a point—illuminating. The argument begins thus:

> The central principle of Protestantism is the doctrine of justification by grace alone, which means that no individual and no human group can claim a divine dignity for its moral achievements, for its sacramental power, for its sanctity, or for its doctrine. If, consciously or unconsciously, they make such a claim, Protestantism requires that they be challenged by the prophetic protest, which gives God alone absoluteness and sanctity and denies every claim of human pride. This protest against itself on the basis of an experience of God's majesty constitutes the Protestant principle. This principle holds for Lutheranism as well as for Calvinism and even for modern Protestant denominationalism. It is the principle which made the accidental name "Protestant" an essential and symbolic name (p. 226).

And then Tillich says:

> The consequences of the Protestant principle for intellectual, moral, and social life are obvious. Protestantism is a highly intellectualized religion. The minister's gown of today is the professor's gown of the Middle Ages, symbolizing the fact that the theological faculties as the interpreters of the Bible became the ultimate authority in the Protestant churches. But professors are intellectual authorities—i.e., authorities by virtue of skill in logical and scientific argument. This sort of authority is the exact opposite of the kind that is sought by the disintegrated masses, whose disintegration is to some extent an echo of the endless arguments and counterarguments among their leaders. Bishops, priests, and monarchs have a sacramental authority which cannot be taken away by arguments and which is independent of the intellectual and moral qualities of its carriers. It is a character which can by no means be lost. This sacramental basis is denied by the Protestant protest. The minister is preacher, not priest; and sermons are intended, first of all, to appeal to the intellect. But the masses that are dis-

integrated need symbols that are immediately understandable without the mediation of intellect. They need sacred objectivities beyond the subjective quality of a preacher. . . . More and more individuals become unable to endure the tremendous responsibility of permanently having to decide in intellectual and moral issues. The weight of this responsibility became so heavy that they could not endure it; and mental diseases have become epidemic in the United States as well as in Europe. In this situation, psychoanalysis has seemed more desirable for educated people than religion, especially Protestant religion. In Catholic countries the situation has been different because the confession has been able to overcome many tendencies toward personal disintegration (pp. 227–228).

Then, in a footnote, Tillich refers to the "success of psychoanalysis in Protestant countries" which he attributes to the assistance it gives the individual to "bear responsibility and guilt without the help of confession and the related forgiveness which comes from the outside" (p. 228). Here, it would seem, is where Paul Tillich took the wrong turn in the road. Today we can say, without fear of contradiction, that psychoanalysis has *not* been a "success," in this or any other country. Yet many theologians, including Tillich, continue to preach and write as if Freudian theory and practice were the Alpha and Omega. When, as in the Tillich sermon cited in the preceding section, theologians today expound the psychoanalytic doctrine of false guilt, they simply do not, from a secular and scientific point of view, know what they are talking about. This, among other reasons, is why I say that secular students of this problem have no choice, at the moment, but to strike out on their own in this domain and make the best sense of it they can. And the only way the present writer can understand the situation is along lines suggested at the outset of this paper, namely, in terms of the absurdity of the Reformation doctrine of human guilt and divine grace. This, as I have already argued, places man in an intolerable predicament, from which psychoanalysis purportedly rescues him but, in point of fact, only plunges him into the deeper. The time has come, if we are not to march straight to perdition, to make an about-face and return to principles which a perilous and arrogant theology has led us to ignore and despise.

12

Protestant Christianity:
II. Challenge and Change*

If, as the last section of the preceding chapter suggests, the Protestant Reformation was, in certain important respects, deviant and incomplete, there is urgent necessity for continued exploration, new insights, and social inventiveness. But in an area as intricate and vital as the one presently under consideration, "research"—in the conventional sense of that term—is not very meaningful. What is needed, instead, is broad trial and error, actual experience, or "action research" as it is sometimes called. In the present chapter we review "experiments" of this type that are already under way and suggest certain other possibilities that deserve a hard try.

Surely one of the main reasons why, as Pauck (Chapter 11) says, the Reformation "must go on" is the need to bring science and religion into a common, or at least compatible, universe of discourse. There is at present some lack of sanguinity on this score, borne of the consequences—already apparent to many—of our having tried to make religion mesh with the pseudoscience of Freudian psychoanalysis. We are now in process of getting a clearer vision of psychological and social realities; but Reformation theology has made its own distinctive contributions to present confusion and has an obligation to put its house in order, as well. To repeat a truism, a sound psychology and a sound theology will show congruence, not conflict, and should generate personal practices and institutional forms decidedly superior to those we currently follow.

In this lecture I shall make no systematic attempt to summarize the preceding one but will, instead, go directly

---

* Delivered, in somewhat abbreviated form, at North Park College and Seminary on May 3 as Part II of the David Nyvall Lectures for 1960 and also presented, as a Geehns Lecture, at the Southern Baptist Theological Seminary.

on with the main argument and analysis. However, I shall try to do this in such a way that those who may not have heard the first lecture will, by inference, quickly identify the assumptions on which we are operating and the objectives toward which we are aiming.

I. FALSE QUESTS FOR IDENTITY AND INTEGRITY

In the first lecture I mentioned having attended, a few months ago, a very remarkable three-day conference. The group consisted of ten or twelve eminent seminary professors and parish ministers, with a sprinkling of psychologists and psychiatrists. And although I thought I knew something of the specialized, as well as common, language of the professions thus represented, by the end of the first day I was thoroughly mystified by what was being said and done, especially by the theologians. Obviously some new type of "group dynamics" was at work, which I did not at all understand—or, I confess, like. We had been called together (and were being *paid*!) to consider ways and means whereby the modern church can become more intelligent and effective in helping modern men and women live confidently, meaningfully, and creatively (in the best sense of that vastly overworked term). But this group was obsessed by a cultus which was foreign to me personally and, as I perceived it, irrelevant and negative as far as the stated objectives of the meeting itself was concerned.

By the end of the second day, with everyone picking at and on everyone else, as well as himself, and generating an impenetrable intellectual and emotional fog, a little light began to dawn. Here, I surmised, were the Existentialism of Paul Tillich and the I-Thou philosophy of Martin Buber *in action*. My fellow conferees were, it seemed, trying to put into effect, in their personal and professional lives, what they understood these two speculative giants to be advocating. But then a chance remark provided a more specific cue; and when I returned home I hurried to consult a book which I had owned for some time but had not previously read: *The Meaning of Persons* by Paul Tournier (1957). At once it was clear that here was the manual which was inspiring and guiding the strange demonstration I had witnessed—a sort of Latter-

Day Pentecost, but with the thunder and bolts of fire
on a vastly reduced scale. The Fire, in fact, was mainly
smoke and the thunder, just "noise."

At this meeting a sort of pass-phrase which I heard
repeatedly, in slightly varied versions, was: "But I want
to get to know *you*, the *real* you." On the second page
of his first chapter (which has as a title what Harvey
Cox has recently characterized as "that hardly helpful
question, Who Am I?"), Tournier says:

> Day after day men and women of all ages and conditions,
> the healthy as well as the sick, come to see me in order to
> learn to *know themselves better*. They tell me the story of
> their lives. They take great trouble to get the details abso-
> lutely right. They are seeking to know the person that they
> themselves *really are*. . . .
> What matters in this search for the person is not so much
> historical facts as the *way* in which we see and feel them.
> If our memories deceive us, the distortion that they have
> undergone is by no means accidental; it tells us as much
> *about ourselves* as do the facts themselves [italics added].

And a few pages later the author also says:

> The reader will see now why it is that this problem of the
> person has for twenty years been of such absorbing interest
> to me. It has a general significance which is of vital im-
> portance for all thought and all civilization: what is man?
> But it also has a particular significance, which is equally im-
> portant for my life: who am I, really, myself?
> It is a question which haunts each one of us, whether we
> are aware of it or not. It is there in every consultation I give.
> It is there for the man who comes to see me, and for me as
> well. This frank and living contact with people is the very
> substance of my professional life. It is for me, quite as much
> as for the man who consults me, a means of discovering
> myself. I seek to attain it not only in my consulting-room,
> but all the time, in every meeting with another person, in
> my own family, with my friends, in conferences, and on a
> holiday (p. 14).

And *my* friends were doing it, *too*, at the conference
—where, objectively, at least, they were *supposed* to be
doing something else! But objectivity, we soon discover,
is passé:

> When we evoke our memories, we can never be quite sure
> that we have banished all illusion from them, however

sincere we are. What we call to mind is not the facts themselves but their appearance, the way in which we saw and
felt them. All that we have seen and felt—images and sensa-
tions—remains more or less distorted in our memories (p.
12).

There was a time when legend, poetry and music counted
for more than science in the making of a cultivated man.
. . . One of Pirandello's *Six Characters in Search of an Author* declares that an imaginary being like Sancho Panza is
more real than any real man. . . . Where then is the
frontier between what I am and what I can become? (p. 13).

Even Sancho Panza is not identical for everybody; my idea
of him is not the same as yours, or as that of Cervantes.
. . . The same thing happens with all these people who
come to see me, and take so much trouble over their efforts
to describe themselves to me with strict accuracy (p. 14).

Twenty years earlier, we discover, Buber in his booklet
What Is Man? was making substantially the same point:

When imagining and illusions are over, the possible and
inevitable meeting of man with himself is able to take place
only as the meeting of the individual with his fellow-man—
and this is how it must take place. Only when the individual
knows the other in all his otherness as himself, as man, and
from there breaks through to the other, has he broken
through his solitude in a strict and transforming meeting.
It is obvious that such an event can only take place if the
person is stirred up as a person (pp. 201–202).

And precisely how is this to transpire? The answer:

In real conversation, . . . a real lesson . . . , a real em-
brace and not one of mere habit, a real duel and not a mere
game—in all these what is essential does not take place in
each of the participants or in a neutral world which includes
the two and all other things; but it takes place between them
in the most precise sense, as it were in a dimension which is
accessible only to them both. Something happens to me—
that is a fact which can be exactly distributed between the
world and the soul, between an "outer" event and an "inner"
impression. But if I and another come up against one another, "happen" to one another, . . . the sum does not
exactly divide, there is a remainder, somewhere, where the
souls end and the world has not yet begun, and this remainder is what is essential. . . .
On the far side of the subjective, on this side of the objective, on the narrow ridge, where *I* and *Thou* meet, there
is the realm of "between" (p. 204).

This reality provides the starting-point for the philosophical science of man; and from this point an advance may be made on the one hand to a transformed understanding of the person and on the other to a transformed understanding of community. The central subject of this science is neither the individual nor the collective but man with man (p. 205).

What, then, can one say to all this? There is something undeniably appealing and wistful about it, but can it be put to work in the everyday world? In the same context from which the foregoing passages come, Buber refers to "something ontic," and there is now in Chicago and one or two other cities in this country an Onto-Analytic Society. And various forms of Existential Analysis have been practiced in Europe for some years. But is their record any better than that of psychoanalysis? In an oblique criticism of the latter, Buber writes:

> We have seen that an individualistic anthropolgy, an anthropology which is substantially concerned only with the relation of the human person *to himself*, with the relation *within* this person between the spirit and its instincts, and so on, cannot lead to a knowledge of man's being (p. 199, italics added).

The emphasis on the relation of man-to-man is, surely, an improvement upon Freudian doctrine; but is there not still a serious ambiguity here? The emphasis, as Tournier's phrasing especially suggests, is still upon one's coming to *know himself.* Don't we, in fact, know ourselves only *too well* and sicken of this knowledge, yet are loath to let *others* know, in the same sense, *who we are?* I do not mean "others" in the sense of a professional listener who is paid to keep our secrets, but in Sullivan's sense of the significant, *ordinary* others in our lives: relatives, friends, colleagues, neighbors. *Here* is where the real "break-through" to community and personal authenticity comes; and anything which falls short of this is, I submit, a pious hope.

II. PERSONS OR PRINCIPLES?

For the atmosphere created at the conference and the prevailing tone of the quotations from Tournier and Buber in the preceding section, there is surely only one apt word: mystical. And since Orientals, rather than Westerners, have cultivated the occult so much longer, it is no accident that we should now be turning to them for real expertness in these matters. Zen Buddhism has already achieved at least a minor vogue in this country; and recently a full-page ad by Harper and Brothers in the *Christian Century* was headed: "Books on Eastern Religions for Western Readers." A few weeks ago a former student, as a pleasant gesture, sent me a copy of *The Wisdom of Laotse* (Lin Yutang, 1948). Laotse was a Taoist, and Taoism is one of the direct and dominant tributaries of Zen. Open the Laotse book, almost at random, and here is the sort of thing one finds:

Life arises from death, and *vice versa*. Possibility arises from impossibility, and *vice versa*. Affirmation is based upon denial, and *vice versa*. Which being the case, the true Sage rejects all distinctions and takes his refuge in Heaven (p. 49).

And to this intellectual nihilism is added moral negativism or at least neutrality. For example, we read:

The man of character lives at home without exercising his mind and performs actions without worry. The notions of right and wrong and the praise and blame of others do not disturb him. When within the four seas all people can enjoy themselves, that is happiness for him; when all people are well provided, that is peace for him. Sorrowful in countenance, he looks like a baby who has lost his mother; appearing stupid, he goes about like one who has lost his way. He has plenty of money to spend, and does not know where it comes from. He drinks and eats just enough and does not know where the food comes from. This is the demeanor of the man of character (p. 129).

Now it is a good thing, surely, to have international trade, both in the realm of material things and in ideas. But when we start importing and extensively appropriating notions which by traditional Western standards are patent nonsense, we need to look well to our condition. If the line of thought we have pursued in the preceding lecture and thus far in this one is sound, the facts run something like this: The Calvinist doctrine of the guilt of man and the grace of God (or what Tillich has called the Protestant Principle) has been a heresy which has produced despair, anger, and madness. Freud, with a great flourish of scientific objectivity and logic, pretended to deliver us by going all the way and taking from us responsibility *both* for our sins and our salvation. The result: moral collapse and chaos! Now, feebly, in a sort of hebephrenic languor, we are toying with Asiatic abstractions that make about as much sense as does modern abstractionist art. Is *this* the best we can do? Perhaps, but I believe there is an alternative way of approaching the problem which we should consider very seriously: namely, to assume that there are *principles*—universal, consistent, knowable principles—in the domain of human personality and social process which transcend "persons," and that we can *know others* and *be ourselves*, in the ultimate sense, only in terms of these principles.

Today we are hearing a great deal, in some quarters, about God *as person*.[1] But from the personal emphasis, we easily move to the subjective; and, as we have just seen, it is also but a short step from the subjective to mysticism and chaos. For myself—and here I think I speak for many others—what *I* want is a clearer knowledge

[1] For example, Hordern (1955), in describing the theological position of William Temple, Archbishop of Canterbury, writes: "The supreme revelation is given in the life and person of Jesus. The revelation is not his teaching or his acts but himself. . . . Christianity is not a dedication to a system of rules or of thought, but a dedication to a person. This is unique among the religions of the world" (p. 190). This emphasis upon God-as-person is likely to strike the skeptic as a patent absurdity; and it is also, it seems, of doubtful practical assistance to the nominal believer when he is in emotional difficulties. One can rebuild his life, in a constructive and satisfying manner, along lines laid down by Christ's *ethical* teachings; but the notion of the "mystical" union with Christ has, I submit, little value save as a topic for endless theological disquisition. I once took a young Polish psychologist (who was, I presume, also something of a Communist) to the first Christian church service he had ever attended; and afterwards, he was quiet for a few minutes and then thoughtfully asked, "And what are all those people going to *do* now?" What could I say? The truth is there isn't much that a person *can* do about much Protestant preaching, except to go back next week and hear more of it. The de-emphasis on preaching and stress upon action, deeds, works in the Catholic Church surely has something to recommend it. (Cf. a similar emphasis in the Mormon and Moslem religions.)

of *principles*, which we can learn to obey and thereby live abundantly or, if we choose, disobey and suffer the consequences. A friend who is a state mental hospital chaplain tells me that a point which he often makes with patients is this: "We don't *break* God's laws. They break *us*, if we disregard or defy them." Isn't *this* what we need to know, more about how the Universe is constructed and operated, in the psychological and moral realm, so that we can conduct our lives more intelligently and more meaningfully? If, in the physical realm, we observe the Laws of Gravity, we get along nicely; if, on the other hand, we disregard them, we may have a broken neck to show for it. But do we "break" the principles of gravity? Not in the least, *they* break us.

There is thus, as I see it, no place for Calvinistic logic in the modern world: we have, it seems, a completely symmetrical choice between observing natural principles and prospering, on the one hand, and disregarding them and getting into trouble, on the other. And we have just as much responsibility—and deserve just as much "credit," positive or negative—in the one case as in the other. If we are to end the wasteful and undignified conflict between scientific and religious world views, it must surely be along these lines; and it is, I submit, along the very same lines that the ecumenical movement within religion itself also has the best prospects of success. As long as different religious groups focus upon personages, which are of necessity unique, they will remain apart; but when they begin to look at the *principles which they have in common*, reconciliation and union are by no means improbable.

Especially interesting in this connection is another passage from the article by Richard Niebuhr which I have already [Chapter 11] cited. It reads as follows:

Experience and study [over the past 25 years] both have led to some changes in the theological formulation of [my] convictions. The complex, dynamic, interhuman as well as the human-divine interaction of trust and loyalty has excited my wonder and challenged my efforts to understand faith more than ever. Perhaps it is this concentration on faith as trust and loyalty which had led me farther away from the road that many other postliberals—particularly Karl Barth— have taken. So many of them seem to me to have gone back to orthodoxy as right teaching, right doctrine, and to faith as *fides*, as assent; they tend, it seems to me, toward the definition of Christian life in terms of right believing, of Christianity as the true religion, and otherwise toward the assertion of the primacy of ideas over personal relations. When I think about this I have to say to myself that important as theological formulations are for me they *are not the primary one*. I discover further a greater kinship with all *theologians of Christian experience* than with the theologians of Christian doctrine. So I find myself, though with many hesitations, closer to Edwards and Schleiermacher, to Coleridge, Bushnell and Maurice than to Barth and the dogmatic biblical theology current today in wide circles. To state my understanding of our theological situation briefly: I believe that the Barthian correction of the line of march begun in Schleiermacher's day was absolutely essential, but that it has become an over-correction and that Protestant theology can minister to the church's life more effectively if it resumes the general line of march represented by *the evangelical, empirical and critical movement*. Some new studies in modern theology have convinced me that the movement from Schleiermacher to Troeltsch was by no means so humanistic as its critics have asserted. Existentialism also has served to reinforce my *concern for the personal*, for the religiously experienced, for I-Thou relations between God and man and between men. Among contemporary theologians it is Bultmann who above all seems to me to represent *this empirical and ethical strain in theology* (pp. 249–250, italics added).

Here, as I see it, is an attempt to dissociate religion from theological arrogance and abstraction and to relate it to on-going human and social experience and need, in a way which is immediately attractive to the person with naturalistic, scientific, and humanistic predilections. Here there is hope of finding principles of living on which parish ministers and social scientists can deeply agree. Here is an attempt, as Niebuhr explicitly states, to make religion empirical, to validate it by its accomplishments, instead of reducing it to a set of dogmatic asseverations which are to be taken purely on faith, without any reference to the consequences which flow from them in the real world.

Niebuhr's emphasis upon the personal and interpersonal is, therefore, a very welcome one—and sound, provided it is interpreted and implemented in terms of definite principles, rather than as a "Cloud of Unknowing" (to borrow the title of the anonymous book on medieval Christian mysticism which Progoff, 1957, has rendered into modern English). The need for a synthesis of science and religion in the psychological and social area is today very great, and here, in the realm of the personal and the interpersonal, is manifestly the place to begin. But this enterprise will not prosper if we rest content with the amorphous utterances of Buber, Tournier, and other Existentialists or if we drift off into the frank anti-intellectualism and ethical nihilism of certain Asiatic philosophies. This is a capital challenge to both contemporary social scientists (see Mowrer, 1961) and to clear-minded and courageous religious leaders, such as Niebuhr.

III. SOME NONSENSE ABOUT SIN AND SINS

It is, of course, painfully clear that the obstacles to a return to principle in the moral and spiritual realm are formidable. From Luther down to this very day, there is a subtle but powerful Protestant doctrine which is the very antithesis of consistent, objective principle in this area. Recently I heard a bright well-educated young minister preach a sermon from which I wish to quote at some length:

> *In the first place, we need to understand what it means to say that we are sinners.* Usually we mean by "sinner" somebody who has broken a rule or violated a law, someone who doesn't conform to accepted moral and social standards. . . .
> But that isn't what sin means in the Bible! Sin is not the accidental breaking of a rule, but the willful violation of a personal relationship. We don't sin against rules, we sin against persons. The Biblical God relates to his people not primarily as a Judge to an offender, but as a Father to a son who has rejected his love and wandered away into a far country. Sin is what we were talking about last week. It is the condition into which men meet each other from behind masks, afraid to be known for what they are. Sin is when we build walls of isolation and security to avoid the demand of men to be loved as ourselves. Sin is the "thingification" of persons—the using of human beings for what good they can do us, rather than the seeking of genuine human community. Sin is the ritual that allows us to glad-hand and smile and

date without ever knowing the person we so casually "contact." Have you ever been talking with someone and then realized that you hadn't really heard a word he or she was saying? Have you perhaps lived with a person and gone through the motions of friendship or marriage and suddenly realized you didn't really *know* him?

And now it isn't so easy to slough off our responsibility, is it? We may never violate the commandments, but we may know very well what it means to treat persons as things. Listen to our poets, our dramatists, our sociologists, our philosophers, our beatniks. They all speak with one voice, and ask: "How can we stop brushing by each other the way we brush by a blackboard or a bush? How can we start being *human* to each other?" That question shows that, by whatever name it is called, sin is a reality to modern man.

Here we have it! Sin is not the grubby, mean, vicious, duplicitous, self-defeating and socially destructive things we *do*. It can't be that simple—otherwise, we would not perhaps need so much preaching, so much explaining to understand it. No, it is something much more complicated, which only the professional theologian can fully fathom. And this is what he preaches and teaches to the laity, despite the fact that, as we have seen, when he personally gets into emotional hot water, he finds it precious little help, judging by the alactrity with which he is likely to resort to a secular therapist of some sort [see Chapter 11].

This distinction between sins and Sin was, of course, stressed by Luther, during the Reformation, in his attack upon the opposite emphasis of the Catholic Church. But it has extensive roots back in the New Testament itself in the writings of the Apostle Paul; and it is no accident that the sermon from which the foregoing quotation is taken was buttressed by texts from the Letter to the Ephesians, wherein the familiar Pauline doctrine of justification by faith is expounded as follows:

But God, who is rich in mercy, out of the great love with which he loved us, even when we were dead through our trespasses, made us alive together with Christ (by grace you have been saved), and raised us up with him, and made us sit with him in the heavenly places in Christ Jesus, that in the coming ages he might show the immeasurable riches of his grace in kindness toward us in Christ Jesus. For by grace you have been saved through faith, it is the gift of God—not because of works, lest any man should boast. For we are his workmanship, created in Christ Jesus for good works, which God prepared beforehand, that we should walk in them (2:4–10).

But now in Christ Jesus you who once were far off have been brought near in the blood of Christ. For he is our peace, who has made us both one, and has broken down the dividing wall of hostility, by abolishing in his flesh the law of commandments and ordinances, that he might create in himself one new man in place of the two, so making peace, and might reconcile us both to God in one body through the cross, thereby bringing the hostility to an end (2:14–16).

Here, clearly, is Biblical authority for Luther's enigmatic injunction to "Love God and sin boldly" (since our sins are already forgiven before we commit them) and, equally, for Calvin's doctrine of predestination ("which God prepared beforehand"). Paul (Ephesians 3:4) concedes that all this is "the mystery of Christ" but claims he has "insight" into it. Can it be that the mystery is largely of his own making and that although *he* perhaps understood it, few have since been similarly blessed.

It is not surprising, perhaps, that Lloyd C. Douglas, while he was still a Congregationist minister, and before he became a great novelist, often referred to Paul as "that noisy troubadour from Tarsus!" Even though his mellifluous phrases have rumbled on down through the centuries, it is still not certain whether they make any real sense. In Paul's own time, he had a trenchant critic in the writer of the Epistle of James, who needs only three and a half pages to refute the essence of what Paul takes 88 pages, or nearly a third of the New Testament (RSV), to say.

> What does it profit, my brethren, if a man says he has faith but has not works? Can faith save him? If a brother or sister is ill clad and in lack of daily food, and one of you say to them, "Go in peace, be warm," what does it profit? So faith by itself, if it has no works, is dead (2:14–17).
>
> Show me your faith apart from your works, and I by my works will show you my faith (2:18).
>
> You see that a man is justified by works and not by faith alone. And in the same way was not also Rahab the harlot justified by works when she received the messengers and sent

them out another way? For as the body apart from the spirit is dead, so faith apart from works is dead (2:24–26).

Fundamentalists, literalists, and revelationists sometimes make a great point of the *internal consistency* of the Bible. One need not be a Biblical expert to know that James was in direct and emphatic disagreement with Paul. And K. W. Lowther Clark, in his authoritative *Concise Bible Commentary*, adds: "The impulse [which prompted the Epistle of James] was supplied by the desire to recall Christians to reality in religion; [the author] had seen the unfortunate impression made on some minds by reports of St. Paul's teaching and wished to *counteract it*" (p. 915, italics added).[2]

[2] Since the above was written I have received a letter from a clergyman of Calvinist persuasion which reads in part as follows: "Ever since your opening address [see Chapter 8], I have also wondered about something else which maybe you could answer for me. If I remember correctly, it was your belief that many times we make forgiveness too easy. Man has worked his way into sin; he must somehow be given the opportunity to work his way out. Your reference to the old-fashioned mourners' bench especially intrigued me. Could it be, however, that this is due to the fact that we have separated the doctrine of the substitutionary atonement from the offer of forgiveness? I mean that if we preached, what I believe to be the teaching of the Bible, that Christ was bearing the wrath of God against sin, that he was being punished for my sin, that we would not think of it as cheap and easy? I can never atone for my sin, but Christ has done that for me. He has paid the price. He bore the punishment due me; and my union with him through faith means that my sins have been punished and I can now have a clear, clean conscience." Here is an epitome of the Great Idea which Reformation theologians spread abroad in the world! If one is *pleased* with the present status and prospects of Protestantism, after four hundred years, one should by all means persevere in this ambiguous and bloody doctrine. But for a growing minority (or is it now, in fact, majority?), it just won't do. The discrepancy between the beliefs professed by many modern ministers from their pulpits and their personal practices when in emotional difficulties has been commented on in some detail in the first lecture of this series. And a little later in the present discussion, we shall allude, at least sketchily, to the much over-worked concept of forgiveness. However, no attempt is made here [or elsewhere in this volume] to deal in any systematic way with the whole

Although the Catholic Church has made a mystery and a muddle of many things, in this issue between Paul and James it has been clear-headed—and thoroughly Jamesian. It has stressed the importance of good works (as a means of correcting *sins*, without much reference to *Sin*), with implicit recognition of a "balance sheet" on which our sins and virtues add algebraically. As Tillich (1959) observes in the sermon previously cited:

> Our moral balance sheet is not so bad as it would be without these acts! And did you ever see a preacher of what is called the "total depravity" of man who did not show in his own behavior a reliance on a positive moral balance sheet? (p. 17).

But the emphasis in the writings of Paul, and in Protestant theology generally, has been on a very different note, namely, that in the Substitutionary Atonement (Christ's crucifixion), God wiped the "balance sheet" clean for all time and for all men, provided only that they say, "I believe. . . ." In "accepting Christ as our personal redeemer," sin is supposedly banished in our lives and we are, from this point on, "saved." This is what Deitrich Bonhoeffer, in his book *The Cost of Discipleship*, dubs the doctrine of *cheap grace*, a doctrine which has been a *disgrace* and a scandal to Christendom. It is a doctrine which holds the deep natural wisdom of the Judeo-Christian ethic in contempt—and prevents us from coming to grips effectively with the most profound personal problem of our time, mental illness.

IV. RETURN TO CONFESSION, WITH A DIFFERENCE

The crux of our present predicament, then, is that Protestantism has embraced a theology which put the

---

notion of *sacrifice*, as a therapeutic force. Although Christ undoubtedly made a great personal sacrifice (of allowing himself to be crucified for his conviction, rather than quietly slipping off into the desert, as he easily could have), I believe a wholly unjustified cult has grown up around this act which completely distorts the historical facts and blinds our present-day perception in some vitally important areas. However, this topic is so complex, and vital, that I am reserving it for special treatment in a lecture to be given shortly at the Allan Memorial Institute of Psychiatry, at McGill University, in Montreal. It will be published separately, at a later date.

problem of personal guilt beyond the scope of religion and thus fostered the development of secular psychotherapy in general and Freudian psychoanalysis in particular. But analytic treatment and theory, far from lessening our woes, have exacerbated them; and we are today looking to religion, once again, with renewed hope and urgency. We have tried to believe that personality disorder is basically an *illness—mental* illness; but we are now increasingly persuaded that the problem is fundamentally *moral*, that the guilt which is so obviously central in psychopathology is *real* rather than false, and that only a moral attack upon this problem can be successful. We had hoped that an easy solution might be found for personal evil; and we have tried both the doctrine of "cheap grace" (in religion) and the strategy of denying the reality of sin and guilt altogether (in psychoanalysis), but neither has worked. And so today there is a growing readiness to accept the verdict that "therapy," or "salvation," is possible only at great cost: the cost of self-revelation, deep contrition, and a radically changed way of life.

The injunction to engage in auricular confession is still to be found in the Protestant Episcopal Book of Common Prayer; and a similar admonition is also present in most forms of Lutheranism. However, the actual practice of confession has largely fallen into disuse in these denominations; and among more radically Protestant groups, confession has long been regarded as papish and hence to be shunned like the plague. In the pastoral counseling movement, there has, of course, been a sort of half-hearted, disguised return of confession. But this movement has been so dominated by ideas and techniques which have been appropriated from secular forms of psychotherapy that the results have been quite ambiguous. Protestant churches must, I believe, rethink and revitalize their efforts in this direction.

Luther, we should recall, was not protesting against the institution of confession as such, but against its *abuse*. Over the years, however, the assumption seems to have developed that the only way to prevent this abuse is to eliminate the institution itself. This is like arguing that because surgery, in incompetent or unscrupulous hands, can be misused, it should be eliminated altogether. Mani-

festly some means must be found whereby ordinary
mortals can work through the problem of personal guilt
in a way which is more effective than anything which is
at present generally available. And the indications are
that confession, in a moral and religious context, is the
logical starting point. In his book, *Life Together*, Deitrich
Bonhoeffer devotes the last chapter to the topic of "Confession and Communion." Here he says:

"Confess your faults one to another" (Jas. 5:16). He who
is alone with his sin is utterly alone. It may be that Christians, notwithstanding corporate worship, common prayer,
and all their fellowship in service, may still be left to their
loneliness. The final break-through to fellowship does not
occur, because, though they have fellowship with one another as believers and as devout people, they do not have fellowship as the undevout, as sinners. The pious fellowship
permits no one to be a sinner. So everybody must conceal his
sin from himself and from the fellowship. We dare not be
sinners. Many Christians are unthinkably horrified when a
real sinner is suddenly discovered among the righteous. So we
remain alone with our sin, living in lies and hypocrisy. The
fact is that we *are* sinners! (p. 110).

In confession the break-through to community takes place.
Sin demands to have a man by himself. It withdraws him
from the community. The more isolated a person is, the
more destructive will be the power of sin over him, and the
more deeply he becomes involved in it, the more disastrous is
his isolation. Sin wants to remain unknown. It shuns the
light. In the darkness of the unexpressed it poisons the
whole being of a person. This can happen even in the midst
of a pious community. In confession the light of the Gospel
breaks into the darkness and seclusion of the heart. The sin
must be brought into the light. The unexpressed must be
openly spoken and acknowledged. All that is secret and
hidden is made manifest. It is a hard struggle until the sin
is openly admitted. But God breaks gates of brass and bars
of iron (Ps. 107:16) (p. 112).

In his book *The Riddle of Roman Catholicism*, Jaro-
slov Pelikan writes:

Through the administration of these three steps—contrition, confession, and satisfaction—the church has a splendid
opportunity to apply the healing power of the gospel to the
concrete needs of the penitent. In the hands of a conscientious pastor, the sacrament of penance makes divine grace

meaningful without minimizing the individual's responsibility for his sin. It is, at its best, a truly evangelical means for "the cure of souls," one whose benefits Protestantism has discarded too easily, and one for which a friendly chat with the minister is not a satisfactory substitute. Psychologically, too, private confession is sound, enabling a person to "come clean" about his feelings and to know that he has forgiveness from God in spite of anything he may have done. The therapeutic value of this is difficult to overestimate (pp. 120–121).

And Meehl et al. (1958), in their book *What, Then, Is Man?*, take a similar position. They say:

> One of the facets of confession which is often viewed superficially in pastoral practice, or even ignored, is the detailed or specific confession of actual sins. Many of the Lutheran clergy do not minister to the needs of their parishioners adequately because they are content when their people participate in general confessions instead of insisting upon the health-giving function of specific confessions, as the Lutheran Catechism and standard works in Lutheran pastoral theology recommend. The result has been that the act of confession has become secularized. Educated people especially seem more often to feel that their needs are better met by psychoanalysis than the Word of God. Our pastors ought to re-examine both the healing power of the Gospel and the apparent self-sufficiency of their parishioners.
>
> If the non-Christian psychotherapeutic effort has become vastly greater in our society and has obtained enormous recognition among our own people, it is in part the consequence of superficial pastoral care. Though it must not become exaggerated, so that it confers upon the pastor the role of grand inquisitor, there is nonetheless such a thing as penitential discipline to which *all* Christians ought regularly to submit. Self-knowledge really exists only to the extent that one does, or is able to, communicate it in speech to another person. The psychotherapeutic value of making specific, or even detailed, confessions is therefore very great (pp. 68–69).

As it happens the three writers just cited are all Lutherans. But men in other Protestant denominations have made similar statements, some of them very much earlier than the ones we have just reviewed. For example, Holman (1943), in a review of H. E. Fosdick's book, *On Being a Real Person*, wrote:

Away back in 1927 Dr. Fosdick, then pastor of the Park
Avenue Baptist Church, New York City, gave an address
before the Greater New York Federation of Churches which
immediately brought expressions of angry resentment or warm
approval from Protestant ministers in all parts of the country.
Said Dr. Fosdick:

"We modern Protestants fail in some things. Our
Roman Catholic brethren in keeping the confessional
have pretty nearly wiped us off the stage in one feature
of human service. . . .
"For six years I have conducted—Baptist though I am
—what I call a confessional. . . . I have an office
where people who know they are spiritually sick and
mentally disturbed can come with their problems. Why
shouldn't I minister to them? Never again will I be
without such a place where people can meet me alone.
Week after week I meet nearly as many people as a
priest. They are mentally unbalanced—sick souls who
need ministration" (p. 214).

What, then, has thus far been the fruit of this growing awareness of the need for a return to confession in
the Protestant churches? Fosdick's early interests were, as
we know [Chapter 6], very largely absorbed and diverted
by the pastoral counseling movement, which has been
dominated by ideas taken from Freudian psychoanalysis
and the counseling methods of Carl Rogers. This movement leaves much to be desired; and it is not without
significance that there is a new concern, on the part of
such men as Bonhoeffer, Pelikan, and Meehl, with the
therapeutic and redemptive potentialities of confession.
At the same time, however, there are some deep-seated
and at least partially justified reservations. We have constantly before us the fact that confession has long been,
and is still, practiced in the Catholic Church, with results
which are not entirely reassuring. In later sections we
shall go into this problem in more detail; but here the
following considerations are in order.

Whenever confession as a means of personal redemption and change is under discussion, the question is sure
to be asked, and not unreasonably: Do Catholics enjoy
any better mental health than do members of other religions or, for that matter, nonreligious persons? Mental
hospital statistics are likely to be quite ambiguous on this

score. The religion of an entering patient, if any, will ordinarily be recorded without much reference to whether the individual has recently been religiously active or inactive, thus obscuring the effects of the conscientious observance, or disregard, of the tenets of his faith. But there are independent indications—such as lower suicide rates, lower divorce rates, and greater resistance to "battle fatigue"—that Catholics do have some advantage in this connection. However, the difference is not dramatic.[3] Catholics, laymen and members of the monastic and priestly orders alike, suffer from personality disturbances both mild and severe, thus indicating that confession either does not have the redemptive and therapeutic powers sometimes attributed to it or that—and here is the point of special interest—there are serious weaknesses in the way confession is practiced by Catholics. I wish to discuss these weaknesses in the following order.

1. *Catholic confession is often little more than an empty, perfunctory formality.* I have a friend who, when the occasion offers, makes a practice of sitting in Catholic Churches throughout the country and noting the time which penitents spend in the confessional booth. On the average it turns out to be about 60 seconds. And a Catholic chaplain in a V. A. hospital recently volunteered the information that the confessions he hears from the patients who are entrusted to his care usually run from 40 seconds to three minutes. Unless extensively supplemented by interviews outside the confessional, this type of procedure can hardly be adequate to the needs of even ordinary persons, to say nothing of those who are in personality crisis.

Priests vary enormously in the extent to which they are interested in the confessional. Many are frank to say that they get through with this duty just as speedily as possible, in order to have more time for other concerns. On the other hand, there are priests who give major attention to this aspect of their work and who become widely known and sought after as confessors. These are the men who are likely to become known as "spiritual directors." But there is apparently no great pressure upon

[3] There is, moreover, some indication that in Catholic countries the incidence of suicide is not accurately reported, because of the great opprobrium associated with this act.

priests to emphasize the confessional, except in its sacramental aspects; and there is also, it seems, no scarcity of Catholic laymen who are as willing to handle their confessions every bit as routinely as are many priests.

2. *The penance assigned is often not psychologically adequate.* Although I have not yet located documentary proof for it, Catholic priests tell me that there was a time in the history of the Church when penances were much more severe than they are today and were more nearly designed to "fit the crime." Now penance often involves nothing more than saying some extra prayers and perhaps burning a few candles. We know, of course, that individual human beings, when overwhelmed by remorse and guilty fear, are inclined to be quite hard on themselves; and it is not surprising, therefore, that the penances assigned by the Church often leave the sinner in a state of unassuaged personal guilt and anguish.

3. *Confession is not an adequate deterrent.* This criticism is most often heard from non-Catholics, but Catholics themselves are not unaware of it as a problem. For example, a young priest once told me the following story, as one that circulates in Catholic circles. A peasant went to the village priest and said, "Father, I have sinned." "Yes, my son," came the reply, "what is your sin?" "Father," said the peasant, "last night I stole a bale of straw. No, make that *two* bales, I want to get another one tonight!"

Those who have been caught in a disgraceful deed or who, from bad conscience, have had to make a painful confession thereof know that having one's failures and shortcomings become known by significant others is, in fact, an extremely powerful corrective of behavior. But the fact that confession is not expected to go beyond the priest and commonly involves a mere token penance can hardly fail to limit its effectiveness both as a means of assuaging guilt and of deterring action when inner controls are weak.

4. *Absolution and forgiveness are questionable procedures.* Protestant churches do not, of course, lay claim to "apostolic succession" in the power to forgive sins; but they do preach a doctrine of divine forgiveness and absolution of sorts. Let us examine this concept in a strictly human, interpersonal light. A few months ago, partly as

an inadvertence and partly out of slight exasperation, I made a very unfortunate remark to a woman of my acquaintance. I immediately realized that she was embarrassed, and I was deeply remorseful. But I didn't attempt any sort of apology, and she never said anything in the way of "forgiveness." Nevertheless, after this incident, she was even more kindly and respectful in her behavior with me than she had been before. I knew, therefore, that she was not going to indulge in the luxury of being resentful toward me or of rebuking me. She, manifestly, had "forgiven" me in the sense of rising above the incident herself; but this made *my* guilt and remorse even greater, not less.

This incident set me thinking about the logic and psychology of forgiveness in general. How *can* another, either in a religious or purely personal setting, forgive us? The misdeed, the sin is *ours*; and who would presume, and whom would we *ask*, to remove this responsibility? If we have erred, do we not wish to make restitution, instead of being "excused"? Forgiveness in the usual sense of the term is, I feel, an act of great condescension and not at all likely to restore either our self-respect or peace of mind.[4]

Therefore, in keeping with a greater emphasis on penance and meaningful restitution, I would like to see Protestant churches, as they reconsider the institution of confession, stress restitution and reform, not forgiveness. If our consciences have enough rectitude to bother us when we act badly, I believe they will also approve and support us when we have done the best we can to correct our misdeeds.

Extensive documentation of the psychological inadequacy of religious confession and assurance of forgiveness as commonly practiced is not readily available. But Meehl *et al.*, in the volume already cited, related the following incident:

> A young woman confessed that she had broken the Seventh Commandment [Lutheran numbering; eighth in the Reformed system] by pilfering ribbons and socks from a

[4] In discussing this matter with a colleague recently, I was much interested in his opinion that forgiveness is "a profound irrelevancy in human affairs."

dime store. She was obviously contrite about the transgression, and the pastor assured her of God's understanding and gracious forgiveness. In a few weeks she was back in the study to confess that she had stolen again, this time a few cents from her mother's purse. Again absolution was pronounced. When, not too many days after this, the girl again came in tears, the pastor began looking more deeply. Professional help was called in to assist the girl. Serious deficiences in her home life were uncovered. It became apparent that she had unexpressed misgivings about whether God had actually forgiven her after her previous confessions. While she had repented of the sin that she knew, she recognized her inability to straighten herself out; this feeling created internal doubts about her confession. As these feelings were brought out and she began to understand them, the urge to steal waned—and the absolution was accepted and believed (p. 284).

Here we see, first of all, the inadequacy of the simple formula of confession and assurance of divine forgiveness.[5] The unfortunate behavior continued, so "Professional help was called in to assist the girl." What more eloquent testimony could one ask of the loss of authority and confidence on the part of the clergy than the tendency to regard *secular* healers as the "professionals" in this area? If, as we now increasingly suspect, moral issues are nuclear to every neurosis, isn't it remarkable that the clergy no longer regards itself as first in competence here? In the particular instance cited, therapy along the familiar lines of insight and understanding was ostensibly successful. But, in the large, we know the picture is not a good one, that secular therapy predicated on the common assumptions about repression, mistreatment, and the like does not have a reassuring record; and this is why there is a growing feeling that we should re-examine, revive, and revise the institution of confession so as to make it psychologically and ethically more meaningful and adequate. This, it seems, is a challenge that is pertinent not only to the Protestant denominations but to Catholicism as well.[6]

[5] See also Weatherhead (1957), especially Chapter 7, on "The Difficulty of Feeling Forgiven."

[6] A recent newspaper report indicates that the Catholic Church has under consideration a proposal to increase the severity of penances, to accord with earlier—and probably sounder—practice.

V. PROTESTANT (AND PSYCHIATRIC) OBJECTIONS
  TO THE DOCTRINE OF GOOD WORKS
  AND RESTITUTION

In the discussion period following another lecture, I
received this written question and comment:

> How would you interpret Jesus' reference to the pharisees
> as whited sepulchres—outwardly made beautiful and inside,
> old bones and dead men's bodies? The outward beauty ob-
> viously refers to the pharisees' assumed goodness and the
> old bones and dead men's bodies must refer to repression
> and undeveloped life.

The reference is here, of course, to Matthew 23:27;
and on many other occasions Christ rebuked the Pharisees
for their tendency to pray and give alms in public and
otherwise exhibit their piety. "They *have* their reward,"
was his summary evaluation.

Those who are looking for it can, of course, easily find
here an apparent repudiation of the doctrine of good
works. But how, then, are we to interpret the story of the
Good Samaritan and dozens of other similar incidents
reported in the New Testament? No, clearly the objection is not to good deeds as such—far from it!, but to
boasting and exhibitionism with respect to the virtue or
credit thus achieved. But to this aspect of the problem
Christ himself gave the solution: when you perform
charity, do it, as often as possible, *in secret:* "Let not
your left hand know what the right hand doeth." Is this
so hard to understand and practice?

As if the Bible itself were not sufficiently explicit on
this score, Lloyd Douglas, in both *Magnificent Obsession*
and *Doctor Hudson's Secret Journal,* elaborates and
dramatizes this point for us around the idea that real
"power," as he calls it, comes only when we do good
by stealth. Dr. Hudson (the central character in both
these books) holds that most of us live lives which are
blighted by chronic insecurity, doubt, and despair because
we characteristically display our virtues, and good deeds,
and hide our sins and shortcomings. We are, so to say,
chronically in debt and in danger. How, then, can we
resolve the situation? It is obvious, says Dr. Hudson:

Display, admit, confess our sins and *hide* our good works. Such a strategy, he argues, helps us, slowly but surely, to move from anxiety, depression, and indecision to confidence, inner strength, and joy—or, as he calls it, "power."

Another argument which we often hear in this connection is this: "But many of our sins are of such a nature that we *can't* atone for them." This, in the literal sense, is, to be sure, often true. But we can *try*—and if we persevere long enough, knock hard enough, the door eventually opens. The atonement or restitution doesn't, of course, have to be "in kind," i.e., made precisely to the person who has been wronged or hurt, or be precisely on the point of the original misdeed. There is always need for service of other kinds in the world; and who is to say that sacrifice for a good cause is less worthy as "justification" than is a specific reparation?

Sometimes psychologists and psychiatrists who do personnel assessment work for seminaries and mission boards will damn a candidate on the grounds that he is "motivated by personal guilt." Is this necessarily bad? How many men and women, one wonders, have saved themselves from mental illness or worse by this very device? The important thing, I suspect, is that the individual be clear-headed about *what* he is doing and *why* he is doing it. If these conditions are met, I should be inclined to expect such a motivation to augur for success rather than the reverse. What other type of motivation would we regard as sounder? Or what better means of dealing with personal guilt would we suggest?

Of course, the whole idea of atonement is foreign to our modern way of thinking about personality disturbances. Such disturbances, we have been told and told again, come from false guilt, from lack of insight, from over-conscientiousness; so what is there to confess, much less realistically atone for? The "need for punishment" in neurotic individuals has, of course, long been recognized; but it has been largely dismissed as the "masochistic" aspect of neurosis itself. In other words, it too was seen as irrational, a form of sickness rather than a sensible and healthy striving toward wholeness.

But the times are changing. Recently *The Psychiatric Bulletin* of the University of Texas carried a feature article entitled "Retribution and Neurosis," the introductory paragraph of which reads as follows:

> In many kinds of emotional illness or maladjustment, guilt, whether conscious or unrecognized, coexists with an assumption of punishment. Sometimes any disorder or event is interpreted as such. Patients may feel doomed or fated to undergo some tragedy or committed to a course of action that will culminate in disaster. Others may explain a chronic illness or develop a functional one as a retributive measure. Two related versions of this manifestation are described as the *talion principle* and the *nemesis concept* (p. 16).

There then follows a discussion of the talion and nemesis principles, which I assume are well known. But in a section entitled "Treatment," a new note is struck. Here there is no reference to the classical Freudian doctrine of false guilt as basic to neurotic difficulties. Instead we read:

> Patients may be anxious, phobic, or obsessive, for example, but their basic fear is also their method of coping with the discomfort caused by their unresolved guilt.

And in conclusion the author says:

> A nineteenth-century physician Abraham Coles, wrote of "the inappeasable Nemesis within." He was speaking of the guilty conscience. In this way the individual meets his own guilt feelings; ideas of retribution may figure strongly. Patients require psychotherapeutic help, both for their psychosomatic ailments and for alleviation of such fears as may be explained away. In obsessional cases or in severe instances in which the concept of retribution affects all phases of the patient's living, referral for psychiatric treatment is needed (p. 17).

If the reader senses some ambiguity here, it will not be surprising. What is the author really saying? On the one hand, he seems to be saying, or at least implying, that in neurosis, guilt is (always?) real, with a justifiable expectation of impending punishment or retribution of some sort. But also he is suggesting that such fears may sometimes be "explained away"; and if not, that they can be dealt with by established psychiatric methods. It is not clear what methods modern psychiatry *has* for dealing with real guilt. But the title of this article at least carries the implication that restitution might be an alternative to the retribution which is often associated with neurotic tendencies. Here is a new trend in contemporary psychiatric thought, which is further underscored by the following lines, quoted by the author, from Byron's "Childe Harold's Pilgrimage":

> Meantime I seek no sympathies, nor need;
> The thorns which I have reap'd are of the
>   tree
> I planted,—they have torn me—and I
>   bleed;
> I should have known what fruit would
>   spring from such a seed.

It sounds as if at least some psychiatrists are beginning to take guilt seriously. This is a hopeful and constructive sign.

VI. CONFESSION: SACRAMENT OR THERAPY?— THE CATHOLIC POSITION

In the Catholic Church, confession and the associated acts of contrition and attrition (remorse and penance) are first and foremost *a sacrament*: means, that is, of bringing one's immortal soul from a state of sin to grace and thus averting the dangers of Hell. But on the question of whether confession is also emotionally and psychologically helpful *in this life*, the Church is officially silent, with the views of individual Catholic writers covering the full spectrum from strong affirmation to emphatic denial.

If present presuppositions are valid, confession and penance should—and in many instances rather clearly do —have a genuinely hygienic effect, limitations in the Catholic system notwithstanding. And among those who, within the Church, emphasize this aspect of the practice, none is more urgent and eloquent than Father Alfred Wilson, C. P., in his book *Pardon and Peace* (1954). Worthy of close study in its entirety, this work ("*Nihil obstat*") can here be considered only in the most cursory fashion. But the author, having paid his respects to the sacramental aspect of confession, comes quickly and clearly to his central thesis, which is that confession is unmistakably and powerfully therapeutic. He says:

Our unfortunate non-Catholic brethren do not know what they are missing, and little realize the blessings that heresy has snatched from them (p. 2).

No one goes to the doctor or the dentist for fun, unless he is mad. No one goes to Confession for fun. From the nature of the case, confession cannot be easy. The result, not the process, of confession is consoling.

After serious sin, however, we have no alternative but to confess if we desire to regain undisturbed peace of mind and safeguard our sanity. We must lift the burden from our minds, or become a burden to ourselves and risk becoming a burden to others. Confession is then—if you like to put it that way—the lesser of two evils (p. 3).

Why is this relief necessary? Why must we tell our misery to at least one representative of the human race? Because until we confess we feel hypocrites. We feel that we are being taken for a hundred percent good and we know we are not. We feel that we are obtaining respect and love under false pretences. If, however, we can find one member of the human race who will listen to us sympathetically, who can know the worst and still respect and love us, we feel that our self-respect and social status are somehow restored. We can then reasonably hope for the respect of our fellow-men, despite our fault.

Sin sets up in the mind a conflict between our self-respect and our social sense. That conflict can be terminated only by some form of confession. "Confess, therefore, your sins one to another that you may be healed" (p. 5).

There then follow some well-chosen phrases especially meant for Protestant ears:

Confession is the only remedy. It is no use to say, as many non-Catholics do: "I confess my sins directly to God, and that is quite good enough for me." First of all, it is the common experience that confession to God alone does not bring the fullest measure of relief of mind. It is no argument against this to say that it is not your experience. It is the common experience, and it is safe to presume that Christ legislated for the rule and not the exception.

In any case, adequate mental readjustment after sin requires readjustment of our relations with our fellow-men as well as with God. If you insult a friend, it is not enough to apologize to God—you must apologize to your friend as well. . . . Sin is an offense against society as well as against God, and for both offenses adequate reparation must be made. . . .

All these unrealists (who pout incessantly and suspiciously

about their realism) are heading for a nervous breakdown (p. 6).

And then, again in a more general vein, Father Wilson continues:

> Confession of serious sin is necessary for the restoration of health of mind and soul, redundantly, even for health of body. "Suppressed sin, like suppressed steam, is dangerous. Confession is the safety-valve" (Weatherhead, 1929, p. 88).
> Modern psychologists have rediscovered this. They have found from practical experience that many nervous breakdowns can be traced to a sense of guilt from unconfided and unforgiven sins (p. 8).
> I don't think the majority of Catholics realize how much they owe to the Sacrament of Penance. One of the greatest of Viennese psychologists, a man bitterly anti-Catholic [presumably Freud], had the honesty to admit that, among his cases of serious psychological disorder, he had never had a genuinely practising Catholic (p. 10).

Now, in stark contrast, we turn to a recent article by Father Richard P. Vaughn, S. J., entitled "Mental Illness among Religious." Here the whole emphasis of the Wilson book upon the relationship between unredeemed sin and emotional disturbance is flatly repudiated:

> In spite of research data to the contrary, there still persists a vague suspicion that mental illness is in some way connected with a sinful life or at least that it cannot occur if a person is leading a truly holy life.
> A psychosis is a type of sickness, just as are ulcers of the stomach or cirrhosis of the liver. Whether the cause of the psychotic condition is psychological or organic or a combination of both (which is more likely) has not yet been established. It can, however, safely be stated that a psychosis (with the exception, perhaps, of a condition brought on by alcoholism or drug addiction) is not the result of a sinful life. The idea that it is the effect of sin is simply a remnant of past attitudes which still prevail from an era when little was known about psychiatry and psychology. The fact, therefore, that a religious person becomes psychotic does not in any way imply past moral indiscretions. Religious,[7] even though they follow a more perfect way of life, are no more

_____
[7] "Religous" is the Catholic term for persons who have taken Holy Orders.

immune from severe mental illness than the average lay person (pp. 27–28).

What a remarkable exhibit! Despite the ancient and widespread folk belief that there is a connection between moral integrity and psychological integration, and despite the obvious advantage which accrues to Catholicism if it can be successfully maintained that confession is mentally hygienic (as well as sacramental), here is a Jesuit seriously and insistently arguing *against* this position. The reason for his discomfiture is, however, not far to seek: it is impossible to verify the effectiveness or ineffectiveness of confession as a *sacrament*, and the Church can continue to make great metaphysical claims for it without fear of empirical refutation; but as soon as one makes a claim for confession as an instrument of either prevention or treatment, such a claim immediately becomes susceptible to empirical check—and it is already known that the facts on this score are somewhat ambiguous. Wilson, as we have seen, implies that confession, as prescribed by and practiced within the Church, is virtually a panacea as far as emotional and psychological disturbances are concerned; whereas Vaughn is equally emphatic and categorical in holding that there is no connection here at all! The truth probably lies somewhere in between; but with its doctrine of infallibility, the Church must, of course, take an all-or-none position—partially effective measures not being admissible. Yet, as it functions today, confession apparently has precisely this status, psychologically speaking: although it is or, at least under the most favorable conditions, can be a decided aid to mental health, the mere formal observance of the rules governing confession is no guarantee thereof; and the Church, some writers apparently feel, cannot afford to lay claim to any power which is not absolute.

The situation is further illuminated if we note that in writing for and about religious laymen, as Father Wilson obviously did, it can always be argued that if a Catholic encounters intractable emotional difficulties, this is because he has in some vital respect failed *as a Catholic*— and I am personally persuaded that there is *some* merit in this argument. But once a man or woman has taken *Holy Orders*, the situation, per theory at least, is importantly

modified. Here are *the best,* "the religious," an elite
guard, in whom human frailties have been all but vanquished; and the fact, indeed *prevalence,* of serious mental disorder among monastics (especially women) is well
established (cf. Moore, 1936). This problem is, indeed, so
serious that Father Vaughn pleads for "psychological
screening" of individuals entering the orders:

> Many a community has spent thousands of dollars for the
> hospitalization of a single psychotic member, and this at con-
> siderable sacrifice to the other members of the community.
> And then after all this expense, it not infrequently happens
> that the religious is finally diagnosed as incurable. In such
> cases one might well ask whether such a diagnosis would
> have been reached if the psychotic religious had never been
> subjected to the strain and disillusionment of the religious
> life (p. 29).

Here is an oblique admission that at least for those
entering the special orders, Catholicism, far from being
therapeutic, may have exactly the opposite influence. It
is little wonder, therefore, that this whole matter is at
present a very painful and confusing one for the Church,
from top to bottom. The ambiguity of the situation is, in
fact, excellently portrayed by a current article on "Sin,
Sickness, and Psychiatry," by John R. Connery, S. J.,
which appears in *America,* the official Jesuit journal of
opinion and controversy. Here the author says, by way of
introduction:

> The various aspects of this conflict are best illustrated in
> the different opinions advanced regarding the relationship
> between sin and mental sickness. Besides the opinion that
> would regard sin as sickness rather than an expression of the
> will of the sinner, there is a second opinion that, surprisingly,
> reverses the relationship. According to this opinion, sin, far
> from being the result, is really the cause of mental illness. A
> third opinion refuses to consider sin either as cause or effect
> of mental illness, but tends to regard it as the cure (p. 493).

It is, of course, not surprising that the author of this
article should reject the first and third of these hy-
potheses. The Church, obviously, cannot concede either
that sin is an expression of psychopathology or that it is
a cure thereof ["Have an affair!" "Act single!" cf.]. It
is, of course, the second possibility, namely that uncon-

fessed and unexpiated sin is the *cause* of psychopathology that gives Catholic theorists the difficulty. Connery admits that:

> It is quite true that the act of confessing one's sins, the acceptance of the priest and of his pastoral counsel can have *some* therapeutic value, but this is not the primary purpose for which the sacrament was instituted. The sacrament of penance is primarily a sacrament of forgiveness (p. 493).

Then the author tries to come more specifically to grips with the hypothesis that "neurosis must be traced to sin." He says:

> According to this opinion, it is because the patient has repressed his conscience, rather than because he has repressed his instinctive drives, that he develops a neurosis. Although this position is held by some first-rate psychologists and psychiatrists, it is vigorously opposed by equally competent representatives of these fields. From a religious viewpoint it does not have the objectionable features of the opinions already considered, but it is not necessarily true because it is religiously more agreeable. There are, indeed, good reasons for questioning it. First of all, there are many habitual sinners who to all appearances have average mental and emotional balance. Secondly, the scrupulous conscience, which usually must be classified as neurotic to some degree, does not ordinarily have its origin in past sin. For the most part, the scrupulous individual is as remote from sin as one can get (p. 495).

This is an incompetent and irresponsible statement. The argument that, because all persons who are sinners are not mentally disturbed, there is no relation at all between sin and insanity is a classical non sequitur which I have discussed elsewhere [Chapter 13]. And in the same connection I have cited evidence (as well as another Catholic authority—Stafford, 1950) for the view that scrupulosity is a neurosis precisely because the individual so afflicted prefers this symptom to an honest and thoroughgoing confession.

No, the plain truth is that most Catholic writers do not wish to recognize neurosis as a basically moral and social problem, because they realize that to do so raises embarrassing questions concerning the adequacy of Catholic doctrine and practice, thus underscoring the specific limitations and criticisms which I have enumerated in Section IV. Here, therefore, is a wonderful opportunity and challenge to other religious groups: to develop ways of dealing with personal guilt which are genuinely adequate, psychologically and ethically, and which do not retreat into the realm of metaphysical claims which defy verification. It is also an opportunity for Catholicism to take stock of itself and institute some long overdue reforms.

A curious but not uninstructive drawing accompanies the article by Father Connery, which is also reproduced here. What does it mean? I hold it expresses the ambiguity, the confusion, the sickness of the contemporary Catholic position in this whole matter of sin and psychoneuroses. The figure, ostensibly a monk, is caught in a posture which is both religious and schizophrenic. The Church, which *has* a conscience, is sore afflicted because it is refusing to minister to anxious, depressed people for fear of compromising or having to modify its doctrinal pretensions. If the Church is so rigid and fixated that it cannot act as a physician to itself, the necessary accommodations and changes must be made, as before, outside the Church.

VII. STRAWS IN THE WIND: A CASE HISTORY

With issues as global and controversial as those with which we have dealt in these two lectures, it is easy to doubt, at times, the validity of one's most basic assumptions. There is no simple, direct way of testing or demonstrating them—to others or, indeed, to oneself; and when they represent a marked departure from ordinary beliefs, one wonders, occasionally, if they may not be sheer fantasy. There is, however, a stark reality to which I return in my doubting and always find grimly reassuring. In an era in which physical disease has been spectacularly reduced, the indices of personality disorder, by contrast, have steadily risen. In the two decades between 1934 and 1954, the death rate in this country declined 13.6% (Fagley, 1960, p. 29); but during this same period the likelihood of one's spending some part of his life in a mental hospital—the abode of the *"living* dead"—rose from about one in 20 to one in 10. The evidence that prevailing views and practices in this area are seriously inadequate is thus compelling. And at least small signs keep emerging which point in the direction of alternatives which seem more promising.

Following a lecture which I gave a few months ago in a city in Northern California, a diffident but obviously intelligent middle-aged woman approached me and said that she thought I might like to know that the Church of the Latter Day Saints has always placed a great deal of emphasis upon good deeds—in contrast to the Pauline doctrine of justification by faith—and, as a result, has been a constant target for criticism by Protestant theologians. This bit of information did indeed interest me; and somewhat later I happened to mention it to a social worker who, himself a Mormon, volunteered the additional information that his religion sets aside one Sunday each month for open confession. Then he mentioned a case history recently reported to him by a non-Mormon clinical psychologist known to both of us which indicates the possible therapeutic effectiveness of the Mormon approach in these matters. I immediately wrote for further details; and the psychologist obligingly supplied a copy of the "Social Service Intake" record and of his own "Termination Note." The first of these documents reads as follows:

This 21-year-old female is referred by Dr. —— because of anxiety over sexual adjustment, brought about by long-standing unsatisfactory sexual relationships with her father. She is a rather large, plump girl who brings a long tale of seduction and mistreatment by her father since approximately age 7. She is not a particularly verbal girl, and did not volunteer much during the interview. She has been going with a boy for approximately six months, has thought of marriage, but is physically repelled by him. She states that sex is associated in her mind with sin and pain, and that she would like help to relieve these feelings. Her conversation was flat and unemotional throughout the interview, and she has a rather placid, unemotional face.

Patient is the oldest of four children, having a full sister, a half sister, and a half brother. The patient's mother died when she was four years of age and the father remarried about four years later. —— is a daughter by the stepmother's first marriage, and —— is a son by the present mother and father.

The patient states that the father has forced sexual relationships on her and her two sisters since the patient was 7 years of age, that he has been extremely abusive toward her, that he has never shown any affection except when sexually aroused, and that she has come to think of men as being brutal persons who want nothing but physical satisfaction from their women. She was particularly irked by the fact that her father played favorites, and was frequently quite seductive toward her sisters in her presence. She has tried to work out her problems with her boy friend's help, but feels intensely frigid toward him when he becomes affectionate. Her general attitude toward sex has been that it is dirty, and it has been with effort that she has associated with boys, usually preferring and feeling more comfortable with girls as friends.

Currently, the father is at —— Psychopathic Hospital undergoing psychiatric evaluation, since the girls filed a complaint with the County Insane Commission.* The patient reports that he has been increasingly abusive, suspicious, jealous, and demanding of his daughters. Matters reached a head this spring when the patient returned from her third year of college and refused her father's advances. Currently, the stepmother is attempting to defend him legally. The patient's impression is that the stepmother has known about these affairs for many years, but that she has not wanted to do anything about them.

IMPRESSIONS AND RECOMMENDATIONS: This girl certainly has problems connected with a long-term unsatisfactory relationship with her father. It is understandable that she should equate sex with brutality, and that there should be a distortion in her relationship with men. Significantly, she suspects men of seductive motivations to the extent that she expressed a fear that I might attempt to "seduce" her. It had not occurred to her that such a possibility in a setting like this would be totally unrealistic. There is a question in my mind in regard to her motivation for therapy, but this impression may be imposed by her rather flat manner and affects. The patient should be seen for psychiatric evaluation, and should probably be scheduled for full psychological examination at an early date. This does not appear to be an emergency case, and could be placed on our waiting list following the diagnostic studies.

EXECUTIVE DIRECTOR

* The father was given a long prison sentence subsequent to this evaluation.

This case has many interesting implications and is especially pertinent to the present discussion. It is clear that this young woman's guilt concerning the incest was a barrier to normal marriage and that her coming to the clinic was prompted by the fact that she had become of marriageable age and had some prospects. She felt—quite understandably—that she could not get married with the incest on her conscience; and she was forthright in saying that she "would like help to relieve these feelings."

The intake worker reports that the client—let us call her Marie—"has come to think of men as being brutal persons who want nothing but physical satisfaction from their women," thus implicitly shifting blame and partially rationalizing her own conduct—and somewhat beclouding the reason why she can't get married. But if there were not deep guilt and self-rejection in the situation, it seems that the early introduction to sex and prolonged experience with it would have paved the way for continuation with others. Instead, "sex is associated in her mind with sin and pain." Also it is noteworthy that Marie, while intimating that the stepmother knew of the incest, gives no indication of ever having appealed to her for help. If there had been no complicity in the situation, it seems there would have been a complaint or protest, to someone!

On another occasion [Chapter 8], I have discussed the deep incest guilt of a schizoid girl known as Joan. But in situations where frank psychopathology is present, a skeptic can always dismiss the incest—and, therefore, real guilt as the *cause* of the "illness"—as a fabrication or "delusion" or can interpret the act, if real, as an early expression of the disease itself. (In fact, the counselor who initially reported the Joan case, anonymously, has recently written to me and expressed—apparently for theoretical rather than empirical reasons—some doubt of the validity of Joan's report of the experiences with her father.) But in the present situation, there is no question of "schizophrenia" or any other well developed mental disease; and the fact of the incest seems established beyond doubt (cf. the prison term given to the father for the offense). Hence, the "dynamics" of the case seem particularly clear, unambiguous, and instructive.

Let us now examine the "Termination Note" dictated and generously provided by the psychologist to whom Marie was assigned:

Marie was referred by Dr. —— in September, 1957, because of extreme fears regarding sexual relations, in part stemming from long-term incestuous relations with her father. She was seen for a total of 12 interviews (primarily psychotherapeutically) from November 31, 1957, to April 19, 1958. Marie is being terminated since she will be leaving for —— to obtain work and probably resume College after a while.

Marie had a very strong fear of the close relationship with a man in psychotherapy which resulted in her extreme tension with me at the beginning of the treatment process, wanting to quit treatment several times, and finding different excuses not to make regularly scheduled appointments. At first my interest in her was interpreted by her as having sexual implications. Slow and careful work with her resulted in excellent progress for the relatively few short interviews considering the nature of her problem. Marie has begun to show greater initiative and less extreme submissiveness; there was a definite decrease in her extreme feelings of being "so different and so inadequate," now she can allow herself to try many things, whereas before she would have been convinced prior to any attempt that she could not accomplish the task. There was the beginning of a greater feeling of being at ease with all people including men, plus less sinful and guilty feelings regarding sex. She was able to lose weight more quickly than ever before in her life, probably a reflection of her decrease in fear of being attractive to men.

However, though the progress was excellent, it is felt that much more psychotherapy need be undertaken prior to her ability to deeply enjoy a close relationship with a man, such as in marriage. We had just begun to directly work on the very disturbing sexual area when Marie got this fine opportunity to go to —— and live with persons whom she felt at home with in her new-found religion, that of the Latter-Day Saints.

Her definite need for further treatment when she gets to —— appeared to be fairly well emotionally accepted by Marie. Perhaps more than any insight, the one thing that was most helpful to her was the beginning of the development of some deep trust in one man. However, whoever works with her in psychotherapy should anticipate a pretty stormy relationship with her, including such things as wanting to terminate treatment many times, and finding excuses for not coming to interviews.

TYPE OF SERVICE: Diagnosis and treatment.

CONDITION ON TERMINATION: Improved.

DIAGNOSIS: Phobic reaction (intense fear of close relationship with all men) in a passive-aggressive personality, passive-dependent type.

DISPOSITION: Patient withdrew from Clinic service. Clinic notified. (moved)

PROGNOSIS: Good for continuation of above described gains; need for further psychotherapy after she moves.

—————————————, Ph.D.
CHIEF PSYCHOLOGIST

The orientation of the staff of the clinic to which Marie resorted for help was rather clearly Freudian; and we may conjecture that in therapy an attempt was made to get her to feel that not all men were like her father and that she therefore had no justified reason to fear them—and sexual relations. But if we assume, as we reasonably may, that Marie's problem was not simply one of traumatic conditioning against sex but rather an incontestable personal guilt, then her "fear of men" (as authority figures) was justified, in a very different way; and sensing that the therapy was not addressed precisely to her need, it is perhaps not surprising that Marie was restive, dissatisfied, and eventually "withdrew." A letter from the therapist, which accompanied the materials already presented, is particularly illuminating. It reads, in part, as follows:

> I am happy to share with you some details of the case of a young woman with whom I worked and for whom the membership in the Mormon Church seemed to be a constructive change. . . . This young woman had been a member of a fundamentalist Protestant church, in which she apparently frequently felt terribly guilty when she was present at their services. I have the feeling that therapy may have helped her to reduce enough of the neurotic guilt so that she was able to seek out a religion, which was guilt reducing, paternalistic and supportive, the Mormon religion. Then perhaps the Mormon religion in turn is helping her to reduce the neurotic guilt and thus handle normal guilt, and life in general, more constructively.

It is not clear why reference is made here to "neurotic" guilt. Surely the assumption is not that this young woman should have emerged from her situation with *no* guilt, or that the guilt she felt was unjustified or disproportionate. The circumstances were, to be sure, somewhat extenuating; and it is much to the girl's credit that she eventually took it upon herself to do what she could to rectify matters. But it is hard to see how anyone with even a semblance of character and social awareness could have gone through what this girl had and be more normal or symptom-free. Here, if it was ever the case, guilt was a *fact*, a tragic and inescapable reality, and not just a "neurotic" *feeling*. And it is no accident, surely, that secular therapy was characterized by the girl's "wanting to terminate treatment many times, and finding excuses for not coming to the interviews." We can hardly escape the inference that she sensed her problem was not understood and that no real help would be forthcoming.

Here we also have an excellent example of the common failure of Protestant churches to cope with desperate personal guilt on the part of its members. There is no indication that this girl went to her minister about her problem at all; and if she had, the chances are he would either have been horrified and made a quite nonfunctional scene of some sort or, if more considerate, would have immediately admonished the girl to "seek God's forgiveness in prayer." If, on the other hand, the church had been liberal (rather than Fundamentalist), the minister might have tried to be more enlightened and to "counsel" with her along essentially secular lines, with a reaction similar to the one she gave to the therapy she received at the clinic.

The moral of this case is, therefore, clear: it indicates that neither Protestant theology nor Freudian psychology is at all adequate to the needs of deeply guilty people and that we must instead seek and utilize the healing power of human community and good deeds, rather than ignore and despise them.

VIII. CONFESSION, COMMUNITY, AND CHARACTER

In February, 1960, I spent a few days on the campus of the State College at Corvallis, Oregon, and while there Professor Lester A. Kirkendall told me of the following observation. Professor Kirkendall has done a great deal of counseling with college students, particularly with young men; and over the years he says he has found a striking correlation between a student's general social adjustment and the degree of normality in his sex life. If the man has good social relations, the chances are very high that he will report no serious conflict, perversion, or the like in the sexual realm. But if there is seclusiveness and uneasiness with people, there is likely to be some anomaly in the matter of sex.

Intuitively this relationship is not surprising, but it is useful to look at it somewhat more analytically. If there is perversity or evil in a man's sexual practices, it stands to reason that he should be socially ill at ease: if he has any character at all, he will, as a matter of course, feel guilty and will be uncomfortable in the presence of others. But this perception of the situation, valid as it probably is, leaves unanswered the question of why some young men are sexually normal, others perverse and deviant. Dr. Kirkendall is inclined to believe, and I certainly share his impression, that good control in the matter of sex is most likely to be achieved in an individual who, as a matter of policy and habit, is socially open, has a strong sense of community, and shuns secrecy and duplicity.

We are likely to think of strength of character and so-called will power as something we have or exercise deep down inside us. And we are likely to try to improve this capacity in others by admonishing, scolding, lecturing them. I am increasingly persuaded that will power or self-control is not nearly so much of an individual matter as we sometimes think. Instead, is it not basically a *social* phenomenon? Here, in society, is where the norms and values reside, and the person whose life is open to social interaction and influence has the benefit of social supports and sanctions. But the individual who embarks upon a policy of covertness and secrecy does not have this source of strength and soon finds himself the victim of uncontrollable temptation and, as he is likely to experience it, a "weak will." Superficially, the difficulty lies in the area of his sexual drives and practices; but more fundamentally the problem is one of social integration or the lack of it.

The pertinence of confession and community here is obvious. A few years ago I was discussing this general problem in a summer-school class, and a student spoke up and said that some of the banks in Chicago regularly give their employees lie detection tests. Not immediately seeing the point of this comment, I must have looked a trifle puzzled, so the student added: "It helps them *stay* honest." I then realized that the purpose of this procedure is not so much to detect anyone who has already done something wrong; rather it is to create a feeling that if anyone *begins* a dishonest practice, it will soon be known. This amounts, in effect, to periodic "confession." And if one knows that whatever he does is going to be *known*, one usually finds that he has the "will power" not to do it. Often we think of confession solely as a mechanism for relieving us of guilt associated with acts already committed. If confession is not made artificially easy, I am persuaded it has not only this redemptive function but also a strongly prophylactic one as well.

Sin, as Bonhoeffer aptly observes, demands to have a man *alone*. As long as as a man is in community, in free and open touch with others, he will have a vivid sense of the consequences of wrong acts which gives him the strength, and wisdom, not to commit them—or, if he does, to move rapidly toward their rectification. But if he has committed himself to the path of hypocrisy, of being with people but not *of* them, he does not have this advantage and is almost certain to get into moral predicaments of one kind or another.

The great Protestant emphasis has been, of course, not upon the relation of man to man but on the relation of man to God. By-pass human intermediaries and take our sins and concerns directly to God in prayer, that has been the sovereign Protestant strategy. For the morally and religiously well-developed person, I am sure this is often sufficient. The man of character so prizes a clear conscience and free communion with that immanent or transcendent something called God that he is extremely careful of his conduct, without any necessary reference to whether it will or will not be known to others. But this is the end, not the means, of a long developmental process. In children openness and integrity have to be taught and experienced first in the context of the family; and when, in an adult, there is an inadequacy or failure of character, personal reconstruction seems far more likely to occur in the horizontal than in the purely vertical dimension.

What is the place of ordinary church attendance and public worship in the lives of men and women? Again, for the religiously and morally mature and the emotionally healthy, I have no doubt that corporate confession is helpful and ordinarily sufficient. But in extraordinary circumstances, it is often seriously inadequate and urgently needs to be supplemented by procedures which are generally lacking in the typical Protestant church.

One of the great problems of our time is said to be that the average man doesn't "know who he is." This is a sign of neuroticism. Feelings of depersonalization and a sense of unreality are typical of the experience of severely disturbed persons. How else would we expect it to be? If our thesis be correct, the essence of psychopathology is systematic *denial* of who one is; and if we misrepresent ourselves to others, it is not surprising that we soon begin to appear alien, strange, and "unfamiliar" even to ourselves. Francis Thompson ends the first stanza of his great religious poem *The Hound of Heaven* with the trenchant thought, "All things betray thee who betrayest me." We cannot, it seems, escape the fact that we can be true to ourselves only if we are first true to others. At a very profound level, Shakespeare was right, of course, when he said that if we are true to ourselves we cannot be false to any man. That is to say, one's own long-term self-interest is consistent with his social interest. But in ordinary day-to-day practice, we are undoubtedly on sounder ground if we seek to find ourselves in the life of the group than if we attempt to fashion the group according to our own image and designs.

IX. CONCLUDING COMMENTS
AND RECOMMENDATIONS

Increasingly it appears that the central fact in personality disorder is *real* guilt and that it can be radically resolved only by confession that has at least a quasi-public character. But, as we have seen [cf. Chapters 4, 5, 8, and 13], this always involves, at least in well developed personalities, the danger of a catastrophic reaction, which may take the form of psychosis, suicide, or other forms of "acting-out." Assurance of God's love, grace, and forgiveness are to no avail in such a crisis. What, then, should clergymen do in the face of an eventuality of this kind? Here I have only tentative suggestions to offer; but I am convinced that sound and effective measures can and will be found if religious leaders and dedicated laymen take seriously the moral basis of personality disturbance and allow themselves to feel the full force of the responsibility which thus logically devolves upon them. My suggestions, listed more or less randomly, are these:

1. Clergymen and pastoral counselors need to have at

their disposal facilities for providing continuous care and supervision for persons during periods of acute disturbance. If the acute stages of a personality crisis can be handled in this way, more protracted institutionalization can, I believe, often be avoided. I know a church in Philadelphia which is in the process of establishing such a facility, to be staffed, as occasion requires, by regular church members, its ministers, and Christian physicians.

2. A special effort should be made to elicit the interest and assistance of persons who have themselves had personality disturbances and have made a good recovery therefrom. They are likely to have less fear of other disturbed individuals than does the ordinary person; and they often also have deep insights and are highly motivated. Care of and concern for others is powerfully therapeutic in its own right.

3. Ministers need to band together in their community for a sort of "group practice." In this way the individual counselor can be made both more cautious and more courageous, with group consultation and supervision available to him. A project in Kokomo, Indiana, which has been inaugurated by Granger Westberg, with support from the Lilly Endowment, offers a model for this type of development.

4. Ministers with specialized training and experience in counseling can be of great assistance in guiding, teaching, and supporting other ministers in their efforts in this area. Russell Dicks has recently established himself, in a community in Florida, in a unique kind of "private practice." His plan is to accept referrals from other ministers and to deal with them, on a fee basis, while at the same time encouraging the ministers making the referrals to follow developments and thereby extend and improve their own competence. Such a procedure, if widely adopted, is almost certain to evoke a protest from the psychiatric profession (see Joint Committee on Relations between Psychology and Psychiatry, 1960). But if its effectiveness can be demonstrated, social and legal protection will follow.

5. Young Protestant clergymen with whom I have recently talked complain of their "lack of authority" in dealing with problem persons. They lack, they say, the sanctions of both priest and physician and feel quite

helpless in asserting any kind of decisive influence upon others in time of crisis. My conviction is that as their competence and confidence in this area grow, ministers will find that so also have "authority." Clinical psychologists, in a somewhat similar predicament, have found that making continued psychotherapeutic contact contingent is often effective in inducing client compliance.

6. The individual undergoing acute personal crisis needs to see the potentially constructive, growth-inducing potentialities of the experience. Here the writings of Anton T. Boisen can be particularly helpful. I believe in encouraging the disturbed person to see his situation as involving what Old Testament writers referred to as the Wrath of God. At the same time it should be pointed out that the Wrath of God is the form in which those who defy Him experience His *Love*. The chastisement of an unruly child by loving parents is a meaningful analogy.

7. While accepting the self-condemning and self-punishing tendencies of the "sick" individual as understandable, reasonable, and even right in a certain sense, an effort should be made to help him move as rapidly as possible from expiation to restitution, from self-laceration to a program of service, self-discipline, and meaningful sacrifice. In my judgment the reason electroshock convulsions are often "therapeutic" (especially in depressions) is that they aid and expedite the work of self-punishment. In the preceding lecture we have alluded to the extent to which charity has become secularized and, in a sense, even commercialized (as "insurance" of various kinds). In Zborowski and Herzog's recent book, *Life Is with People*, an interesting picture is given of traditional Jewish life in the now all but vanished "stetl" villages of Eastern Europe. There philanthropy was continuously practiced, by almost everybody, as an everyday aspect of ongoing social and religious life. Many of the traditional occasions for generosity have, of course, disappeared in modern society; but there are always important and deserving "causes" to which one can contribute time and money. It is thus not so much the *opportunity* for generosity which has disappeared as the logical and psychological rationale therefor. The latter desperately needs to be recovered.

8. The Apostle Paul has warned against attempted "justification" through good works, "lest any man should boast." Then let us *not* "boast" but rather make restitution and perform good deeds *without* publicity and self-acclaim. Attempts to pray, analyze, or tranquilize ourselves out of sin have been ineffective. A more *active* form of "therapy" seems our only remaining option.

Somewhat parenthetically I want to say that I am not unaware that the approach here proposed is at least superficially paradoxical: it might be characterized as a sort of irreligious religious approach to the problem of personality disturbance. More accurately, one might say that the approach is actively religious but minimally theological in the conventional sense of that term. The approach is religious in the sense that it accepts the reality of unconfessed and unredeemed sin as central in psychopathology and holds confession and restitution to be commonly necessary for recovery. But it involves a minimal theological emphasis in that it stresses the interpersonal dimension as more crucial for therapeutic movement than the man-God relationship because it is the former that has been most palpably ruptured and can be repaired, in many instances, only by the individual's working hard at modifying and improving his everyday conduct.

Some years ago I heard a Park Avenue minister, in New York, take the position that if man's relation with God goes wrong, he is soon in trouble with his fellow men, and that when this happens he is automatically in trouble with himself; so, by implication, the place to start "therapy" or redemption is in the vertical, man-God dimension. Empirically, this assumption does not seem to be well borne out. And the psychoanalytic assumption that we have to work on our relationship *with ourselves* has also been a disappointment. The possibility that remains is the *interpersonal* approach, and it is the one which is now attracting most interest from secular students of the problem. It is also the one which holds greatest promise of a genuine rapprochement between science and religion in this area. Dr. Gordon McKay, President of McCormick Theological Seminary, has a talk which he sometimes gives to ministers entitled, "Don't Pray Too Soon." I have not personally heard this talk, but Dr. McKay has recently written concerning it as follows:

> The general notion behind the talk is that prayer is too frequently employed as a *substitute* for action. Beyond that, the resort to prayer is frequently among ministers little more than a cover-up for their ignorance and/or unwillingness to employ such community recourses as are available to serve the needs of men and women whose lives are blighted by such problems as alcoholism, marital discord, and mental illness.
>
> It seems to me that a full understanding of the Pauline concept of salvation requires us to recall that Paul's strong insistence on justification by faith was always coupled with the admonition that we are to *work out* our salvation with fear and trembling. Every great theological discourse in Paul's writings is followed by a chapter or two on moral teaching.

And recently I heard Dr. Roy Burkhart, of the First Community Church in Columbus, Ohio, say that salvation is a *social* operation. Certainly there is a growing disposition on the part of sensitive and perceptive clergymen to emphasize this approach. It is, I believe, extremely promising; and if metaphysical assumptions can be, at least for the time being, held in abeyance and a renewed emphasis put upon the interpersonal dimension, I believe something of a "break-through" can be achieved.

13

Footnotes to a Theory
of Psychopathology*

*As the title indicates, this chapter repersents an attempt
to pick up loose ends of fact and logic and tie them into
the general argument with which this book is concerned.
Here we see, again, the internal weaknesses of psychoanalysis, both as formal structure and as a system of
practice, and the ambiguity of a theology which finds it
congenial.*

*Not long ago, in talking with a Lutheran minister,
I remarked of a certain church practice that it might be
theologically necessary and sufficient but that it was
manifestly not psychologically adequate. To which my
friend replied: "In my opinion, if a practice is not psychologically adequate, it's not theologically adequate!"
Here, surely, is a fine spirit, which can go far toward
forging the new, unified conception of man in which we
today stand in such need. But in this chapter we see,
with special clarity, that before a valid synthesis of this
kind can come about, we must have both a psychology
and a theology which are in certain important respects
different from what we have recently known. In other
words, our explorations, here and in other chapters of
this book, suggest reform in contemporary theology as
well as in psychiatry and clinical psychology.*

In a series of recent papers [Chapters 2, 8, and 9],
I have delineated that conception of personality disorder which seems to me logically most compelling, empirically best supported, and therefore most promising
in terms of new and more radically effective methods of
personal (and social) reconstruction. Here it will be

* Presented April 20, 1960, before the Los Angeles Society of
Neurology and Psychiatry and independently published in
Progress in Clinical Psychology (D. Brower & L. E. Abt, edi-
tors), Grune & Stratton, 1960.

neither possible nor necessary to restate that conception in any comprehensive way. Instead, the present paper will take for granted a general familiarity with this theoretical framework and will advance some additional considerations in the nature of footnotes or marginal jottings and comment.

I. CHANGING PERSPECTIVES

Viewed in retrospect, how truly remarkable was that conception of psychopathology which dominated theory and practice two or three decades ago! Genuine guilt, justified self-loathing, and realistic interpersonal uneasiness were given little or no weight in the genesis of the so-called psychoneuroses, where *false* conscientiousness was assumed to be capable of playing veritable havoc. In other words, a supposedly overly severe superego, stemming from unduly strict childhood training and totally unsupported by ongoing experience and social or legal realities, was assumed to be *more powerful* and therefore more likely to disturb or destroy our peace of mind than was a sound, realistic, normal conscience which the individual had outraged by engaging in palpable, unacknowledged, and unredeemed misconduct. Such a thesis is clearly contrary to common sense and what we know about the principles of reinforcement and extinction (in learning theory) and is controverted by all sorts of clinical evidence; yet it was seized upon and proclaimed as a great scientific discovery and cultural achievement.

Now, within the last five or ten years, the picture has changed considerably. No longer is it maintained that the Freudian doctrine is universally applicable but only, perhaps, in *some* cases. For example, Jourard (1958) interprets the present situation as follows:

Clinical experience suggests that neither Freud nor Mowrer is wholly correct or wholly incorrect. Rather, it can be found that some neurotic patients do indeed have a conscience that is too strict; in order to remain guilt-free, they must refrain from *all* pleasurable activities, including those which society condones. Other patients may be found with the makeup which Mowrer has regarded as nuclear to all neurosis

—they repress conscience so they can break social taboos without conscious guilt (p. 366).

This is not necessarily an illogical position, but there is reason to doubt its factual validity. If, a generation ago, psychoanalysts were unable to recognize the presence and operation of real guilt in persons fairly devastated by it and so treated *everyone* as if they suffered only from false guilt, why should we now trust them to make exactly the right distinction between the two classes of "neurotics" which Jourard and many others are today suggesting? Diametrically opposed types of "therapy" would presumably be called for in the two different situations; and it is of some importance, obviously, that the "differential diagnosis" be made with precision and discernment. In the one instance, the goal of therapy presumably remains that of reducing the severity of the superego, i.e., attempting to close the painful discrepancy between a person's moral aspirations and his performance by lowering the level of the moral aspirations; whereas, in the other situation, the therapeutic objective is that of helping the patient become a better person, i.e., to improve and *raise the level of his performance*.

When did psychoanalysts or, for that matter, secular therapists in general, acquire special skill and competence along these latter lines? Their formal professional training and theoretical orientation has been almost exclusively in the reverse direction. When did they suddenly discover, *if* they have, that they are also uniquely equipped to work with this *other* type of personality disturbance? Even if the secular therapist were wise enough to be able to tell in advance of treatment ("diagnostically") whether a given person falls into the one category or the other, and even though he admitted he had no special competence in dealing with the individual suffering from *real* guilt, there is still an interesting question as to what he would then *do* with such persons. When the secular therapist today discovers that a patient is suffering from a genuine moral dilemma or ambiguity, rather than an imaginary ("neurotic") one, what does he typically do—meticulously "refer" such a person to pastoral counselors? Are secular therapists, who in the past were so insistent that parish ministers and chaplains

recognize their "limitations" and know when to "refer,"
now recognizing *their own* limitations and making coun-
ter-referrals? Or is the flow, for economic reasons, still
largely in the one direction?

We cannot here hope to settle the question as to
whether there is indeed a residual class of persons who,
as Freud insisted, suffer from over-conscientiousness,
rather than justified and realistic pangs of conscience.[1]

[1] A somewhat different way of approaching this problem has
been suggested by Dr. H. J. Eysenck in his book, *The Dynamics of Anxiety and Hysteria:* "In closing this chapter [on
Socialization and Personality] we may fittingly return to the
difference in opinion we noted in our second chapter between
Mowrer on the one hand and Dollard & Miller [1950] on the
other. It will be remembered that in their theories of neurosis
these writers were in sharp contradiction, Mowrer advocating
a theory according to which the Id was too powerful as opposed
to the Super-Ego, while Dollard & Miller [with Freud] advocated a theory according to which the Super-Ego was too
powerful as opposed to the Id. We can now see that these
theories are relevant, not to neurosis, but to extroversion-introversion. What we have called excessive degree of socialization,
due to strong conditionability, these writers call Super-Ego;
what we have called insufficient degree of socialization, due to
weak conditionability, these writers call Id. Mowrer appears
to be dealing exclusively with the extroverted symptoms and
syndromes, Dollard & Miller with the introverted symptoms
and syndromes. If there is any truth in our theory, then it will
be clear that both sides fail to come to grips with the problem
of neurosis, or excessive emotionality, i.e., that which is in
common to both hysterics and dysthymics, and deal rather
with a continuum which is orthogonal to neuroticism. Thus
our theory appears to reconcile the apparently contradictory
observations of these men in a larger synthesis. It also succeeds
in getting away from the reification inevitable in the use of
such concepts as Id and Super-Ego, and it provides a mechanism causally responsible for individual differences in these
respects which has a solid experimental foundation and whose
laws of functioning are reasonably well known. For all these
reasons we venture to offer this theory as not only an alternative to, but as an improvement on, those of Mowrer, and
Dollard & Miller" (pp. 221–222). Like Jourard, Eysenck is
here suggesting that there may be psychopathology on "both
sides" of what he calls the extroversion-introversion scale, taking
the form of hysteria in the one case, anxiety (dysthymia) in the
other. Normality and abnormality then depend upon another

But it will be useful to examine a few of the circumstances which do, to be sure, often give a superficial impression of justification for the Freudian perception of the situation. Typically, when adult human beings present themselves for therapy, they *are* inhibited, depressed, anxious, conscience-stricken. But this, manifestly, is not their "normal" state of mind and being, to which they long to return. Quite regularly, when we get into the situation, we discover that a little while back these persons have been something very far from inhibited, repressed, unexpressive. A psychoanalytic friend of mine used to be fond of saying: "There is just one thing wrong with the people who walk through the door of my office: they haven't been having any *fun*." They were, to be sure, at the moment too depressed and too anxious to enjoy life. But when we go into the question of how they *got* that way, information is usually forthcoming which clearly suggests a very different interpretation of the situation.

But what of the person who is more or less *chronically* over-conscientious: the so-called obsessive-compulsive or the victim of religious scrupulosity? These are certainly driven, tortured people; what is *their* underlying "dynamics"? We can, of course, assume that Lady Macbeth had a hand-washing compulsion because her mother (or nurse) was too zealous in "cleanliness training" and thus gave to My Lady spuriously high standards in these matters. Or we can assume, as Shakespeare obviously did, that the excessive preoccupation with "hand-washing"

---

variable, termed "excessive emotionality," which is independent of (orthogonal to) the first dimension. All of which, it seems, tends to beg the question: What determines the proneness to this excessive emotionality? Dr. Eysenck has, I believe, too quickly and for logically insufficient reasons dismissed the matter of id-ego-superego balance as irrelevant to the problem of neuroticism. And informal reports from his laboratory indicate that the empirical justification for his attempted re-interpretation may not be as substantial as it appeared to be (in 1957) when *The Dynamics of Anxiety and Hysteria* was published. But it is, of course, very much to the good that Dr. Eysenck and his co-workers have been willing to attack this problem in terms of evidence other than that provided by mere clinical observation and impression.

was energized by a *displaced guilt* which, in its own right, was only too terribly real. In the case of the Catholic who must confess and confess, without deriving any relief therefrom, may we not also reasonably suspect (with Stafford, 1950) that this compulsion continues precisely because the individual is careful to see that his "confession" never goes all the way, never really gets to the heart of the matter? It is, of course, not at all difficult to find instances of displaced—and therefore seemingly unrealistic, unjustified—guilt. We must be careful not to accept a superficial perception of the situation as basic and ultimate.

In light of considerations such as those just advanced, some may ask: But is it not possible that the picture has *changed?* Perhaps it is true that the majority of clinical problems today involve real moral inadequacy or failure; but during the so-called Victorian era, in which Freud made his original observations and formulated his theories, may not the picture have been typically otherwise? We cannot, of course, say categorically that such an interpretation is untrue, but it is improbable. Freud, we must recall, lived and worked in Vienna, which was never exactly famous for its prudery or restraint in sexual matters. Besides, as Progroff (1956) has recently pointed out, Adler, Jung, and Rank (also Stekel and many others) broke with Freud, not on personal grounds, but because *they* could not find in the clinical data justification for the inferences which Freud boldly drew. The data to which these men had access were essentially the same as Freud's, yet they could not agree with him, even then (see also Ichheiser, 1960).

There can, of course, be little question that sexual morality was somewhat stricter and probably better observed 60 or 70 years ago than it is today. But the question is: Was it excessively *high* then or is it dangerously *low now?* Many astute observers of the contemporary scene (LaPiere, 1959; Fitch, 1960) are suggesting that the latter assumption comes closer to the truth of the matter.

It is, of course, clear that man is more susceptible to self-condemnation and therefore "neurosis" (if he handles his guilt badly) when he holds high standards for himself than when his standards are low or nonexistent.

And as I have suggested on another occasion [Chapter 9], Freud's "mission," as he conceived it (see Fromm, 1959), was to introduce a new era of "psychological liberty" (Bakan, 1958). We are now far enough into this "era" to have both a retrospective and a prospective view of it, which we do not seem to like. In simplest terms, it involves a level of morality and responsibility comparable to that of beasts in a jungle, each of which "thinks" essentially of himself and his "natural" needs and has a minimum of social awareness.

Recently an intelligent woman told me of a conversation she once had with an analytically-oriented child-guidance expert. She said one of her teen-age sons' chores around the house was that of emptying the waste baskets. Sometimes he was dilatory or refractory about doing this. Now, asked the mother, "Should we *require* him to perform this task or should we let him do as he likes about the matter?" The reply was, "But why *should* the boy have to do this if he doesn't want to. He didn't *ask* to be born into your family." This may be *one* way to avoid inner conflict in human beings, to let children grow up as mere "blobs" (Robert Fitch's term!); but socially and, in the long run, individually (see Link, 1937), it is surely a form of "treatment" that is worse than the original "disease."

In light of the developments which have been alluded to here, present-day apologists for psychoanalysis and kindred "therapies" are fond of saying: "Yes, to be sure, there were some inadequacies and errors in Freud's original formulations and prescriptions. But there have been *great advances* in our science since Freud's time." However, on close inspection, these alleged "advances" turn out to be more nearly in the nature of retreats. One of the allegedly great new developments in psychoanalysis is the shift from the original emphasis upon unconscious mechanisms to so-called "ego psychology," which involves, essentially, a new emphasis upon what has always been known as ego strength, character, or "will power." One of the distinguishing features of Freud's doctrine was its emphasis on "The Unconscious," and now this is being abandoned in favor of "ego psychology," which analysts are frank to say they as yet know very little about "because it is so new to us and we are only beginning to investigate it." Common sense has been concerned with these matters for a very long time!

The most seminal and indigenous movement in American psychiatry during this century has unquestionably been the emphasis of Harry Stack Sullivan (following leads suggested by Adolph Meyer) upon the *interpersonal* nature of psychiatric problems, an emphasis which has been echoed, in one form or another by virtually all of the so-called neo-Freudians, notably including Eric Fromm and Frieda Fromm-Reichmann. But is this *new*? Throughout history, the world over, it has been assumed that there is a connection between "sin" and "sickness," i.e., between how one deals with others and what happens to oneself. The apostle Paul gave this principle its classical Christian formulation when he proclaimed that the "wages of sin is death," a psychological and spiritual death (as opposed to the abundant life which comes from the reverse of evil); but the principle itself is a universal one and by no means exclusively Christian.[2]

No, the modification and revisions which Freud's followers are having to make in their theories and practice are not extensions in the direction which Freud originally took, but are rather "advances to the rear." They are

---

[2] Since the above was written, Dr. Perry London and I have conducted a graduate seminar on "The Nature and Management of Guilt," in which many of the foregoing issues were considered. In response thereto, pro-Freudian students made the following points: (1) Psychoanalysis is still a "young science" and has perhaps not yet had a fair chance to demonstrate what it can do. If one will pursue the references cited in this paper, I believe he will come to question the grounds for such optimism (if one can *call* it that!). And (2), a related consideration: Granted that, during the half century or so that psychoanalysis has been with us, the world has not greatly improved, may this not be due to *other factors*—such as urbanization and loss of primary-group contacts, the automobile and television, two world wars, etc.? In other words, why blame psychoanalysis (the "Freudian Ethic") for *all* our ills? Historical progression (or retrogression) is, of course, always complicated, intricate, multi-faceted; and there is surely no disposition on the part of anyone to hold psychoanalysis exclusively responsible for the pervasive "sickness" of our society. But, in the light of the varied evidence now available, let's at least be very cautious about the continued assumption that psychoanalysis is *the cure*.

reversals, which are euphemistically—and misleadingly —called "progress."

II. IF ALL B IS A, IS ALL A, B?— OR "THE LORD IS SLOW TO WRATH"

On numerous occasions, a supposedly devastating criticism has been leveled against the hypothesis that there is a connection between moral failure and psychopathology. Phrased in various ways, its basic form is this: If all neurotic and functionally psychotic individuals have a history of unacknowledged and unredeemed real guilt, are all sinful, guilty persons neurotic or psychotic? Manifestly the latter is not true, and the stratagem underlying this question involves an effort to discredit the whole emphasis on moral considerations in mental illness by means of a classical *non sequitur*. Elsewhere [Chapter 3] I have called attention in this connection to that class of persons who engage in thoroughly evil, antisocial behavior but who simply do not have the character—or, as one may say, the "common decency"—to go crazy. It takes a fairly adequate personality to be seriously "disturbed"; in fact, the very *power* of neurotic and psychotic affects attests to their strength of character.

Also, some persons have the good sense to rectify personal mistakes shortly after they occur and thus do not allow themselves to fall into a chronic state of sin, disgrace, "neurosis." But over and beyond these considerations [cf. Chapter 10], there is another phenomenon about which I should like to speak in a little more detail.

Imagine, if you will, a sort of "teeter-totter," such as shown in Fig. 1. A child, let us assume, is normally born on the left side. He does not at first have to "*prove*" himself. He is loved, accepted, "respected" because he is *our* baby—and can, at first, do no wrong. But then, as the months and years pass, we begin to make demands upon him to "be good." Our approval is no longer automatic, unconditional. In a word, the child's *socialization* begins. Let us assume that all goes well in this connection and that, despite occasional mischief or naughtiness (i.e., light forms of "sin"), this child remains basically good, i.e., learns how to *earn* approval, respect, trust. We say the child is developing well and deserves a good

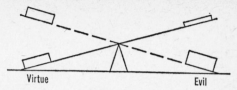

Fig. 1. *Diagram suggesting how a gradual impairment of self-respect (through continued wrong-doing) may lead to a sudden emotional "imbalance" or "breakdown." Only by again getting the virtue in one's life to outweigh the evil can the "balance be righted" and "equilibrium" restored.*

deal of "credit"—which is represented by the "box" shown on the left end of the teeter-totter and which is experienced subjectively as self-respect.

The years pass. This child becomes an adolescent and is no longer under close parental supervision and guidance. Now he (or she) begins to try his wings a bit, to "reality test." What would happen, our youth wonders, if he tasted the "forbidden fruit." And he makes, let us say, a brief excursion out on the wrong or "evil" end of the teeter-totter and then retreats again to the good end. Our young adventurer may have a little apprehension or "guilt" afterwards; but if he is "discreet" and doesn't "advertise" his foray, he may very well find, as did Adam and Eve, that nothing happens! He then begins to wonder even more: perhaps he has been swindled—by his parents, by society. Perhaps, as we were fond of saying in the 1920's, morality *is* "the bunk" and that by observing it one loses out on all manner of good things.

The rest of the story follows a familiar script. Our hypothetical youth returns to the wrong end of life's teeter-totter again and again, and eventually decides to remain there "in his heart" but to deny this overtly. Now the "credit" begins to pile up on the *other* end. And eventually a day comes—perhaps relatively soon, perhaps only after many years—when something very "mysterious" happens: the teeter-totter *tips* into the position shown by the dotted lines; and we say of our young (or now perhaps not-so-young) friend that he has had a nervous "breakdown," that he has lost his *balance*, become *unstable*.

What, now, can a person in such a predicament do to

be "saved"? It would appear that two equally misleading answers have been given to this question in our time. Protestant theology has preached a doctrine of "justification by faith." Place your *trust* in God and *believe* on Jesus Christ, we have been urged, and your sins will be immediately *forgiven*. And for those who prefer a "scientific" rather than a "religious" approach, there has been the doctrine of "justification by insight." In the latter approach, one comes to see that his sins are not real and that he doesn't really *need* forgiveness. It is hard to determine which of these doctrines has been the more pernicious. Bonhoeffer, in his book *The Cost of Discipleship* (1958), has eloquently condemned the conventional Protestant approach to personal salvation and change as a doctrine of "cheap grace"—and hence no grace at all. And although psychoanalysis can hardly be accused of being "cheap" in the monetary sense, its great appeal has surely likewise arisen from the assumption that one could *buy* his way out of perdition, without being otherwise unduly inconvenienced or anguished.

For those who are now disillusioned regarding both of these *easy* ways to "salvation," it is beginning to appear that "the way" is indeed hard and the gate narrow. Emotionally disturbed persons have not *talked* themselves into their difficulties; they have acted, mis*behaved*; and many are now persuaded that one likewise cannot talk (or pray) himself *out* of them. It is surely unrepented and unredeemed evil actions that destroy our self-respect and moral credit; and one can hardly escape the conclusion that these cannot be recaptured by any means other than compensating good actions and deeds [cf. Chapter 12].

A number of interesting and important implications flow from this way of viewing sin and psychopathology. To continue with the same physical analogy, it follows that just as one does not immediately become neurotic upon departing from virtue, so does one not immediately become "well" by "being good" for a little while. One has to *work at it*, perhaps for a very considerable time. But just as conscience eventually condemns and turns against ("attacks") us for pursuing an evil life style, so will conscience eventually approve and reward us for a better type of conduct. To many modern-minded men and women, traditional religious talk about the wonders of "faith" is not very intelligible or convincing. But, in the present analogy, we nevertheless see the relevance of faith, at least of a somewhat different kind. Just as the fully destructive consequences of sin are not immediately experienced, neither are the redemptive consequences of virtue immediately forthcoming; and one has to *have faith, confidence* that redemption will eventually come if one is only persevering. Many have tried to have faith in conventional religion or in psychoanalysis and been sorely disillusioned. But these are both purportedly *easy* forms of redemption. Genuine deliverance is, by contrast, arduous but never, I believe, eludes those who steadfastly pursue it.

But what, one may ask, of those who "never had a chance"? In illustrating the operation of the teeter-totter principle, we deliberately selected an individual who had been born to and reared by parents who were themselves of good character, loving yet firm. But psychoanalysis explicitly teaches that neurotic difficulties arise from an excessively strong and unrealistically severe superego which is created by the hostility, rejection, and moral irrealism of parents. Hence, every neurotic is presumably a person who "never had a chance"; and would-be therapy all too often, therefore, takes the form of encouraging the patient to wallow in self-pity and resentment, thus nurturing the paranoid tendencies which are already present in so many "sick" individuals. Is it any wonder that the accomplishments of such curative strategies are not impressive?

Later in his life Freud was forced to admit that the supposed correlation between neurosis and harsh training in childhood could not be empirically confirmed. He said: "If the parents have really ruled with a rod of iron, we easily understand the child developing a severe superego, but, contrary to our expectations, experience shows that the superego may reflect the same relentless harshness even when the up-bringing has been gentle and kind" (1933, p. 90). And when Freud then adds, candidly, that he has not "fully understood" this paradox, we see how shaky is the whole theoretical and therapeutic edifice which he erected. The doctrine of what might be called "justification" by "circumstances over which one has no control" is thus pragmatically questionable and leaves both the cause and cure of personality disturbance completely up in the air [see Mowrer, 1961].

Also, I wish to call attention to a question which a student raised when I lectured a few months ago at a West Coast university. He said he wanted to know, quite simply, what could be done to "save" persons who are living on the wrong end of the teeter-totter but who have not yet broken down, fallen. I had to tell him that I, frankly, did not know. It is clear that "salvation" has two aspects. One may speak of saving a fallen, manifestly sick person in the sense of helping him to "rise again"; *or* one can work preventively, to try to "save" people in the sense of *sparing* them the anguish of an acute personality crisis. But most of the efforts which we psychologists have directed along supposedly hygienic or preventive lines have probably been as misguided as our more specifically therapeutic, or redemptive, efforts have been. The leaders of Alcoholics Anonymous insist that an alcoholic can't be "helped" until he "hits bottom"; and it may be that much the same view is justified with respect to other types of "confirmed sinners." But ideally there *ought* to be something that could be done of a preventive nature. This, of course, is the age-old problem of "evangelism"—the hope of conversion *prior* to crisis, of calling the "hard-of-heart" to repentance and reformation before it is "too late." Certainly it should make *some* difference what the prevailing ideology of a society is. So long as we continue to assume that there is no relationship between sin and psychopathology and that if, by some mischance, one happens to crack up, one can always hire an expert to put him back together again, wrong living will hardly hold the implications of danger (and this is an important part of what *makes* it "wrong") that it ought to have. But the repudiation of the notion of such a relationship has now proceeded so far that it is very difficult to see precisely what steps can be taken to alter either the specific modes of would-be therapy or the general tenor of what passes for "mental hygiene."

In passing, it may be noted that there is today a revival of interest on the part of religious leaders in the concept of conversion, but with an attempt to avoid the emotionalism of the traditional "revival" meeting.

III. WHAT HAPPENS WHEN PSYCHOANALYSIS IS "SUCCESSFUL"?

A variety of studies (Ausubel, 1960; Cartwright, 1959; Dollard, 1945; Eysenck, 1952; Masserman & Moreno, 1959; Ubell, 1958) have indicated that no form of secular psychotherapy which has been around long enough and practiced by a sufficient number of persons to have a "record" can boast of anything very substantial in the way of accomplishment [see also Chapter 1]. When the likelihood of spontaneous remission is taken into account, the accomplishment is, in fact, almost exactly nil. In other words, untreated controls (to the extent that such controls are possible) seem to fare about as well as treated groups.

All this, of course, is well known in professional circles (e.g., see Fromm-Reichmann & Moreno, 1956)—and is gradually leaking through to the public. But I was quite unprepared to have an analyst tell me, a few years ago, the following concerning the findings of the psycho-analytic institute of which he was a member. Typically, he said, he and his colleagues have found that psycho-analysis has one of two outcomes: either the analysis is technically unsuccessful, which means that it fails to lessen the presumed over-severity of the superego, with the result that the patient continues to be neurotic; *or* the analysis is technically successful, i.e., the superego is softened-up and inner conflicts are resolved, but the patient then develops a "character disorder" and begins "acting out."

Manifestly such a picture is not reassuring and confirms more systematic reports of negative therapeutic outcomes and the growing popular disillusionment. But it was only recently that the theoretical implications of the report of my analyst friend dawned upon me. More than a decade ago, I began suggesting that analytic theory is wrong in at least one important respect: namely in its insistence that repression goes in the "direction" of the id, rather than (as I had come increasingly to suspect) toward the superego. And if this surmise is sound, it has important implications for the theory of character types. If, as Freud insisted, the neurotic is a person with an excessively severe, over-developed superego or conscience, the three major character types—criminal psychopath, normal, and psychoneurotic—could be aligned as shown in Fig. 2. Such an arrangement or conceptualization is neither unreasonable nor unattractive, in some ways. It permits us, for example, to draw a standard, bell-shaped distribution curve over these three personality classifications, with the normal type of personality being "average," model, and therefore most frequent, and with the two deviant forms of personality—psychopathy and psychoneurosis—trailing off in opposite directions. In such a frame of reference, the therapeutic objective is, logically enough, to help the patient move away from his position of excessive superego severity, in the *direction* of psy-

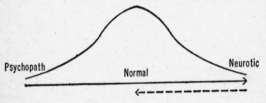

Psychopath   Neurotic
                          Normal

Fig. 2. *Character typology inherent in Freudian psychoanalysis. Therapy (broken arrow) in this system consists, logically enough, in trying to get the neurotic individual to "move" in the direction of psychopathy but to stop in the region of normality.*

chopathy, but to stop somewhere in between, in the general area of normality (see short broken arrow). This, of course, is in the direction *opposite* to that in which the efforts of the home, church, school, and other socializing (character-building) institutions are largely directed (see long solid arrow). And so it was that psychoanalysis became a self-appointed and strident critic of socialization (cf. Freud, 1930), on the grounds that it is precisely those persons in whom this process has been most effective and proceeded furthest that neurosis is most likely to arise.

If, on the other hand, the neurotic's basic difficulty is not that his superego is excessively severe but that the superego has itself been repudiated and "repressed" [cf. Chapter 2], a very different character typology results, as schematically portrayed in Fig. 3. Here the neurotic, rather than being seen as over-socialized, over-controlled, over-inhibited, falls somewhere in between the criminal psychopath or sociopath, on the one hand, and the normal type of person, on the other. Here it is assumed that such a person has an essentially normal, basically adequate superego but that it has been muted, disregarded, dissociated. This constellation or arrangement of character types might at first seem improbable, in that it can be encompassed "statistically" only if one uses a J-curve of the kind shown in the figure. To some this type of distribution may seen anomalous; but the work

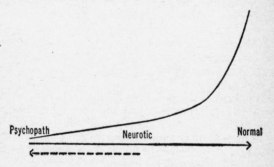

Fig. 3. A more realistic character typology. Here it becomes evident why a form of "therapy" which pushes the neurotic individual to the "left," if it succeeds, produces a psychopath rather than a normal person.

of F. H. Allport (1934) and his students has demonstrated, more than 25 years ago, that the J-curve, far from being anomalous, is *typical* of social phenomena; and since character is manifestly a social product, we should not be in the least surprised to find that it is distributed or varies, not according to the bell-shaped curve, but in conformity with the J-curve.

Especially significant is the bearing all this has upon the report of psychoanalytic failures and "successes" cited at the outset of this section. If the conceptual scheme shown in Fig. 3 is valid, then a form of "therapy" which attempts to push the individual *toward* psychopathy would be expected to "work" in precisely the way reported: either the therapy would be unsuccessful and the individual would continue in his neurotic state *or*, if the procedure did "move" the individual characterologically, it would be over into psychopathy, not normality!

A few weeks before writing this paper, I happened to sketch the foregoing considerations to a clinical psychologist who has long been in private practice in Southern California—probably the most thoroughly analyzed area in the world; and his comment was that he could cite innumerable instances both of clear failure of psychoanalysis and of its negative "success," i.e., instances wherein it had been actively countertherapeutic—and very few cases in which it had had a genuinely beneficial effect.

As Bakan (1958) points out, psychoanalysis has, however, had its greatest impact, not as an individual therapy (great as *that* has, of course, been), but as a broad social ideology and personal philosophy. The Stanford sociologist, Professor Richard LaPiere, in his book *The Freudian Ethic* (1959), advances cogent and numerous reasons for thinking that, *as* a social ideology and philosophy, analysis has been even more mischievous than as an individual "therapeutic" procedure, if for no other reason than that it has in this form affected so many more persons.

IV. PARANOIA AND SOCIOPATHY

If one adopts the view that neurosis arises, not from personal irresponsibility and immaturity (see Fig. 3), but from excessively high moral standards which harsh and unreasonable parents (and other socializers) have drilled and dinned into the individual as a child (see Fig. 2), it follows, ineluctably, that the individual is not "to blame" for his so-called neurotic difficulties. It is rather his father, mother, siblings, teachers, minister—*anyone* but himself. And soon the analysand, under this pernicious tutelage, is luxuriating in self-pity and smoldering resentment. If there are any paranoid trends already present, how else could they be more effectively fanned and fed? The distinguishing feature of the paranoid is that, unlike the depressive, he typically projects his own outraged conscience out upon others and then perceives *them* as "after" him, and *against* him.

Thus, it seems reasonable to infer that psychoanalysis, in its classical form and strategy, would drive individuals toward *both* sociopathy (psychopathy) and paranoia. We have already seen that the first of these outcomes does in fact occur. In "successful" individual analysis and in the movement of society as a whole which has been encouraged by the "Freudian Ethic," we see the trend toward the "psychological liberty" which we first thought was going to be our salvation but which we are now beginning to view instead as a scourge. While in Southern California I repeatedly heard stories from clinical psychologists, ministers, and social workers concerning the youth of the "best families" in their communities: i.e., families with money, education, leisure, and extensive psychoanalytic therapy. And what was the picture? The youth of such families, with distressing frequency, present a picture of demoralization: little personal ambition, self-centeredness and selfishness, dope addiction, general defiance and insubordination, illegitimate babies, and the rest.

The situation came particularly close to me in the following incident. At the home of one of my friends, I was casually watching a little girl (perhaps four years old) and her mother in an adjoining yard. The child was throwing a ball for a kitten to chase and having some difficulty with her coordination. Presently she made a particularly awkward throw; and I heard her say, "Oh, God! God *damn* it!" as casually as a child of an earlier generation might have said, "Oh, my!" or possibly "Drat it!" Her parents have very likely had the benefit of our best schools and colleges; and if they have not personally "had therapy," they know well the direction in which one is supposed to "move" therein and how, according to therapeutic doctrine, to bring up children without neurotic scruples and inhibitions. The difficulty is that we thus also bring them up *without character*.

Following a lecture in another state, a middle-aged woman tearfully spoke to me about her grown son: he is now, she says, himself trained as a social worker but has been "in analysis" for several years and still is; and as a part of his therapy he has been encouraged to blame his mother for all his difficulties, has little or nothing to do with her, and seems to be increasingly paranoid and hostile in his general outlook. Recently a psychologist told me (I unfortunately have misplaced the reference) of a factor-analytic study in which paranoid and socio-pathic traits come out as a single factor. This is hardly surprising, since both types of individuals perceive their trouble as "out there," as indeed it is for the sociopath; and although the paranoid individual has, more than the sociopath, internalized the norms of the culture, he *rejects* them so strenuously that he can experience them only in projected (delusional) form. How astonishing that we should have adopted as "therapy" an ideology and interpersonal strategy which we are now beginning to see moves us away from the more benign forms of personality disturbance (depression, anxiety states, etc.), not toward normality, but toward the two most malignant forms of personality deviation known to man! [3]

[3] Here I wish also to comment upon a question which is posed by the underlying logic of this paper. As we know, the prospect of recovery is always good in the depressions but, at least with present methods of treatment, poor in schizophrenia. Why should this be the case? Many contemporary students of the problem are inclined to agree that depressions are pre-dominantly "psychological," i.e., involve a "working through" of personal problems but assume, because of its greater chron-icity, that schizophrenia has a more constitutional, or endog-enous, basis. In his 1936 book, *The Exploration of the Inner World*, Anton Boisen advanced an intriguing hypothesis which has, I feel, received too little consideration: namely, that schizophrenia tends to be chronic and, not infrequently, "pro-gressive" because the individual manifesting this disorder "re-fuses" to admit his guilt and undergo appropriate remorse or make fitting restitution. Perhaps sociopathy and schizophrenia are, therefore, presently "untreatable" for much the same reason: in both conditions the individual does not take *respon-sibility* for his antisocial and immoral acts; but the symptom-ology is different because, as indicated above, the sociopath (as a type) *has* no conscience whereas the schizophrenic has one but *projects* it. The depressive, by contrast, "gets well" because he has a conscience *and*, through the depression, comes to terms with it. If this understanding of the situation is valid, it might lead to important innovations in treatment: notably, an approach which would help the schizophrenic move, not toward sociopathy, but toward the depressive syndrome.

Elsewhere (p. 163) I have quoted Schiller to the effect that "Life may not be the highest possession, but guilt is the greatest evil." Nietzsche's "Superman," we recall, was to live beyond good and evil, without guilt; and Adolf Hitler, World War II, and the mass extermination of Jews were some of the horrid manifestations of this dream. More subtle but nonetheless insidious and deadly, the Freudian Ethic implies the same philosophy in another guise. And it is no accident, surely, that it has prepared the way in this country for the widespread and growing interest in Zen Buddhism. One of the Chapters in Alan W. Watts' (1959) book, *The Way of Zen*, opens with this Zen Buddhist poem:

> The perfect Way is without difficulty,
> Save that it avoids picking and choosing.
> Only when you stop liking and disliking
> Will all be clearly understood.
> A split hair's difference,
> And heaven and earth are set apart!
> If you want to get the plain truth,
> Be not concerned with right and wrong.
> The conflict between right and wrong
> Is the sickness of the mind.

On the front of this book is a Buddha, arms folded, eyes closed, and countenance inscrutable. How different are the outspread arms and open countenance of Christ! Why this abandonment of the Judeo-Christian faith for Nietzsche, Freud, and Zen? The answer, I believe, can only be found in certain features of the Protestant Reformation, especially as they were shaped and expressed by John Calvin. His doctrine of predestination and human helplessness paved the way for the despair of Kierkegaard and the anger of Nietzsche. Roger L. Shinn in *The Existentialist Posture* (1959) credits Nietzsche with saying that "The churches are the tombs of God" and Kierkegaard with accusing "the churches of making a fool of God" (p. 70). It would appear that some revisions in the realm of theology are quite as urgently needed, if our civilization is to survive, as are called for in the area of secular "therapy."

Bibliography and Author Index

The numbers appearing in brackets after a bibliographic item indicate the pages on which that item is cited in the text. Non-specific reference to the ideas or work of others are likewise shown in brackets, after all the specific references have been listed or, if there are no such references, directly after the individual's name.

Abulafia, A. B. S. (*See* Bakan, 1958a) [113].

Adler, A. [21, 24, 227].

Allport, F. H. (1934). The J-Curve Hypothesis of Conforming Behavior. *J. Soc. Psychol.*, 5, 141-183 [237].

American Psychiatric Association, Committee on Relations between Psychiatry and Psychology (1954). Resolution on Relations of Medicine and Psychology. *Amer. Psychiat. Ass. Mail Pouch*, October [50].

Anderson, Camilla M. (1957). *Beyond Freud*. New York: Harper & Bros. [132].

Anderson, G. C. (1959). *Man's Right to be Human*. New York: William Morrow & Co. [67, 74, 126].

Angell, J. R. (1907). The Province of Functional Psychology. *Psychol. Rev.*, 14, 61-91 [8]. — (*See* Boring, 1950 [4].

Anonymous (1958). A New Theory of Schizophrenia. *J. Abn. & Soc. Psychol.*, 57, 226-236 [84, 104].

Anonymous (1960). Retribution and Neurosis. *Psychiatric Bulletin*, 1, 16-17, University of Texas [200].

Ausubel, D. (1960). The Proper Domain of Psychotherapy (a review). *Cont. Psychol.*, 5, 134-135 [235].

Bailey, P. (1956). The Great Psychiatric Revolution. *Amer. J. Psychiat.*, 113, 387-406 [131-132, 133, 138].

Bainton, R. H. (1950). *Here I Stand: A Life of Martin Luther*. New York: The New American Library [105].

Bakan, D. (1958a). *Sigmund Freud and the Jewish Mystical Tradition*. Princeton, N. J.: D. Van Nostrand Co. [112, 114, 115, 116, 122, 228, 238]. — (1958b). Moses in the Thought of Freud. *Commentary*, 26, 322-331 [115].

Barth, K. (*See* Niebuhr, 1960) [183, 184].

Berg, C. (1948). *The Case Book of a Medical Psychologist*. New York: W. W. Norton [120].

Berg, R. H. (1960). Psychiatry, the Troubled Science. *Look Magazine*, 24, 33-60 [141].

Blake, J. A. (1955). Happiness Versus Reality. *Understanding the Child*, 24, 44-45 and 59 [1].

Boder, D. P. (Personal communication) [163].

Boisen, A. T. (1926). Challenge to our Seminaries. *Christian Work*, 120, 110-112 [61, 62, 72]. — (1936). *The Exploration of the Inner World*. New York:

Harper & Bros. [24, 25, 26, 37, 39, 63, 72, 84, 101, 126-128, 163, 240]. — (1944). Niebuhr and Fosdick on Sin. *Chicago Seminary Register*, 34, 12-14 [66]. — (1945). *Churches of Crisis and Custom*. New York: Harper & Bros. [140]. — (1952). The Genesis and Significance of Mystical Identification in Cases of Mental Disorder. *Psychiatry*, 15, 287-296 [32]. — (1958). Religious Experience and Psychological Conflict. *Amer. Psychol.*, 13, 568-570 [98, 99, 104]. — (Personal communication) [65-66]. — [64, 68, 71, 73, 79, 127, 128, 153, 157, 168].

Bonhoeffer, D. (1948). *The Cost of Discipleship*. New York: The Macmillan Co. (original German edition published in 1937). [100, 107, 149, 189, 232]. — (1954). *Life Together*. New York: Harper & Bros. [107, 147, 191, 193, 216].

Boring, E. G. (1950). The Influence of Evolutionary Theory upon American Psychological Thought. In *Evolutionary Thought in America* (Stow Persons, ed.) New Haven, Conn.: Yale University Press [4, 5, 6].

Brengle, S. L. (1948). *Helps to Holiness*. London: Salvationist Publishing & Supplies, Ltd. [135].

Bridgman, P. W. (*See* Boring, 1950) [5].

Brower, D. and Abt, L. E. (Eds.). (1960). *Progress in Clinical Psychology*. New York: Grune & Stratton [222].

Buber, M. (1938). What is Man, in *Between Man and Man* (R. G. Smith, translator). Boston: Beacon Press (1957) [150, 179, 180]. — [150, 177, 185].

Buchman, F. N. D. [124].

Buddha [241].

Bultmann, R. K. (*See* Niebuhr, 1960) [184].

Burkhart, R. A. [221].

Bushnell, H. (*See* Niebuhr, 1960) [184].

Byron, G. [201].

Calvin, J. [159, 160, 165, 241].

Cartwright, D. S. (1959). Psychotherapy tomorrow: The Age of Conscious Strategy. Read at a symposium on "Psychotherapy and Values" at Ohio State University. (Mimeographed) [235].

Catholic Almanac (1959). Felician A. Foy, ed. Paterson, N. J.: St. Anthony's Guild [108].

Cattell, J. McK. (*See* Boring, 1950) [4].

Cervantes, S. [179].

Christ [9, 12, 125, 149, 169, 187, 189, 241].

Clark, K. W. L. (1952). *Concise Bible Commentary*. London: S. P. D. C. [188].

Clark, W. H. (1951). *The Oxford Group*. New York: Bookman Associates, Inc. [35, 109].

Coleridge, S. T. (*See* Niebuhr, 1960) [184].

Coles, A. (*See* Anonymous, 1960) [200].

Come, A. B. (1959). *Human Spirit and Holy Spirit*. Philadelphia: Westminister Press. [124].

Conant, J. B. [136].

Connery, J. R. (1910). Sin, Sickness and Psychiatry. *America*, 102, 493-495. [205-207].

Corsini, R. J. and Rosenburg, Bina (1955). Mechanisms of Group Psychotherapy: Processes and Dynamics. *J. Abn. & Soc. Psychol.*, 51, 406-409 [12, 13].

Cox, H. (1959). An Address to the National Student Councils of the YWCA and YMCA [44, 63, 72, 134-135, 138, 139, 178].

Cressey, D. R. (1953). *Other People's Money: A Study in the Sociology and Psychology of Embezzlement*. Glencoe, Illinois: The Free Press [152].

Dallenbach, K. M. (1955). Phrenology versus Psycho-analysis. *Am. J. Psychol.*, 68, 511-525 [70].

Daniel, The Prophet [29].

Darwin, C. (*See* Boring, 1950) [5]. — [8, 112, 122].

deGrazia, S. (1952). *Errors of Psychotherapy*. Garden City, N. Y.: Doubleday & Co. [119].

Descartes, R. [6].

Dewar, L. (1959). *The Holy Spirit and Modern Thought*. London: Mowbray & Co. [124].

Dewey, J. (*See* Boring, 1950) [4, 66].

DeWire, H. (1958). Personal Communication [111].

Dollard, J. (1945). The Acquisition of New Social Habits. In *The Science of Man in World Crisis* (R. Linton, ed.) New York: Columbia University Press [148-149, 235]. — [148].

Dollard, J. and Miller, N. E. (1950). *Personality and Psychotherapy*. New York: McGraw-Hill Book Co. [225]. — (*See* Eysenck, 1957) [225].

Douglas, L. C. (1929). *Magnificent Obsession*. Boston: Houghton-Mifflin [139, 198]. — (1939). *Dr. Hudson's Secret Journal*. Boston: Houghton-Mifflin [139, 198]. — [14, 139, 187].

Edwards, J. (*See* Niebuhr, 1960 [184].

Eglash, A. (1958). Offenders' Comments on Creative Restitution. *J. Social Therapy*, 4 [168]. — (1960).

Creative Restitution: Guidance and Rehabilitation of Offenders (in preparation) [102].

Eglash, A., and Papenek, E. (1959). Creative Restitution: A Correctional Technique and a Theory. *J. Indiv. Psychol.*, 15, 226-232 [168].

Eliot, T. S. (1959). *The Elder Statesman*, a play. New York: Farrar, Straus & Cudahy [75].

Ellis, H. [25, 148].

Eysenck, H. J. (1952). The Effects of Psychotherapy: An Evaluation. *J. Consult. Psychol.*, 16, 319-324 [235]. — (1957). *The Dynamics of Anxiety and Hysteria*. New York: F. A. Praeger [225-226]. — (1960). What's the Truth about Psychoanalysis? *Reader's Digest*, 76, 38-43 [132].

Fagley, R. M. (1960). *The Population Explosion and Christian Responsibility*. New York: Oxford University Press [208].

Federn, P. (1952). *Ego Psychology and the Psychoses*. New York: Basic Books [34].

Fenichel, O. (1945). *The Psychoanalytic Theory of Neurosis*. New York: W. W. Norton & Co. [27].

Fingarette, H. (1955). Psychoanalytic Perspectives on Moral Guilt and Responsibility: A re-evaluation. *Psychoanal.*, 4, 46-66 [1].

Fitch, R. E. (1960). Rake's Progress in Religion (unpublished manuscript: Berkeley, California: Pac. Sch. Rel.) [227, 228].

Fliess, R. (1957). *Erogeneity and Libido*. New York: International Universities Press [102]. — [113].

Foote, N. N. & Cottrell, L. S., Jr. (1955). *Identity and Interpersonal Competence: A New Direction in Family Research*. Chicago: University of Chicago Press [12].

Fosdick, H. E. (1943). *On Being A Real Person*. New York: Harper & Bros. [64, 65, 192]. — (1955). Redigging Old Wells, in *What is Vital in Religion?* New York: Harper & Bros. [61, 154]. — (*See* Holman, 1943) [78]. — [71, 170, 171, 193].

France, A. [119].

Frankl, V. (1955). *The Doctor and the Soul*. New York: Alfred Knopf [4].

Freud, S. (1900). *Die Traumdeutung*. Vienna [116]. — (1915a) Repression. In *Collected Papers* (1934), *Vol. 4*, 84-97. London: Hogarth Press [18-21]. — (1951b). The Unconscious. In *Collected Papers* (1934), *Vol. 4*, 98-136. London: Hogarth Press [18-21]. — (1923). A

Neurosis of Demoniacal Possession in the Seventeenth Century. *Collected Papers, Vol. 4,* 436-472 [116, 118, 125]. — (1927). *The Problem of Lay Analysis.* New York: Brentano [49]. — (1928). *The Future of an Illusion* (W. D. Robinson-Scott, translator). London: Hogarth Press [10, 112, 159]. — (1930). *Civilization and its Discontents.* London: Hogarth Press [236]. — (1933). *New Introductory Lectures on Psychoanalysis.* New York: W. W. Norton [32, 54]. — (1935). *The Ego And The Id.* London: Hogarth Press [153-154]. — (1935). *Autobiography.* New York: W. W. Norton [49, 82, 110]. — (1937). Analysis Terminable and Interminable. In *Collected Papers* (1950) *Vol. 5,* 316-357. London: Hogarth Press [22, 45, 121]. — (1939). *Moses and Monotheism* (Katherine Jones, translator). London: Hogarth Press [115]. — (*See* Steiner, 1958) [70]. — [8, 11, 14, 15, 22, 26, 36, 43, 49, 55, 70, 83, 86, 88, 111, 112, 113, 114, 115, 116, 117, 122, 128, 131, 132, 136, 148, 153, 157, 158, 160, 161, 164, 165, 170, 171, 181, 203, 223, 225, 227, 228, 233, 241].

Fromm, E. (1947). *Man For Himself.* New York: Rinehart & Co. [27]. — (1955). *The Sane Society.* New York: Rinehart & Co. [107]. — (1956). *The Art of Loving.* New York: Harper & Bros. [148]. — (1959). *Sigmund Freud's Mission.* New York: Harper & Bros. [228]. — [229].

Fromm-Reichmann, Frieda and Moreno, J. L., Eds. (1956). *Progress in Psychotherapy.* New York: Grune & Stratton [3-4, 235].

Fromm-Reichman, Frieda [229].

Galdston, I. (1955). *Ministry and Medicine in Human Relations.* New York: International Universities Press [4].

Galileo [111, 112, 122].

Gall, F. J. (*See* Steiner, 1958) [70].

Gallagher, J. J. (1956). Rejecting Parents? *Exceptional Child,* 22, 273-276 [1].

Gandhi, M. [145, 146].

Gilkey, L. B. (1960). Calvin's Religious Thought. *Motive,* 20, 5-6 [165].

Glover, E. (*See* Kubie, 1956) [121].

Goldbrunner, J. (1955). *Holiness is Wholesome.* New York: Pantheon Books [10].

Gutheil, E. (1958). Pseudoneurotic Symptoms in Psychosis. *Amer. Psychol.,* 13, 350 [45].

Haak, N. [140, 141].

Haitzmann, C. (*See* Freud, S., 1923 [118].

Hawthorne, N. (1850). *The Scarlet Letter*. Boston: Ticknor, Reed & Fields [53].

Hegel, G. W. F. [143].

Hepburn, Katherine [140].

Hitler, A. [241].

Hobbs, N. (1956). Curing Unreason by Reason: A review. *Contemporary Psychol.*, 1, 44-45 [1].

Hoch, P. and Polatin, P. (1949). Pseudoneurotic Forms of Schizophrenia. *Psychiat. Quart.*, 23, 248-276 [90].

Hoch, P. H. (*See* Fromm-Reichmann and Moreno, 1956) [3].

Hocking, W. E. [66].

Hollingshead, A. Redlich, F. (1958). *Social Class and Mental Illness*. New York: John Wiley & Sons [149].

Holman, C. T. (1943). On Being A Real Person (by H. E. Fosdick): A Review. *J. Religion*, 23, 214-215 [78, 192-193].

Hordern, W. (1955). *A Layman's Guide to Protestant Theology*. New York: The Macmillan Co. [182].

Huss, M. [9].

Ichheiser, G. (1960). On Freud's Blind Spots Concerning Some Obvious Facts. *J. Indiv. Psychol.*, 16, 45-55 [227].

James, The Apostle [109, 189].

Jellinek, A. (*See* Bakan, 1958a) [114].

Joint Committee on Relations between Psychology and Psychiatry (1960). Report on Relations between Psychiatry and Psychology. *Amer. Psychol.*, 15, 198-200 [218].

Jones, E. (1953-57). *The Life and Work of Sigmund Freud, Vols. 1-3*. New York: Basic Books 21 [49].

Jones, E. S. [139].

Jourard, S. M. (1958). *Personal Adjustment—An Approach Through The Study of Healthy Personality*. New York: The Macmillan Co. [26, 27, 35, 126, 223-224, 225].

Jung, C. G. (1938). *Psychology and Religion*. New Haven: Yale University Press [27]. — [21, 24, 227].

Kant, E. [124].

Kierkegaard, S. A. (1849). *Sickness Unto Death* (W. Lowrie, Trans., 1941). London: Oxford University Press [160]. — (1855). *Attack Upon Christendom.*

(W. Lowrie, trans., 1956). Princeton, N. J.: Princeton University Press [160]. — [170, 241].

Kirkendall, L. A. (1960). A Viewpoint on Morality (Mimeographed: Corvallis, Oregon) [148]. — [214-215].

Kubie, L. S. (1956). Some Unsolved Problems of Psychoanalytic Psychotherapy. In *Progress in Psychotherapy* (Fromm-Reichmann & Moreno, eds.) New York: Grune & Stratton [45, 69, 121]. — (*See* Fromm-Reichmann & Moreno, 1956) [3].

LaPiere, R. (1959a). *The Freudian Ethic.* New York: Duell, Sloan & Pearce [133, 134, 136, 138, 139, 157, 227, 238]. — (1959b). The Apathetic Ethic. *Sat. Rev.*, August 1, 40-45 [133-134].

Lee, Katie [53, 77].

Levitsky, A. (1960). *An Approach to the Theory of Psychotherapy.* Unpublished [27].

Levy, D. (Personal Communication) [151].

Lifton, W. M. (1953). Counseling and the Religious View of Man. *Personnel & Guid. J.*, 31, 366-367 [1].

Lin, Yutang (1948). *The Wisdom of Laotse.* New York: Random House [181].

Link, H. C. (1936). *Return To Religion.* New York: Macmillan Co. [11, 228].

London, P. [229].

Lowy, S., and Gutheil, E. A. (1956). Active Analytic Psychotherapy. In *Progress In Psychotherapy* (Fromm-Reichmann & Moreno, eds.). New York: Grune & Stratton [23].

Luther, M. [9, 105, 106, 109, 185-187, 190].

McCann, R. V. (1957). *Delinquency: Sickness or Sin?* New York: Harper & Bros. [52-53].

McKay, A. R. (1960). Personal Communication [220-221].

Macalpine, Ida, and Hunter, R. A. (1956). *Schizophrenia, 1677: A Psychiatric Study of an Illustrated Autobiographical Record of Demoniacal Possession.* London: W. Dawson [116].

Marx, K. [173].

Marzolf, S. S. (*See* Shoben, 1957) [39].

Maslow, A. H. (1956). Defense and Growth. *Merrill-Palmer Quart.*, 3, 36-47 [1].

Masserman, J. H. and Moreno, J. L. (1960). *Progress in Psychotherapy: IV. Social Psychotherapy.* New York: Grune & Stratton [235].

Maurice, F. D. (*See* Van Dusen, 1958) [128]. — [184].

Maves, P. B. (ed.) (1953). *The Church and Mental Health*. New York: Charles Scribner's Sons [4].

May, R. (1953). Historical and Philosophical Presuppositions for Understanding Therapy. In *Psychotherapy, Theory and Research* (O. H. Mowrer, ed.). New York: Ronald Press [138]. — (1955). *Toward A Science of Man* (Unpublished manuscript) [13].

Mead, G. H. (1934). *Mind, Self, and Society*. (Charles W. Morris, ed. and intro.) Chicago: University of Chicago Press [13, 140, 150]. — [66, 150].

Meehl, P. E., et al. (1958). *What, Then, Is Man?* St. Louis: Concordia Publishing House [107, 192-193, 196-197].

Menninger, K. (1958). Personal Communication [90, 126].

Mesmer, F. A. (*See* Steiner, 1958) [70].

Meyer, A. [229].

Michalson, C. (1959). *Faith for Personal Crises*. London: Epworth [53, 67].

Michelango [115].

Milans, H. F. (1945). *God At the Scrap Heaps*. Chicago: Salvation Army, Inc. [135].

Miller, A. (1949). *Death of a Salesman*. New York: Viking Press [53].

Miller, A. (1955). In *The Renewal of Man* (R. Niebuhr, ed.). New York: Doubleday [14].

Million, E. [154].

Mills, C. W. (1959). *The Sociological Imagination*. New York: Oxford University Press [134, 135, 138].

Montague, M. F. A. (1955). Man—and Human Nature. *Am. J. Psychiat.*, 112, 401-410 [132].

Moore, T. V. (1936). Insanity in Priests and Religious. *Amer. Ecclesiastical Rev.*, 95, 485-496 [205].

Moses [114, 115].

Mowrer, O. H. (1947). The Problem of Anxiety. In *Learning Theory and Personality Dynamics* (1950), pp. 531-561. New York: Ronald Press [26]. — (1950). *Learning Theory and Personality Dynamics*. New York: Ronald Press Co. [68, 83, 127]. — (1951). Anxiety Theory as a Basis for Distinguishing between Counseling and Psychotherapy. In *Concepts and Programs of Counseling* (R. F. Berdie, ed.) Minneapolis: University of Minnesota Press [26-27]. — (1953). *Psychotherapy—Theory and Research*. New York: Ronald

Press Co. [102, 127]. — (1959). Religion as Thesis and Science as Antithesis. *The Hanover Forum*, Hanover, Indiana, Vol. V, No. 1, 37-46 [143, 154]. — (1960a). *Learning Theory and Behavior*. New York: Wiley & Sons [5]. — (1960b). *Learning Theory and The Symbolic Processes*. New York: Wiley & Sons [8, 32]. — (1961). Guilt in the Social Sciences, or The Conflicting Doctrines of Determinism and Personal Accountability. In *The Effect of Psychiatric Theories on Modern Society* (J. W. Wiggins & H. Schoeck, eds.). In Press [32, 42, 58, 185]. — (*See* Eysenck, 1957) [225]. — [26, 223].

Muenzinger, K. [31].

Nebuchadnezzar, King [29].

Nestrov, J. [121].

Niebuhr, H. R. (1955). Introduction to Alexander Miller's *The Renewal of Man* (1955) [14]. — (1960). Reformation: Continuing Imperative. *Christian Century*, 77, 248-251 [172-173, 183].

Niebuhr, H. R., Williams, D. D., and Gustafson, J. M. (1957). *The Advancement of Theological Education*. New York: Harper & Bros. [62, 72, 74].

Nietzsche, F. (1887). *The Genealogy of Morals* (F. Golffing, trans., 1956). Garden City, N. Y.: Doubleday & Co. [163, 170]. — [241].

Packard, V. (1957). *The Hidden Persuaders*. New York: D. McKay Co. [146].

Pauch, W. (1960). The Christian Faith and Historical Thinking. Earl Lectures, Pacific School of Religion [172, 173, 176].

Paul, The Apostle [14, 109, 170, 186, 187-189, 220, 229].

Pelikan, J. (1959). *Riddle of Roman Catholicism*. Nashville, Tenn.: Abingdon Press [135, 120-121, 191-193].

Perkins, Sara E. (1956). My 4½ Years in a Chinese Communist Prison. *Presbyterian Life*, Feb. 18, pp. 8-12 [11].

Pfeutze, P. E. (1954). *The Social Self*. New York: Bookman Associates [150].

Pfister, O. (*See* Bakan, 1958b) [115].

Pike, J. A. (1954). *Beyond Anxiety*. New York: Charles Scribner's Sons [13-14].

Pirandello, L. [179].

Progoff, I. (1956). *The Death and Rebirth of Psychology*. New York: Julian Press [21, 24, 227]. —

(1957). *The Cloud of Unknowing*. New York: Julian Press [185].

Rank, O. [21, 24, 227].

Richards, I. A. [149].

Riese, W. (*See* Shoben, 1957) [39].

Roberts, W. H. (1956). Psychologists Are Getting Religion. *The Dalhousie Rev.* (Nova Scotia), 36, 14-27 [1, 12].

Robinson, H. W. (1928). *The Christian Experience of The Holy Spirit*. New York: Harper & Bros. [80].

Rogers, C. R. (1951). *Client-Centered Therapy*. Boston: Houghton-Mifflin Co. [164]. — [54, 164, 165, 193].

Runestam, A. (1932, republished in 1958). *Psychoanalysis and Christianity*. Rock Island, Ill.: Augustana Press [84, 127].

Russell, Anna [49, 53].

Schiller, J. C. F. [163-164, 170].

Schleiremacher, F. E. D. (*See* Niebuhr, 1960) [184].

Schneiderman, L. (1954). Anxiety and Social Sensitivity. *J. Psychol.*, 37, 271-277 [1].

Shakespeare, W. [88, 217, 226].

Shinn, R. L. (1959). *The Existentialist Posture*. New York: Association Press [241].

Shoben, E. J., Jr. (1955). Anxiety vs. Immaturity in Neurosis and its Treatment. *Amer. J. Orthopsychiat.*, 25, 71-80 [1]. — (1956). Work, Love, and Maturity. *Personnel & Guild. J.* 34, 326-332 [1]. — (1957). Toward a Concept of the Normal Personality. *Am. Psychologist*, 12, 183, 189 [34, 39].

Shrader, W. (1956). Why Ministers Are Breaking Down. *Life* (August 20, pp. 95-104). See also *Readers Digest*, 1956, November issue, pp. 55-58, and *Christian Century*, 1956, November 7 and 28 [158].

Smith, H. (1960). Toward a Socially Responsible University Curriculum. Faculty Forum Address, University of Illinois YMCA, March 11 [157].

Solomon, H. C. (1958). The American Psychiatric Association in Relation to American Psychiatry. *Amer. J. Psychiat.*, 115, 1-9 [76].

Stafford, J. W. (1950). Psychology and Moral Problems. *Homiletic Rev.*, 57, 118-124 [102, 206, 227].

Standal, S. W., and Corsini, R. J. (1959). *Critical Incidents in Psychotherapy*. New York: Prentice-Hall [91, 97, 104].

Steiner, L. R. (1945). *Where Do People Take Their*

Troubles? Boston: Houghton-Mifflin Co. [69]. — (1958). Are Psychoanalysis and Religious Counseling Compatible? (Paper read to Society For The Scientific Study of Religion, Harvard University, November meeting.) [69].

Stekel, W. (1938). *Technique of Analytical Psychotherapy* (1950). New York: Liveright [21, 22, 23, 24, 25, 26, 29, 37, 68, 84, 127]. — (1950). *Autobiography of Wilhelm Stekel.* New York: Liveright [21]. — [22, 227].

Stuber, S. I. (1952). *The Christian Reader.* New York: Association Press [9].

Sullivan, H. S. [150, 229].

Szasz, T. S. (1960). The Myth of Mental Illness. *Amer. Psychologist, 15,* 113-118 [51].

Temple, W. [182].

Thompson, F. (1922). *The Hound of Heaven.* Baltimore: Norman, Remington Co. [155, 217].

Tillich, P. (1948). *The Protestant Era* (Abridged, 1957). Chicago: University of Chicago Press [110, 174, 175, 181]. — (1959). The Good I Will, I Do Not. *Union Seminary Quart. Rev., 14,* 17-23 [169-170, 189]. — [142, 170, 177].

Tournier, P. (1957). *The Meaning of Persons.* New York: Harper & Bros. [177, 178, 179, 180, 185].

Troeltsch, E. (*See* Niebuhr, 1960) [184].

Ubell, E. (1958). Psychoanalysis—Report on 9,000 Case Histories. *Chicago Sun-Times, Sunday,* July 13; Section 2, p. 3 [235].

Van Dusen, H. P. (1958). *Spirit, Son and Father.* New York: Charles Scribner's Sons [123, 124, 125, 128].

Vaughn, R. P. (1959). Mental Illness among Religious. *Rev. for Religious, 18,* 25-26 [27-28, 29, 85, 195, 203, 204, 205].

Virgil [116].

Waelder, R. (1960). *Basic Theory of Psychoanalysis.* New York: International Universities Press [34].

Walters, O. S. (1955). Freud, his Philosophy of Life. *His—Magazine of Campus Christian Living, 16,* 8-11 [14].

Watson, J. B. (*See* Boring, 1950) [4, 5].

Watts, A. W. (1959). *The Way of Zen.* New York: New American Library [241].

Weatherhead, L. D. (1929). *Psychology In The Service*

Of The Soul. London: Epworth Press [203]. — (1957). *Psychology, Religion, and Healing.* Nashville, Tenn.: Abingdon-Cokesbury Press [197].

West, R. F. (1959). *Light Beyond Shadows.* New York: The Macmillan Co. [79].

White, E. (1955). *Christian Life and the Unconscious.* New York: Harper & Bros. [4, 11].

White, R. W. (1952). The Dangers of Social Adjustment. *The Medical Pr.*, 228, July 2, pp. 9-15 [1].

White, V. (1956). Guilt: Theological and Psychological. In *Christian Essays in Psychiatry.* New York: Philosophical Library [107].

Whitehorn, J. C. (*See* Fromm-Reichmann & Moreno, 1956) [3].

Williamson, E. G. (1956). Counseling in Developing Self-confidence. *Personnel & Guid. J.* 34, 398-404 [1].

Wilson, A. (1954). *Pardon and Peace.* New York: Sheed & Ward [109, 201, 203, 204].

Wortis, J. (1954). *Fragments of an Analysis with Freud.* New York: Simon & Schuster [132].

Zborowski, M., and Herzog, Elizabeth (1953). *Life Is with People.* New York: International Universities Press [219].

Zilboorg, G. (*See* Fromm-Reichmann & Moreno, 1956) [3].

Subject Index

254